The
Survival
of the
Coolest

an addiction memoir

by

William Pryor

I play it cool and dig all jive;
that's the reason I stay alive.
(Langston Hughes)

First published in Great Britain in 2003
by Clear Press Ltd
Unit 136
3 Edgar Buildings
George Street
Bath BA1 2FJ

Page makeup by Clear Books

Cover Design by Jerry Goldie
Printed and bound in Great Britain by Creative Print and Design Wales, Ebbw Vale

British Library Cataloguing in Publication data available

Library of Congress Cataloguing in Publication data available

ISBN 1 904555 13 6

CONTENTS

1 The Devoted Scapegoat 1

2 Girls and Nights Errant 25

3 Morning Glory in Paris 41

4 Moral Sciences and Total Art 59

5 It's All Happening 69

6 Margareta and Wholly Communion 77

7 Melodious Thunk 87

8 'Pataphysics* and the Asylum 101

9 Jamaica, Holes & Coltrane 115

10 Back Down the Dilly 129

11 Natural Deselection 139

12 India – an Oasis in the Desert 153

13 Bookselling and Marriage 161

14 The Geographical Cure 171

15 The Trials of Torquay 189

16 Totterdown and First Steps 197

Epilogue 221

REALITY CHECK AND ACKNOWLEDGEMENTS

Soon after I stopped taking mind-altering substances 28 years ago, this book was born, as a mirror in which I could try to see myself. It was long and self-indulgent and was soon shuffled into a drawer. When 9/11 compounded the demise of the dot com bubble thus deflating my dreams of entrepreneurial millions, I opened the drawer again and set to reinventing myself as a writer.

The book is entirely organic: nothing but real places, events and people (99.9% of whom retain their real names) have been used in baking it - no artificial additives. If the dramatic style I use in places has lead to historical distortions, I beg forgiveness of those who might feel themselves thus maligned, but my goal has been to put emotional and conceptual truths before their historical brethren.

Without the generosity of those involved in events described in the book, directly or indirectly, I would have got nowhere. My mother and my sisters were essential players and I thank them for putting up with my urgency and braggadocio, likewise my various Barlow, Cornford, Darwin, Hambro, Keynes, Pryor and Wedgwood cousins. Also crucial were the following whom I thank unreservedly: Broadway Lodge, Matthew Chapman, David Gale, Jenny and Nigel Lesmoir-Gordon, Andrew Rawlinson, Faith Singh, Anthony Stern and Marina Warner. Thanks are also due to Judy Ryde and to my agent Liz Puttick who invested editorial discrimination and encouragement way beyond the call of duty, enabling me to believe there might be an audience for the book. For their support and help, I am also grateful to Brian and Shelagh Bocking, Jani Brenn, Professor Peter Cohen, Robert Derrick, Matthew Dodson, Helen Donlon, Susan Howard, Mike Jay, Ann and Bill Kahn, Francesca Longrigg, Michael Mann, Anna Rawlinson, Geoff Roberts, Matthew Seal, Frances Spalding, Sheila Stern, Carl Stickley and Professor Richard Velleman.

But most of all I must thank Baba Ji for his persistence and my wife Joy, whose trust, generosity and enormity of heart have underwritten every word of this book.

1 THE DEVOTED SCAPEGOAT

We will now discuss in a little more detail the Struggle for Existence.
(Charles Darwin, *On the Origin of the Species*)

One fine summer day, as I languished in the belly of the behemoth that was Cane Hill Lunatic Asylum, being 'cured' of heroin addiction, my dear friend Nigel came to visit, causing a flurry in reception. They phoned the staff nurse on my ward to let me out. I sloped the miles of linoleum corridors, past anonymous brass-locked doors, the hum of ECT machines, the shuffle of carpet slippers and the crash of state-owned aluminium trolleys of spotted dick and custard. For a great great grandson of Charles Darwin to be shut away in a loony bin was shameful enough, only mitigated by knowing that Charlie Chaplin's mother had been committed here at the turn of the century as had David Bowie's half brother in the recent past.

Nigel in his *Granny Takes a Trip* finery.

A vision in his *Granny Takes A Trip* lamé boots and flounced shirt, Nigel Les-moir-Gordon waited for me in reception as the flat-hatted functionaries eyed him and he them. The many hundreds of inmates of Cane Hill Hospital were, in the main, forgotten, written off, not talked about, and didn't get visitors. For an Acid London Beau to visit this corner of Victorian Britain was unknown and the cause of mutual amazement. But Cane Hill's sheer size and gloom was an overwhelming Hades, so we went out onto the lawns.

"I've brought you a present." Nigel rummaged in his pocket and produced a small envelope. Out of it came two small squares of blotting paper.

"What on earth's that?" I asked.

"Acid, man, the glory juice. All you do is put a drop of acid on each piece of blotting paper and you have it, a truly portable trip." We chewed our blotting paper there and then and penetrated the corridors in search of a cup of tea. The flux of space-time began to sway in the air of the canteen as we sat amongst those patients coherent enough to be allowed out of their wards. We couldn't help but look at them, bravely insouciant, stirring their teas, some dribbling, some mumbling, others with mutated consciousness.

We could feel their madness, see that it wasn't. I got scared that someone, a doctor or a nurse, would notice our tripping. I leaned towards Nigel's coiffed locks and whispered.

"Isn't someone going to notice what's happening with us?"

"In a place like this, they won't notice a thing. They'll take us for just another pair of lunatics, which of course we are, lunatic, I mean."

We were walking down one of the endless corridors. A man with no teeth, trousers that were far too short and careworn carpet slippers on his feet, stopped in his shuffling when he saw us coming and grabbed me by the arm as we tried to pass.

"Young man, I can see, you're just off to the big city." We stopped. He hesitated, hand to chin, remembering.

"I was in the big city once. It's where people float, isn't it. Yes, of course it's where they float. Got no weight to them, that's what it is. They're quite without any preponderance." He was a lovely old man. I thought he recognised where we were in our acid perceptions.

"Right on, yeah, we're just off to the big city, where it's definitely preponderances that are the problem." We looked at each other, pupil to pupil, until something reminded him of his mission. He started shuffling again. We walked on.

"You see Nigel, my brother, we're all mad, but it's *all* right. It's all right, all right. It's all, all, all right. They can't contain your mind, after all." I wasn't sure that was correct. Maybe they could.

"No," I grabbed Nigel's shoulder and turned to face him. "First they *institutionalise* you. Then they give you a lovely label all of your own. Mine's 'addict'. That's what it's about. They are rendering people's unacceptable behaviour impotent through language labels and then, drugs."

I left myself in a hopelessness with this, but Nigel was with me.

"It's OK man. You tread a lonely path, but you'll get there. Antonin Artaud spent years in one of these places. Hey, yes, he did," he remembered something and stopped me in my tracks, hand on shoulder.

"I've got this quote from him." He fumbled through his velvet jacket pockets. Triumphantly he produced a piece of notebook on which he'd scribbled these lines:

The truth of life lies in the impulsiveness of matter. The mind of man has been poisoned by concepts. Do not ask him to be content, ask him only to be calm, to believe that he has found his place. But only the madman is really calm.

We walked down the corridors, through the small courtyards, right round the hospital, the human refuse tip, where awkward human beings were managed.

Down one corridor we heard an intriguing cacophony. We followed it and found ourselves in a great hammer-beamed hall. Why did the Victorian burghers of Greater London build a hall like this in an asylum? So the lunatics may dance?

Fifty innocents and educationally-challenged persons were banging away on tambourines, side drums and triangles, with the pattern and pulse of chaos. It was mesmerising. We grooved to the free improvisation of madness. One or two of them dared to look up and smile at our enjoyment.

"I'm not this, am I Nigel?" I broke the reverie.

"No, you are a poet, dear man," said Nigel.

We stood for an enraptured age beholding this theatre of the absurd. Eventually we had to make our way back to something more closely resembling reality and a parting. After much corridor we found our way up the asylum's oesophagus into the mouth it used to swallow rationality. Nigel had to leave me to my padded cell of spotted dick, custard and carpet slippers. He went back to his Brave New London, I to my charade of a cure.

I was nineteen and locked in a nineteenth century lunatic asylum to have my heroin addiction corrected. I had already completely adapted to the cliché of crazed addict, a rat in a sewer of cravings. Somehow being an addict answered my needs, my pain, my lack of definition. Well, it didn't, but for a short honeymoon of intoxication, it seemed to.

The very concept of addiction has shifted in the last 30 years: when you allow for workaholism, eating disorders, and gambling, sex, shopping and TV addiction, a significant majority of the developed world are addicts. On this hierarchy of degradation, of which street heroin and crack cocaine occupy the basement, the addict plays his part in the reinforcement of the myth that 'normal' people are unaddicted and free. Without this myth we recovering addicts would have nothing to strive to become.

The pyramid of addiction is a tomb: all addictions hover around death, to some degree. Addicts want to kill some part of themselves: the great nostalgia or the black discomfort. Junkies and crack addicts are the extremophiles, attracted to an extreme environment that is savagely toxic to human life. Once there, they take leading roles in a tragedy demanded by the fissures in the ever-developing idiosyncrasy of the 21st century self. This tragedy is heightened because the same addict self seeks comfort, meaning and healing through being cast out.

The idea of 'addict' – someone who cannot control himself – is one of the most potent pieces of voodoo used to keep society functioning. Even in these days of the celebrity druggy, the out-of-control, despicable, destructive and nihilistic addict must be cast out to maintain the myth of the good (controlled) self that maintains 'civilised' society.

Back in the sixties, addicts were a relative rarity. The rejection of society and family, implicit in my addiction, broke deep taboos and could not be ignored. Forty years on and 21st century addicts have a hard time being anything more than a nuisance.

But the queue of what the myth teaches us to regard as self-indulgent inadequates, only too eager to adopt the role of filthy junky, keeps on growing. They can't get no satisfaction. They go to great lengths to be more than a nuisance. We step over them in the streets. They steal from us. They do not wash. Their bodies offer AIDS. And there are fortunes to be made selling them stuff and curing them afterwards, bringing them back into control.

How does a great great grandson of Charles Darwin sink to such depths? The outline of an answer might be found in a broth made with equal parts sociocultural history of sixties Cambridge, cultural nuances of the Darwin-Bloomsbury nexus, mythologies of addiction, my psychological nurture and my family's genetic nature. A rich brew in which to look for an answer! Let us go then, you and I...

My privileged upbringing began with my birth in January 1945, as the last century's second war to end all wars played out. For my mother these were the best times of her life, because everything was so clear-cut and comprehensible. You knew where you were: there was a clearly defined enemy, a shared purpose, and the hardships, privations and danger were rationed out equally to everyone, high and low. You were all facing the

The authorial pram.

same direction with fortitude and self-denial. You all had to eat your powdered eggs with a stiff upper lip. The world became complex and subtle again as soon as the war ended. I couldn't digest the black and white simplicities my parents brought out of the war. I found that moral dilemmas were not that straightforward. Authority had lost its credibility. But part of me still hankers after those clarities: black and white British war movies where chaps are so readily noble in their sacrifices and courage and the enemy was so obviously evil.

My father's wartime record was eccentric. At one point he tried to

join the Home Guard, but was so utterly hopeless with his rifle that they politely suggested he concentrated on his scientific work at the Royal Aircraft Establishment where he was developing epoxy resin glues with which to stick the wood-en frames of Mosquito aircraft together.

He invented these glues from his passionate interest in the molecular chemistry of

My father in his garden.

honeybees. As soon as the war was over, his friend and colleague, de Bruyne, put all the lab equipment in the back of a lorry, took it off to some factory and went on to make lots of money, calling the glue Araldite. But my father considered the pursuit of money vulgar.

He has been dead for more than thirty years now, but I can still picture his hooked nose and bony, slightly hunched frame, brown tweed jackets with leather elbow patches, grey flannel trousers, but that's not him. I have the outer shape of him, but the being, the father eludes me. His enthusiasms were all so private – there wasn't one he could share with me.

He made mayonnaise with scientific passion. He was a wine snob. He created a one-acre, playfully weird garden, with its bog and giant rhubarb, tree peonies, two hundred guinea pigs that mowed the lawn and two asparagus beds. His dinner parties and Guinness and oyster soirées were renowned. But there was no bonding or sharing. There was never, ever, a conversation about how I felt, about how I coped, about how I *was* with the confusions of growing up. No birds and bees. Nor did he ever tell me how *he* felt about anything. OK, middle class British fathers didn't then, but how was I to know?

Mark Gillachrist Marlborough Pryor was the middle son of landed gentry, who own the fertile acres on which their manor houses find themselves. For the last four hundred years, in Hertfordshire's green and rolling hills, Pryors have been quietly reaping and consolidating rich harvests from some initial 16th century fortune. The chaps have been to Eton and Trinity Cambridge since time immemorial, but Mark was the brainy one who stayed on to become an entomologist, don and eccentric pillar of the university establishment.

That 16th century fortune was founded on first the business of carting 'night soil' out of London, and then, after they had converted to Quakerism, on brewing beer in Baldock. A fortune in puritan shit and Quaker beer!

Indeed, though fortunes and money are subjects at the heart of the British middle class way of being, they are never discussed in polite society. The fact that my great great grandfather's face adorns the ten-pound note encourages me to overcome this reticence – indeed we must talk about it because it wraps the core of my addiction. Landed gentry of the Pryor variety are never short of a bob or two. Pryor tentacles not only reached out of the 16th century night soil into brewing and the management of the Bolivian economy, but another branch was one of the founding families of Barclays Bank. And then Sir Stanley Spencer was a friend of my maternal grandmother Gwen Raverat, and the pictures he gave her are worth a...

Oh do stop William, this really will not do! One simply does not talk about the family and money in this way!

Anyway, none of this stopped money being a problem for me – the poor little well-to-do boy syndrome. Those that have never known money focus on the belief that it will solve all their problems, but living *with* money just creates different ones. Even though I've never been at the point of not knowing where the next meal is coming from, the ravages of circumstance have frequently made me feel as though the gutter was the next stop. But even from the depths of injecting heroin in the public toilets of Piccadilly Tube Station I had a bank account to call on.

The substance of this book has proved very expensive to obtain over the last fifty years, yet, somehow, here I am perched in my middle-class, double-glazed writing shed with my online bank overdraft available at a click of a mouse. My pendulum of prosperity oscillates between feeling virtually well off enough to run a Saab and the blues that, if it hadn't been for bad luck, I wouldn't have had no luck at all. Oh yes, right down to the bottom of my hush puppies and up again.

There was some wit about money: my father established a trust fund to pass on his wealth to his four children in a tax efficient manner. He called it the Pelican Fund, because the birds are rumoured to stab at their own breasts to feed their chicks blood when there is no other food.

How the family *held* money only made my addiction more likely. Money was a birthright. I should not have to exert myself to get it. Or to spend it on drugs. I mean: the unwritten Pryor script was that, as the man child, you only have to excel at whatever it is you do, and money will appear. It is one's by right. It was a vulgar misconception that one had to 'work'. One got paid for exercising one's genes.

My father, my father! I would relish being able to extol the warmth of his fatherhood, the guidance, the example, the love. But I can't. He didn't know how to express such things, though sometimes he tried. He took me on a birthday treat once, maybe I was ten. It wasn't a natural occasion. He didn't enjoy it.

He hired a motorboat to take just my mother, him and me down the River Cam to the east of the city. I was allowed to drive. But the rope was left dangling over the back. And – inevitably – it got caught in the propeller and the boat came to a standstill. Daddy had to get into the river, standing in a foot or so of mud to spend what seemed hours disentangling the rope. It was clearly my fault – they wouldn't have gone anywhere near a motorboat if it hadn't been for me. But nothing was said through those pursed lips.

I was allowed to visit him in his lab, to rub the glass of the tank where the electric eel lived and watch him ripple his spine fin as he swam backwards in response. I could marvel at the tanks full of different coloured cockroaches. I was invited to witness the white-coated high priests of science at prayer, talking in their jovial secret language.

A man entranced by the act of discovery, who, if pushed for his metaphysical or religious inclinations, would mutter something about being a stoic, about virtue being the highest good and indifference to pleasure and pain something he strove for.

Indifference to whose pleasure and pain? He was brought up by a nanny and a chauffeur. In his formative years he saw his parents only at the occasional teatime, though they lived in the same manor house. Later on depression got the better of his mother and she spent the last decade or so of her life drugged and zombie-like. A chain of not seeing that dragged me into its hole.

With her dark French good looks, but tendency to self-effacement, my mother put herself in my father's shadow. Not a typical Darwin character trait and maybe my later anger had some ground in her timidity at motherhood, her fear of intimacy with her only male offspring. She has found it hard to know who she is, overshadowed by a well-known mother, an extremely well-known great grandfather and a clever and most accomplished husband. Maybe what I mean is: *I* don't know who she is.

She plays a Steinway grand and the violin. She paints pictures. She gardens. She goes for walks. She takes unusual holidays, walking over the Pyrenees looking at flowers. She has raised four children. She cooks with a simple French subtlety. Moderation in all things: just one glass of sherry, just one hug. She fills her time meticulously – every moment planned and worried over.

Her parents were Jacques and Gwen Raverat. Jacques was a French painter who died aged just 40 from multiple sclerosis. Gwen was a granddaughter of Charles Darwin and a woodcut artist of some repute. They were on the edge of the Bloomsbury phenomenon, counting Eric Gill, Rupert Brooke, Stanley Spencer, Virginia Woolf, cousin Ralph Vaughan Williams, as well as André Gide, among their friends.

Towards the end of her life, long after Jacques' death, Gwen wrote a memoir of her Cambridge childhood, *Period Piece**, first published in 1952 and still in print. Her grandfather, Charles Darwin, was already akin to a god:

> *Of course, we always felt embarrassed if our grandfather were mentioned, just as we did if God were spoken of. In fact, he was obviously in the same category as God and Father Christmas.*

---

*Period Piece, Gwen Raverat, New Hardback edition, Clear Press, 2003.

But *I* wasn't embarrassed for very long if he were mentioned – the family has me by the genes. I have discovered, for instance, that great diligence is required to keep the Darwin arrogance gene from infecting my outlook. This loftiness – that I am somehow immune from the repercussions visited upon ordinary mortals – has also been a key driver of the deep risk taking I was to find necessary to my practice as an addict.

In her recent biography* of my grandmother, Frances Spalding records an example of Gwen's father George displaying this swagger:

> *He was infuriated by the non-delivery of a telegram addressed 'Darwin, Cambridge', as a result of which Maud had missed seeing one of her sisters before her return to America. When the post office explained that he was not the only person named Darwin residing in Cambridge, and the lack of forename or initial had made it impossible to know for whom it was intended, George was so incensed he wrote a letter of complaint to The Times. Emma Darwin sympathised with him and wrote to Maud: 'How vexatious it was about the telegram . . . If Darwins are not known at Cambridge where are they to be heard of?'*

Being the great granddaughter of Charles Darwin has been more of burden than a matter of pride for my mother. Mostly she too has been embarrassed when he, or her mother, are mentioned. My attitude has been different: if I include myself, I can count 32 great great grandsons and 36 great great granddaughters of the National Treasure (his face *is* on the current ten pound note) that is Charles Darwin.

A fellow member of this Club of Thirty Two has recently warned me against the heretical tendency of claiming any direct advantage, loftiness or intelligence from being a descendent of a god of science. It is to be in error, and rather vulgar too. One must be subtle about it, let it happen by inference!

As an Awful Warning, he went on to tell me the story of the Fraudulent Darwin. Sotherby's needed to authenticate a collection of Darwinia. Research revealed that the objects had belonged to an errant member of the family who had left England under a cloud of sexual scandal in the twenties and had set himself up on the Australian lecture circuit as a genuine direct descendant of the great man (which he was) talking about his collection of the great man's scientific stuff (which it wasn't).

The lesson I was being given, I believe, is that one must not even

---

Gwen Raverat: Friends, Family and Affections, Frances Spalding, The Harvill Press, 2001.

contemplate making a living out of being a Darwin. One can write learned tomes about great great grandpapa with more likelihood of being published than most, but a Darwin must not set up shop selling unnatural selections!

The story I put before you is all me, driven, in part, by the weight of the expectations that being a scion of the Darwin dynasty drew upon my head. These expectations, that I be brilliant in whatever I did, can be added to the broth of reasons why I became a drug addict.

The Darwin genes for observation and enquiry were to be put to the one-pointed service of my addiction. In March 1792, Charles' grandfather Erasmus Darwin wrote in a letter: *A fool...is a man who never tried an experiment in his life.*

Charles Darwin was ours after all; we were of him. But Darwinian dogmas do not encourage any challenges being made to the dysfunction endemic in his own family. Everything must fit their ideology, which has little to say about the joys and pains of being evolved or of the illuminations of art. But Virginia Woolf was a central Bloomsbury pillar; my grandmama made elegiac woodcuts and Ralph Vaughan Williams was a Wedgwood and therefore a Darwin. They created sublime art, richly expressing human love and suffering. I have expended much energy, on the one hand, rejecting the rigours of the Darwin orthodoxy, while, on the other, loving the creative wealth into which I was born. It's this ambivalence that has plagued me: love and hate, respect and dismissal, flight and confrontation.

There was so much that seemed pointless and empty at home as well: the need to 'behave yourself' according to some unspoken system of rules that was never explained. Ah! That lack of explanation, that lack of a family myth, of intimacy! We had no religion but Darwin and Bloomsbury, the gods of science and art, no structure of the heart. In my teens it got to such a state that I could only relate to what love, care and affection my family *did* show with confused and aggressive ideas that it was arbitrary, entirely arbitrary that I was born to these particular parents with these particular sisters. The only bond was of irritation and awkwardness.

When sitting in the bath, with the steam around my ears, I would debate with myself why I, William, was not someone else. What on earth (or in heaven) determined that I should be 'I'? It was so lonely being William. Why couldn't I be someone else, why *wasn't* I someone else?

Already, I was not happy in my skin. Already I was adrift. Already I felt the effects of not being seen for what I, me, this was (whatever that was). Already I had an overweening sense of lack, a physical sensation in my belly. I wanted to go home, but I already was home. I wanted my mummy, but she was already there. I wanted to be happy, as I imagined everyone else to be.

Ingrid was our buxom Austrian girl-next-door au pair when I was 2 or 3. She wore dirndls and was well scrubbed. Some forty years later she had become a respected psychotherapist in Vienna and visited my mother when on holiday in England. When my mother told me that Ingrid remembered me fondly, there was an explosion of primal warmth in my heart. The vision of Ingrid's soft mothering breasts, of her loving attention, of her SEEING me, loving me.

It's not as if I was an only child. No, I have three sisters, one older. I am aware that some sibling relations in some families have some degree of warmth, closeness, support and sympathy. Not that we hate each other. Not that we love each other. But that, with the exception of the occasional outburst of extreme exasperation, we are largely indifferent to each other's fate. And sometimes a hand reaches out. And sometimes it is held.

The eldest, Emily, was a tomboy as I emerged from toddling. Was she compensating for the arrival of a boy? She could (and did) beat me hands down in any fight, verbal or physical. Only recently, when gathered to help my mother through a medical crisis and out for a walk along frostily crisp Devon lanes, did Emily tell me how she saw a counsellor once a week for ten years as a young adult. She drifted into her first marriage, she said, because she didn't exist. She thought me so alive! Little did either of us know!

The siblingarity with my younger sister, Lucy, was more nourishing. Such were the dynamics that I didn't take a lot of notice of her until we were in our teens. An attractive girl, a self-possessed artist who produces some extraordinary paintings in the post-naïve mould. Marriage to my friend Andrew transformed her into an occasionally irascible mother of four very tall children and a more determined artist.

And the youngest, Nelly: I was old enough to appreciate the drama of her arrival in the family and to dote on her: she was so sweet. But then the age gap meant we had little to do with each other later on, except around the time she married her filmmaker Philip Trevelyan, son of Julian, the painter, and Ursula Mommens, the potter.

This was the sub-Bloomsburian dynasty spreading, fulfilling its own measure of itself. As the only son, great things were expected of me. My academic prowess, or lack of it, mattered far more than did that of my sisters. They could always, and in fact did, get married and that would be Darwinian enough with regard to genes. Whereas

I had to excel to gain the full measure of my parents', especially my father's, love and approval. And I didn't excel; and I didn't get that love and approval. And I'll never know if there was a causal relationship between the two.

This family of mine! On the one hand you have the royalty of science and Bloomsbury, on the other the fading world of the English landed gentry. Every Christmas there was a gathering of the Pryor tribe at the Park, Uncle Johnny's palatial home in the ancestral village of Weston. With first and second cousins, this meant a crowd of over one hundred sitting down to Christmas cake and crackers and then drifting through to the ballroom where a fifteen-foot Christmas tree from the estate was surrounded by piles of presents. The talk among the grownups was frequently about the hunt ball or the shoot. For instance, how Johnny had accidentally shot his cousin Peter's dog, and he, in a fit of pique, had crept up to the Park early one morning and had shot one of Johnny's cats. For years they wouldn't talk to each other, taking it in turns to attend meetings of the parish council of which they were both members.

As the inevitably useless presents were distributed with much oohing and aahing and 'how simply gorgeous, it's just what I wanted', the uncles would circulate their nephews and stuff five pound notes into their breast pockets. It wasn't on to give actual presents on a man-to-man basis, but the little beggars had to have something didn't they?

One Christmas – I must have been 15 – Johnny had run out of fivers by the time he got to me, but promised he would put one in the post. I remember that I'd made a special effort, despite much protest, and had polished my shoes and had my hair cut. True to his word, the fiver arrived a few days later, wrapped up in a letter.

"Dear William," it opened. "Here is the five pounds I promised, I hope you'll use some of it at the barber's. When I was in the bag [he had been a prisoner of war], we had to keep our hair short in case of lice." And then more about personal cleanliness and respect for one's elders and the disgrace that is CND. I was incensed and returned his fiver with a righteous note. Not least because I had just been on my first CND march *some* of the way to Aldermarston in pursuit of a lovely girl, Cecilia Carter. Uncle Johnny and I didn't speak more than a few words ever again.

The Darwinian authority I had inherited, peering through an upper middle class desert of assumptions and muddled priorities, got me, at a very early age, questioning the mores of the Darwin-Bloomsbury nexus itself. They seemed such hypocrites. So much didn't make sense. I was, unconsciously, applying the principles they held most precious: question everything.

All male Pryors since gentry were gentry had been to Eton and Trinity Cambridge. To break the tradition would be to tempt the wrath of the gods and to suggest we didn't have domain over a reasonable chunk of the empire. To get into Eton you had to take the common entrance exam; common only in that all public schools used it. A key paper in the exam was Divinity: you had to demonstrate a fundamental understanding of the Bible to enter the ruling elite.

At one of my first enforced readings of the New Testament – I was eleven – I noticed that on one page this guy they were wittering on about was called Saul and on the next he was Paul. Obviously a misprint! I took my biro and corrected all the 'Paul's, making them 'Saul's. If a Darwin can't know how to edit the Bible, what can he know?

Uncle Matthew's son Francis, two weeks my junior and now the eminent MBE archaeologist saviour of iron-age artefacts in Flag Fen, had, like me, been put down for Eton at birth. (What a phrase: 'put down for Eton at birth' – like runt kittens!) He was also having problems with his Common Entrance.

A crammer had been found in Cumberland that could guarantee to get even the stupidest boy through. It was the only answer, especially after the results of my Eleven Plus exam had come through. I had been offered a place at Impington Village College. If I'd won a place at the Grammar School or the Perse, things might have been different, but Impington Village College!

The crammer was in a dour stone mansion at the end of a long tree-lined drive. It was near a town really called Aspatria. We would lie awake at night in the draughty, cavernous bedroom plotting our escape through enemy territory back to the South and a hero's welcome. But who would give us such a welcome? That was the problem. They'd only send us back again.

A long, cold winter of endless ploughing through of Latin and Divinity exam papers. So plaintive were the whimpers that penetrated the censorship of our weekly letters home, that my parents battled their way through blizzards and snow drifts to come and see me. This in the late fifties when roads were roads and not motorways, when cars had little sticky-out indicators and struggled over Sca Fell Pass, helped through the blizzards by gallant AA men who saluted, and fathers wore gabardine macs. They took me out for tea in Carlisle, and then bit their top lips and slithered home again, leaving me to work out my term of imprisonment.

And incarceration it was. Not so much being locked away, more being somehow punished for some unknowable sin, some worthlessness, some lack. "You are eleven years old and we, your loving parents, are leaving you here, three hundred miles from your home, in the snow and ice, because you have failed to learn some scripture we don't believe in either, not really." How could I understand this madness? I explained it, through an ache in my belly, as some mysterious, hidden error in the way I was, the marrow of my existence. A punishment that was all for my own good.

This is it: one of the roots of my angst and thus the predilection to addiction. It had a physical reality – a gnawing hole in my belly.

Both Francis and I passed our Common Entrance and were sent away to Eton to become gentlemen. From the start there was an elemental disjoint between the liberal cultured scientific atmosphere of home and the establishment county mindset of huntin', shootin' and fishin' that was Eton. My Cambridge home was about a life of the mind, whereas Etonians thought mainly about the death of pheasants. I could not understand why my father imagined there was any coherence between the two universes. I was miserable.

Non-scholarship boys like me lived in houses known by the initials of the housemaster, in my case P.H. for Peter Hazell. In the private language of Eton one did not talk about one's *house*, but about *m'tutor's*, not about *teachers*, but *beaks*, not about *terms*, but *halves*, not about one's house *matron*, but about one's *dame*.

As long as you were in the lower school (the first two years) you had to 'fag', that is carry out menial tasks for boys at the top of the ladder. Those in the *Library*, a self-elective body which constituted the power elite at the top of the house, had their own personal *fags*, boys who were assigned to cook their teas, warm their lavatory seats, run their errands, and so on.

I was in shock at how ludicrous and outrageous this tyranny was. It was unbelievable that this slavery should still be practised in the 20th century. And yet, and yet, I found it galling that I should fail to rise far enough up the system before I left to have my own fags to order about.

And tyranny it was: if you heard the shout of 'Boy!' after supper it could only mean that someone was going to be beaten. The wretched victim would be summoned before the members of *Library*. His misdemeanour would be read out – no excuses or appeal for mercy were allowed – and the senior boy (usually chosen for his athletic prowess) would point to a wooden chair in the centre of the room.

The culprit would bend over the back of the chair and grasp the wooden rail below the seat, so that his trousers were stretched tight over his bottom. Behind the door was an umbrella stand adapted to take canes. The captain selected a long one from the stand and gave a few practice swishes in the air. Sometimes he would even run a piece of chalk along the cane, so that he could aim for the same spot with each stroke. Sometimes he would move back three paces from the bottom, so he could take a little run at it.

As in my case, most Etonians' fathers had been there before them. They therefore knew full well that their twelve-year-old innocents would be exposed to fagging, beating and all the other barbarities they had experienced themselves (and at huge expense: current fees are in excess of £17,000 a year)! They struggle with rationalisations: "Didn't do me the slightest harm." "Made a man of me." What sort of man is that?

Great loyalty was expected towards the house in all sporting affairs. This was called *team spirit*. Peter Hazell was always telling us few slackers with food stains down our fronts that we never had enough of it. When the house side in any sport was doing badly, we were especially lacking in it, our support from the sidelines had been so pathetic. (I had such trouble with these abstract myths!)

The only nourishing relationship I knew at Eton was with Simon, who was from another house and was eighteen months older than me. In the eyes of the chaps, these two facts were enough to damn our friendship as being queer. It didn't bother us, and only served to harden our conviction that we were the only sane people in an insane institution. He was a fine draughtsman and we would go on long walks down by the Thames with our sketchpads and Gitanes. We were drawn together by our shared disdain for the school and its pursuits, but also because we stuck out like sore thumbs in our acquired shabbiness, apathy and weediness.

In some houses older boys were allowed to have record players, but Hazell, with his stern Quaker outlook, frowned on such decadence. The only way I could get to hear my Gerry Mulligan and Charlie Mingus records was by smuggling them into the music school when out on a 'run' to play them furtively on one of the official gramophones.

This was one thing I *did* learn at Eton: the necessity to go underground to have any contact with life. I was vainly and badly playing the part that had been thrust on me, the part I had been banished to Cumberland to earn. But I wasn't an Etonian. I didn't know what I was, but I wasn't a toff. The black rebellion and vitality of jazz spoke to me as the already developing scapegoat outsider who was devotedly casting himself out of the Darwin nexus, the family uprightness. Jazz's improvised immediacy was the refreshing opposite of the classical stiffness of home.

How strange: my heroes were black Americans: Charles Mingus, Ornette Coleman, John Coltrane, Albert Ayler, Cecil Taylor, Thelonious Monk! The only white was Gerry Mulligan and he was a junky. The vitality and the cerebral but visceral complexity of the pulses, but above all the improvisation itself – these were the excitements of jazz. Improvisation, at its best, say, in the hands of Coltrane, reveals an immediate, godlike creativity on the spot, in the moment. He built a phenomenal technique through hours of practice every day, so that when he launched into an improvisation on the simple but interesting melodic structure of *These Beautiful Things*, an ecstatic keening of pulse would happen in the flash of his soprano saxophone. As though he was uncovering what was there all along. And what was there was a blessedness, an authenticity!

After relentless petitioning, my parents said I could leave as soon as I'd done my O Levels. As a lost cause with the Etonian power brokers I had more time in which I could do as I liked, and was able to escape down to the Drawing Schools, a separate, single-storied building at the back of the Cadet Force's parade ground. Wilfred, the brother of the gay Russian spy and art historian Sir Anthony Blunt, was the Art Master. He provided me with sheets of hardboard and unlimited supplies of acrylic and oil paint with which I could indulge my urge for action painting. My knowledge of the form was limited to what I'd seen in a book of paintings from the New York Museum of Modern Art that had recently been given to my parents. Klee's Twittering Machine, Mondrian's Boogie Woogie and two things by Jackson Pollock grabbed me as visceral and real.

In my innocence, I thought I knew exactly how and why Pollock made his paintings, and decided that I could do it. After all, I didn't need to be a good draughtsman. Of course, it was true, I *did* know how and why he did it, but didn't know how I knew, or what. My first work was predominantly red and was built up by pouring the paint on, swilling it about, flicking it on, scraping with palette knives, and any other trick that occurred to me. I would wipe off most of what I'd done at the end of the day, leaving what struck me as 'good bits' with the rest looking like dirty borscht. I judged it to be finished when there were more 'good bits' than anything else and these had some kind of cohesion. It was an uncomfortable picture, in which some said they saw skulls, bulls and twisted faces.

My action painting was an urgent and abstract form of expression for what couldn't come out any other way. It was a making manifest of the turmoil that was my unconscious so that it might see itself: an intuitive splash of paint in the dark. There was also aspiration: as though I could wail like Albert Ayler[*] without first spending years in a very ordinary R&B band churning out endless twelve-bar blues, as he had. And he ended up dead in the New York East River at the age of 34, a blistering, scorching improviser from whose tenor the white heat of action-playing emotion poured.

The feeling at home was that my painting, my Albert Ayler, was not art, but something dangerous. My mother would ask what it 'meant'? I would make harrumphs of exasperation. If you gathered a thousand Charles Darwins in a room, each with a word processor, and made them type nonstop for ten years, would they eventually come up with the works of William Burroughs? I could not be doing with this constant call for meaning. Can't they simply be themselves, speak for themselves, these saxophone wails and acrylic outcries?

At the end of my last term, after finishing my O Levels, I was carrying the painting back to my room. I had to walk past one of the larger houses, some of whose sporting heroes were sunning their blazered torsos at the windows.

"What is that disgusting thing under your arm?" One of them shouted.

"Oh do come and have a look, Pryor's got some of his, what do you call it, modern art, with him. Which way up is it supposed to be?" Chorused another.

"What's it of, then? Look's like there's been an accident." And so on. Humiliation, but also the source of bitter defiance.

When I got the painting home to Cambridge, it started its stay in my bedroom. But my mother found it disturbing and, in my absence one day, moved it to the garage. And then later, when I came back from my first experiment in adult independence, I couldn't find it. She confessed that she had burnt it. Witches are burnt at the stake; my painting was chucked on the bonfire.

One proof of why I shouldn't be at Eton was Ant Stern, my best friend from prep school. He was the energetic son of a Czech émigré professor of German. He went to the Perse day school. They lived in the most marvellously modern house on the edge of a deep gravel-pit lake, just up the road from our house in Barton Road. He took up the trumpet early on and could play jazz on it – so grown up! With my Norwegian[†] cousin, Christian 'Poly' Hambro, we swam and ca-

---

*One of the giants of free jazz, Albert Ayler was also one of the most controversial. His huge tone and wide vibrato were difficult to ignore and his 1966 group sounded like a runaway New Orleans brass band from 1910.
†My mother's sister had married a Nordic hero.

noed in the boat Grandmama kept for her grandchildren underneath her home, the Old Granary* and later Ant and I shared Charlie Mingus' blasting jazz and the rites of passage towards girls. He was proof of how advanced you could be if you didn't go to Eton or any other public school!

After the Cumberland crammer, I hung out with Ant, feeling a little more grownup. I invited him to the Footlights Review, an annual undergraduate comedy show put on at the end of the academic year. It was keenly anticipated; the tickets were my most prized possessions for weeks.

Come the night, Ant just didn't show up, no phone call, no message, no nothing. I was heartbroken, which was only exacerbated by his ignoring me for some time afterwards. I never did discover what happened, but, at the time, felt it had more than a little to do with me going away to school and not being as cool as him.

When we met up again recently Ant took me out to lunch. After an excited preamble, we both quickly hit the same target: Why didn't he show up? He said he couldn't remember, no reason really. But filed next to a memory of me, was the fact that he didn't show up.

Strangely, it was as I cycled home alone from the Arts Theatre that night that my bicycle lamp picked up something odd on the gravel path on Coe Fen. I stopped and put my bike down. It was a bird. A baby bird, but large. It was hurt, but alive, making a squawking noise. I picked it up, put it my cycle basket and took it home. My father was very clear as to what it was: a baby cuckoo. Its adopted parent must have rebelled and thrown it out of the nest.

I decided to keep it in my room in a shoebox. It was always hungry. Jazz would soothe it for a while. It liked milk, but could never get enough through the syringe I had to use to feed it.

Out of the confusion of culture, science, snobberies and constipation I was compelled to create something new. Luckily there were others in the same rock and roll. Once I left Eton I drifted into a simpatico group back home in Cambridge whose social life revolved around the El Patio coffee bar and the Kenya Coffee House.

Amongst the El Patio regulars were Richard Eyre, an early adopter of the leather jacket route to coolness and now knighted; Syd Barrett, the acid troubadour; David Gale, who was later to start the experimental theatre company *Lumiere and Sons*; Roger Waters, driv-

---

*Just by the Silver Street Bridge, now part of Darwin College.

ing force of *Pink Floyd*; Ant Stern, who was to be an experimental film maker of repute and, later still, a glass blower; Andrew Rawlinson, professional philosopher and concrete poet; and Storm Thorgerson, who would design all *Pink Floyd*'s record covers. But the high priest of our social rituals was Nigel, keeper of the El Patio cappuccino machine and dispenser of the exotic substance in Pyrex glass cups.

In *Light Blue with Bulges,** a novel by a fellow El Patio lounge lizard, Nick Sedgwick, Nigel is lightly disguised as Andy. It was Nigel's vespa that was light blue and had bulges. Nick writes:

> On first sight Andy was a real smoothie, but he had two O levels, knew jazz, and he worked the machine... On the scale of good looks he rated at least a ten, and with a ton of upper-crust charm he gave the impression that butter wouldn't melt in his mouth. Naturally, the impression was false...
>
> We hit it off almost at once. More than anything else he had style. He wore tinted glasses, a leather jacket with proper lapels and a vent at the back, drainpipe jeans, and snakeskin winkle-pickers: all those things my folks wouldn't have me seen dead in. What was the secret, I asked him during an afternoon break.
>
> "Well Ned," he said slowly. "I hope this won't alter your attitude towards me, but you're looking at the product of a broken home..." He got up, smiling broadly, and walked back behind the counter to serve a customer. I watched him work the machine, brewing coffee with untrammelled verve and swagger.

Nigel and I, now in our fifties, are still brothers-in-arms, forty years after we first met. Back then, just as with Nick, Nigel's intelligent, self-assured style went to the core of the matter. With Nigel, it was a calling: his life was his art, a way of being a troubadour. I was invited round to the house he shared with his divorced and glamorous mother. We would get stoned in his room, listen to the muscular music of Mingus, write poems and know stoned transcendence.

Nigel was another errant public school boy, while most of the others had gone to local schools of varying social standing. Unlike me at Eton, Nigel had had a relatively good time at Oundle. He was able to achieve a measure of popularity by being hip. He had actually formed a poetry society there and put on jazz concerts. The greatest irony was that he had put on a gig by Humphrey Littleton, Old Etonian jazzer, who would never have been invited to play at his alma mater.

Along with Gene Vincent, Buddy Holly, Bill Hailey, Cliff Richards and Elvis, we didn't just plop out of childhood as small grownups,

---

*Now out of print, but originally published by Fourth Estate.

complete with trilbies or perms. No, we were teenagers, emulating James Dean in an angst emphasised with purple hearts and grass.

Andrew, Nigel and I, in particular, were also Dadaists, pulled by the Merz of Kurt Schwitters. As Tristan Tzara said in his *Dadaist Manifesto*, we were new men:

> *Rough, bouncing, riding on hiccups. Behind them a crippled world and literary quacks with a mania for improvement. I say unto you: there is no beginning and we do not tremble, we are not sentimental.*

The anarchy, the breaking of bounds, vital expression that could not be codified. We had to overthrow what had gone before: the stiff, uptight, square, inexpressive and repressed world of the BBC Home Service, Bronco waxed lavatory paper and everyone knowing their place. It had to be done, for the hiccups we were riding.

The period of our El Patio revolution, pre Stones, Beatles and Pink Floyd, shouldn't be called the early sixties, even though that is what it was. In flavour it was really the fifties in disguise – grey repressed urges with modernity breaking through in Radio Luxembourg, the Goon Show and the Dansette record player (before this appeared we had to play records on huge things called radiograms). Class and prejudice still ruled and separated, but the El Patio gang hung out with black and white GIs from nearby airforce bases and occasional hip Jamaicans. A revolutionary act. I was what Norman Mailer called a 'White Negro'. I lived to be cool at all times, as were our black friends, man, dangerous and cool!

Pot cost, at most, £7 an ounce. Not many native-born English people had any idea what it was, let alone smoked it. It was associated with jazz musicians, blacks and the dwellers of the edges of the ruling ethos. We were convinced, beyond any question of doubt, that the law was an ass in respect of marijuana, which was obviously far less harmful than the officially sanctioned drug, alcohol. Any law that was so obviously silly deserved to be broken.

But my parents didn't see it that way. My father argued that I shouldn't smoke it simply because it was illegal, quite apart from any consideration of its effect on one's health. I retorted that that was nonsense and used to leave my hash and pot hanging around in my room, quite openly, daring them to have me caught.

The life I was connecting to was not at home, but at the El Patio. We were definitely not going to be younger versions of our parents: science, high art, war, the Festival of Britain were all as dull as spam and chips. We were something entirely new: teenagers who drank cappuccino.

I think it was in Pete Downing's bedsit that I smoked my first joint. He was my driving instructor, fussing that I hold the joint correctly between the knuckles of my cupped hand, showing how the cigarette papers should be stuck together to roll a good spliff and how to make a proper cardboard filter. As I smoked, he would ask how I felt, like a nervous parent watching their child pedal solo on a two-wheel bike for the first time.

DRUG PUSHER CLAIMS ANOTHER INNOCENT VICTIM. Not a bit of it. He was sharing his main delight, his rhapsody, his discovery, so much more health promoting than booze. And it was our own, we were pioneers, found life good, that our eyes could see visions in the weave of a carpet, that our ears could hear convoluted cool in the music of the *Soft Machine* and fairy glens of whimsy in the mad songs that Syd Barrett wrote for our house band, the *Pink Floyd*.

Of course Pete's whole mien only served to heighten this. His role in the group was that of the connoisseur, the dope gourmet, but also that of alchemist prepared to share his philosopher's stone, to open the consciousness of his friends to undiscovered dimensions. He wanted nothing in return, only to be there in the sharing.

He had somehow wangled a subscription to MIMMS, a journal usually restricted to the medical profession that listed all currently available pharmaceuticals as they came on the market. From this he would work out which drugs, still available without prescription, would give a buzz when taken in controlled overdose or in unlikely combinations. He would dole out the pills in their multicoloured combinations: this combination would give an 'impertinent little high', that an 'interesting speed-like effect'.

Not yet seventeen, we were beginning to make connections with the international Beat scene that stretched through London to Paris, New York, San Francisco, Tangiers and later Kathmandu, revolving around such figures as William Burroughs, Brion Gysin, George Andrews and Allen Ginsberg. It was Ian Somerville, a Cambridge connection to Burroughs and Gysin, who had invented the Flicker Machine for use by the international doperati. The one in Pete's room was made from an ancient electric variable speed gramophone in a long-legged wooden cabinet. A silvered cardboard cylinder was placed on the turntable with a powerful spot lamp suspended in the middle. Just below the level of the lamp, vertical slots were cut into the cylinder, their width and spacing being precisely calculated.

By sitting with your lightly closed eyes pressed to the viewing slot cut into the cabinet, you got a strong flickering of light on the retina. By careful manipulation of the speed control it was possible to make the flicker correspond exactly with one's alpha rhythm, the frequency (8 to 12 hertz) at which bursts of electrical energy pass messages from the retina to the cerebral cortex. When an external source of light hits the retina at exactly this frequency, either visual hallucinations of remarkable symmetry and purity of colour occur, or an epileptic fit is sparked off. The idea was to get just nicely spaced out with a joint or two and then sit for as long as one could take it in front of the vision machine.

Despite this infernal machine and drugs and jazz, our social gatherings were not all that different from those of the squares. Instead of blunting our awareness of each other with alcohol, and falling into the usual patterns of wit and common gripe, we indulged in a ritual that to some degree bonded everyone into a coherent communality, able to participate in a shared experience. But this sense of togetherness, which seemed so strong and important, in fact clouded over the fact that we actually did and said very little. It is an observable fact that confirmed potheads are poor conversationalists.

The coherent communality had its dark side too: the horrors or paranoia, an invisible barrier between you and everyone else that was fear, fear that you were missing out, that you were being subtly excluded from the shared experience, or that, worst of all, some shared dislike was being directed solely at you. Such fears are obsessional and bring out the worst effect of pot or hash – that the high is uncontrollable, that it flows where it will, and that, in its heightening of awareness, it is indiscriminating. The mind that is prone to morbid or neurotic fears is expanded to the same degree as the more stable one, and the sensitivity to such fears is correspondingly increased.

But it didn't occur to me to stop smoking the stuff. My need to be thought to belong to the group was too strong, and the group held the smoking of marijuana as their central sacrament.

It has no clear origin, the predilection that became my addiction. Being a beatnik Darwin teenager in sixties Cambridge was one aspect of it, but the imbalances and disquiets, a chronic pain of being, were much older, traceable back to my first months of life.

This whorl of the community – the scientific and cultural elite – that I was growing up in, was too constricting, too hypocritical, too morally ambiguous and I had to adopt the addict position, to vomit in the doors of my tribe's perception and rationality. "But you're so intelligent! You come from such a *nice* family!"

Placing equally passionate emphasis on all three words, I would beseech my parents: "Can't you see?" with a barely restrained hysteria. A rhetorical question, because I knew they couldn't see the need for Munch's Scream or Coltrane's sheets of saxophone. The pain I was showing them had no locus nor rationale. I couldn't see the emperor's clothes; they couldn't see my pain.

I was spoken for, as the word implies. For twelve years I focused on obtaining and putting chemicals – from opium to alcohol – into my body to change how I felt, to blank out the very pain of being an addict. My addiction was inextricably an expression of the unconscious pain, the unrealised fury, the unspoken frustration endemic in the Darwin-Wedgwood-Bloomsbury nexus into which I had been born. I was the scapegoat.

Addiction feeds on itself: you need the stuff to wipe out the pain of needing the stuff. There's plenty of other pain to start with, pain that loves the comfort of the drug. But just as recreational use turns into a habit so all those miseries get subsumed into the one-pointed vexation of being hooked.

I got hooked in 1963 at the age of 18 and plummeted rapidly towards an addict's death until the age of 30, when, somehow, the chemical influx stopped. But the shape of my whole life since has been sculpted by those twelve years.

In a letter to Jacques Raverat, my grandfather, Virginia Woolf wrote: *I feel that for us writers the only chance now is to go out into the desert and peer about, like devoted scapegoats, for some sign of a path.* They didn't know they were doing it. But then they never do. Loading me with the sins of dysfunction, then sending me out into the wilderness beyond the city walls to die. Nor did I know I was acquiescing, but the hurt inside of me *told* me to be devoted.

I could point to my pram and being left to bawl my head off far longer than was required by the baby care book of the day. There's the psychotherapeutic notion of 'being seen' and the anger that I wasn't, at all, and therefore had little notion of who or what I was. But the scapegoat model has far greater emotional truth: I had to cart the family's pain out of the city in a bag marked 'addict'.

How could a member of such a privileged, comfortable and liberal family become a junky? In the end the theories don't do it – it is a mystery that theorising doesn't ever quite satisfy. Judging by appearances, my family and my upbringing were a lot less dysfunctional than most. I wasn't locked in cupboards, beaten, starved, sodomised or otherwise abused. But the pain and the anger were strong enough to drive me to extremes.

The *appearance* of hunky doryness was a large part of the problem. Because it wasn't, and yet family and friends thought it was. And thought I was being unreasonable to suggest otherwise. I would keep on pleading: "Can't you see?" And they couldn't. They were so taken up with being who they thought they were, taking it for granted that I would be excellent at whatever I did. I was a great great grandson of a god, wasn't I?

> Around 3400 BC the opium poppy is cultivated in lower Mesopotamia.
> The Sumerians refer to it as Hul Gil, the 'joy plant'.

Holding a baby chanterelle mushroom in Sweden in 1963.

2 GIRLS AND NIGHTS ERRANT

I was commuting to a crammer in London to do my A levels. We'd moved from Barton Road to a Victorian mansion set in an acre of garden in Chaucer Road, an easy bike ride from the station. I found a shortcut I could take across some shunting yards that saved a good five minutes off the journey. One day a man with a PVC British Rail cap stopped me and asked what I thought I was doing on British Rail property. Did I know that trains were shunted there and I might get knocked down?

"It's quite all right my man, I'm a member of the British Empire," I replied. He looked at me in amazement.

"Oh sorry sir, didn't realise. You should've said." He tipped his cap in deference. I couldn't quite believe it, but obviously my years at Eton had not been entirely wasted.

The evenings and weekends were my own: Miller's jazz club on Fridays, the Dorothy Ballroom on Saturdays, Dave Gale's house. But the main fuelling station was Storm's. Storm Thorgerson was and is another matter. I think his father was Norwegian, hence the name, though he was English enough. Like Nigel, his mother was 'advanced', treated him like an equal, and gave him the run of their small terraced house in the centre of Cambridge. He had a large, sparsely furnished room on the first floor front where we hung out for many hours. Storm was and is an imposing man, not his physical presence, but his biting wit and indomitable self-assurance. I was frightened of him, then. But the boy done good, using his graphic art skills to design all Pink Floyd's as well as other leading bands' record sleeves.

It was his cutting certainty of opinion that I was awestruck by. He knew, I mean *knew*, so much. He led. It was Storm that introduced us to Bob Dylan. Storm, Andrew Rawlinson, Roger Waters and Syd Barrett all went to the same school in Cambridge.

An idyll of the late romantic puberty period: Syd sitting opposite me in a punt with his twelve-string guitar, playing a beguiling fluency of blues-tinged capriccio, as Andrew punted us through the wooded bit of the river behind the Newnham nurses home towards Grantchester Meadows. Fifty years earlier my grandmama's friend Rupert Brooke had written about Grantchester: *Stands the clock at a quarter to three? And is there honey still for tea?*   Such puntings would lead Roger Waters to write this lyric for Pink Floyd's evocative song *Grantchester Meadows:*

> *In the lazy water meadow*
> *I lay me down.*
> *All around me*
> *Golden sunflakes settle on the ground*
> *Basking in the sunshine of a bygone afternoon*
> *Bringing sounds of yesterday into this city room.*
> *Hear the lark and harken*
> *To the barking of the dog fox gone to ground.*
> *See the splashing of the kingfisher flashing to the water*
> *And a river of green is sliding unseen beneath the trees*
> *Laughing as it passes*
> *Through the endless summer making for the sea.*

Nigel organised a series of poetry readings, which he called *Contrasts,* in an upstairs room of the Horse and Groom. He tried to have at least one local poet reading alongside the heavyweight beats he invited from London and Liverpool, all later to be contributors to Mike Horovitz's Penguin anthology *The Children of Albion* – people like Roger McGough, Adrian Mitchell and Pete Brown.

"How would you like to read at the next one, William? I'm running a bit short of local poets," said Nigel one night when walking along King Street. I was knocked off balance. I stuttered. It would give entirely the wrong impression of squareness to tell him I'd not written anything in the seven years since my prep school. Though poetry was, in the sixties, a far more listened-to communication, my experience at Eton temporarily banished any romanticism, any

Nigel and I selling poems at the Cambridge Corn Exchange

thought of poetry. Nigel now enabled me to reclaim that certainty of the heart that is the poet's.

I gathered myself: "Thanks, yes, well, I'd like to." And I was trapped. The creativity worm had found some more compost. The reading was some weeks away. Time enough for me to dash off a few mannered poems.

But they clapped, the audience actually clapped, and from then on I took the role of poet to my bosom. To be appreciated for being a poet: maybe this was the nourishment the cuckoo had been looking for. I began to read Ferlinghetti, Corso, Ginsberg, Carlos Williams and others. The Beats were subversive, spoke for the spirit exploited by a corrupt and materialistic society. They owed it no allegiance. They were of the moment, in the now, celebrating the suchness of the experience before them.

Being a poet was not like having a job or career; more like being a priest, a shaman. For one thing you could never go on holiday, since you could not avoid taking all your poesy with you. It was so easy (that was both the exhilaration and the trouble); it was just words. We all knew the message, but finding the medium was the thing. Cocteau said that the poet never asks for admiration; he wants to be believed.

Hold back the edges of your gowns, Ladies, we are going through Hell, William Carlos Williams wrote in his foreword to Allen Ginsberg's *Howl*:

I saw the best minds of my generation destroyed by madness, starving hysterical naked,
dragging themselves through the negro streets at dawn looking for an angry fix,
angelheaded hipsters burning for the ancient heavenly connection to the starry
dynamo in the machinery of the night...

Girls entered the arena. There was Henrietta Garnet, daughter of one David Garnet who had once been Virginia Woolf's bi-sexual lover Duncan Grant's lover, if you see what I mean. Henrietta was in fact very Bloomsbury to look at: long flowing dresses, long thin face. There was a moment on the grand staircase at Chaucer Road when I was trying to explain how much I loved her, but my sister Lucy kept interrupting.

There was Faith Hardy, the art student daughter of a retired Anglican bishop in Raj India. But that didn't last long. Though we would have much to do with each other in later life.

And then at a rave-up at the Dorothy, very hot and sweaty, I noticed a petite and attractive girl who didn't seem to be with anyone in particular. She wore that futurist style that came from Courreges. We danced for a while. Before very long we went off into the night together. It worked: the interest was mutual. Jenny was her name and we soon became established at the Kenya as a couple. Our first social act together was to visit my good friend Nigel, who was uninvolved at the time. There were pills, some plonk and definitely hash. We talked, enjoyed, talked some more and listened to records.

At about ten, Nigel said he was incredibly hungry and why don't we have some fish and chips. The chippy was just round the corner. I wasn't that eager, what with the amphetamine, and said I'd stay and probably play the new record by a new mind-blowing group called the *Rolling Stones*. Jenny said she could do with some air and went with Nigel. It took them two hours to come back with the fish and chips.

Jenny rang just before our next date to say she had to go to her grandmother's. I didn't go out with her again. Not till a meeting was arranged between the three of us ten days later, did I allow myself to understand what had happened. They have been together ever since.

Now here there be sensual pleasures, yonder a veritable slough of

despond and in the far distance a flickering light. Anita Reeve, above all else, was sexy. Long black hair, slightly turned up nose, a taut, long, delicious body, with heavy eye make-up, as was the style of Dusty Springfield, with false eyelashes. Almost a fantasy woman, with chirpy voice, edgy vitality and street-wise credibility. We met in the Kenya where it took nerve to approach her, sitting in the ambience in which she flowered, blowing her cigarette smoke towards the ceiling, her

Anita (photo by Anthony Stern soon after she left me)

leather overcoat. She stirred my libido with her skilful titillating of the game whose prize would seem to be that we are loved.

She hardly noticed my presence. Her hairdo, eyes, calculated sophistication and high-heeled boots. Oh how those high-heeled boots linger in the memory! It wasn't cool to acknowledge too much. As Langston Hughes wrote for a Mingus jazz poem: *Let me be cool, please let me be cool!* Being cool was everything. To know the right things, to have the hippest opinions, to deeply dig the right music ahead of anyone else, to dress sharply, to have Anita on your arm. This was cool. And to be a poet as well, this was deep cool.

But she did, she noticed me, she went out with me! Although I knew it couldn't really be her scene, she said she would go to Miller's jazz club with me. I would be, I was, the envy of my friends. And could she jive! Even though it was Dick Heckstall-Smith and Art Theman playing beefy post bebop, rather than the *Stones* or *Beatles*, she could jive like she'd invented it. Conversation was difficult. She didn't get what the Beats were about, but what our young and beautiful bodies did for each other was too important for that to matter much. Anyway, she was beat in her attitude, her accoutrement, her style.

We soon became an institution at Dave's, Storm's and the Kenya. It felt good to go into the Criterion with her on my arm. The assorted hipsters, defiant undergraduates, and GIs who packed the place on Saturday nights were impressed. The dynamics of our relationship, apart from the considerable physical chemistry, was that, to her I was deep, classy, an escape from the housing estate, while to me, she was desirable, enjoyable, bringing me social kudos and a fulfilment of my macho delusions. I was well ahead of my peers; that was part of the point. But we couldn't take each other home. Class barriers wouldn't allow it.

Andrew and I began to search for some answers to deeper questions, for some explanations of the whole thing: wisdom, as well as deconstruction, was attractive. And the more exotic, the more other to the great gods of Darwin and Bloomsbury the better. So books like the *I Ching* and the *Tibetan Book of the Dead* became the road maps to the new way of being, the manuals to the unrelenting war. You can hear the *I Ching* in the lyrics of Syd Barrett and of the Incredible String Band; it was in the weft of our explorations. That no less an eminence than Carl Jung had written the preface to it, and indeed had also written *Synchronicity,* a book explaining its mechanics, proved to us that we were right. And, perhaps most important of all, our parents did not understand.

And one day Andrew said that a real live Tibetan Lama, Trungpa Rimpoche, who had escaped from Tibet when the Chinese invaded, would be giving an audience to explain his teachings. This was at the edges of the known universe. Sitting cross-legged in front of a visitor from Tibetan outer mind space was further confirmation that we were forging the right path.

The house in Chaucer Road backed onto Coe Fen, an expanse of grassed flatland with fingers of unspoiltness, cow grazing and willow trees that penetrate as far as Barton Road one way and the Old Granary the other. Both branches of the river run through this common, and we had only to cross the footbridge over the stream that was the boundary of the garden and we were within ten minutes bike ride of the city centre. The house itself was palatial, built in 1895 for an organ-playing academic. This was when dons were first allowed to marry, freeing them to establish themselves in great houses.

My father was a keen, if unorthodox, gardener. He grassed over all flowerbeds, allowing his exotic peonies and bulbs a more natural setting. He built up hillocks with the spoil from the water-garden he dug next to the stream. We called it his bog. In it were delicate concrete bridges with concrete hands protruding from the sides (moulded with washing-up gloves). He matched his delight for food, wine and dinner parties in the decor of the dining room, which had a crimson ceiling and a black end wall with gold griffins embossed on it.

Chaucer Road was a busy place. My mother would put together a delicious ratatouille at the drop of a hat and the bread was usually her own. I could invite anyone to a meal without telling her. My father's elderflower wine was legendary. There was much interplay with the other Cambridge dynasties, academic families of renown, and we would go off on expeditions to places like the Devil's Dyke or the secret wood where the rare oxslips grew.

There were musical evenings. My father played the flute, my mother the piano and violin, and my sisters played piano, cello and flute. They would make up quartets and quintets with friends. I was banished because I 'could not sit still'.

Sounds idyllic! Not a dysfunctional mote in that beam. I know it is difficult to understand how someone from such a privileged and stimulating background could become a heroin addict. But in many ways, that is precisely the point. The anger, the hurt, the lack of being *seen* were well hidden. Saying, "Can't you see?" as I would when trying to explain the truth of the pointlessness of Beckett's tramps or of the harrowing power of Ayler's saxophone screams just went to demonstrate my selfishness, my self-indulgence. The role of scapegoat is a self-fulfilling one: a positive feedback loop.

From the age of about fourteen my instruments were the record-player and the naïve piano. My piano is instinctive and untutored. I can't read music or play a tune. I was inspired to this by the discovery of the music of Cecil Taylor. His playing occupies a space so different from any other pianist, jazz, classical or blues. He is the keyboard Jackson Pollock: his apparent disregard for the rules, his lightening speed and pulse, his way of getting apparently impossible colours, textures and effects from the physical instrument.

So I just sat at my mother's Steinway and doodled and before long the blueish and discordant, but funky shapes showed themselves and the pulse that drove McCoy Tyner and Cecil Taylor was there. Ant Stern would bring his trumpet round when I knew my parents would be out and we would jam. How precociously advanced we were!

"Awful rubbish, dreadful noise," was the response I got. But I enjoyed it. I was becoming a naïve improviser. Later I was to discover that there were others who had the same approach as I did to making music, just playing, no tune, no key, no time signature, whether they had been trained or not. They were playing what is called Improvised Music. I actually got paid for making it once.

They let me leave Eton after my O Levels. I was doing endless A level papers at a crammer in Notting Hill. It was 1962. A fellow crammee and I abruptly realised it was the Fourth of June, the day of the grand gathering of the county and ruling elites at Eton. Nick lent me his oilskin jacket and with our grimy jeans and tatty shoes we looked the very image of early sixties beatniks.

We were soon amongst the flowery hats, the gushing voices, the bloodshot colonels, the champagne picnics, the Rolls Royces and all the other clutter of the upper crust en fête. We made for the cricket where I remembered the heaviest hobnobbing to be. We sat on a bench, enjoying the sun, watching the passing parade of England's top people.

Then, before I could escape, I saw my uncle Matthew with family in

An Etonian family in full bloom, photographed on the day of our visit.

tow. His eldest son, Francis, was still at the school. As he approached, he managed to overcome a fleeting look of despair. He raised his rolled brolly and poked my oilskin jacket.

"Where are all your badges, then?" He asked, amiably enough.

"What badges do you mean?" I really didn't know what he was on about.

"You know, your ban the bomb badge and all that sort of thing."

"I don't belong."

"Oh." He was temporarily lost for words. "Suppose you couldn't stay away? I find most of this such a bore, but one must play one's part, I suppose."

Before long they ambled off into the throng. As we were settling down to a pleasant, sunbaked state of amazement that these people really existed, I noticed a man pointing a camera at us. He was trying to sneak shots of us without our knowing. How rude!

"You were taking photos of us, weren't you?" I asked him with an Etonian aggression.

Über cool on the 4th of June (that's me on the right).

"Yeah." He was American. "I guess so." He didn't look it.

"I'm Loomis Dean." I shook his outstretched hand, suppressing a smirk at his extraordinary name.

"Why were you trying to hide the fact that you were taking photos of us?"

"Well... look, I'll level with you guys, if you give me the dope I'm looking for. I'm from *Life Magazine* and we're doing an article on British High Society in summer. I'm curious, well, why a couple of guys like you, you know what I mean, what you're doing here?"

By the time we got back into the routine of old exam papers again the next day we had forgotten all about the incident. I was amazed when I saw the article in *Life* a few months later. A whole half-page photo of us looking thoroughly disreputable.

My disquiet was forming a hard scar tissue, giving me a bitter confidence as poet, an angry Darwinian authority that was paper-thin. The time had come for me to express my newfound freedom by leaving home. I had done my A levels and would brook no objections from my parents. I would now go out into the world as an adult, while I waited for my results. By a different course, Nigel had come to the same point and had found himself a room in a rabbit warren of a place above the Hang Chow restaurant in Petty Cury.

This was long before they pulled down the whole of that side of the street for redevelopment, also destroying the famous Red Lion Hotel whose ballroom with its bouncing floor was the site of many jazz sessions.

There was another room available, the nearest one could get to a proper artist's garret this side of the channel, and I moved in. I had my jazz records, my *I Ching*, *Howl*, the Don Allen anthology of American Poetry, a Persian carpet borrowed from home, a gas ring, a bed. All I needed to start the adventure-experiment. Anita would come and stay the night whenever she could make appropriate excuses at home. Nigel shared an enormous room at the end of the corridor with Johnny Johnson, a tall, thin, rather haggard American. He was intense in his approach to grass, to poetry, to the whole alternative life style. That this epitome of hip should accept us and want to share our explorations was too much, man.

At one stage I used the desk that sat between the two sets of beams that came up through the floor of the big room. I would sit there, after a good many joints, and churn out poem after poem, handing them to Nigel and Johnny through the beams.

"There, that's another one."

"Jeez, William, don't you ever stop, I mean, man, that's the third this evening." That was what I needed. Johnny knew precisely what a beatnik needed to hear.

"Shall I read it? D'you want to hear it?"

"We can't stop you, can we?" But he would add, "yeah, come on then." I would read them the latest gem, the sparkling raindrop that still dazzled my eyes and they would sit around saying "yeah man, right on," and I would feel I had got it right on and would go on to the next spontaneous poem. Poetry for effect; poetry that, in its successful moments, would catch a meaninglessness that had meaning.

It was a heady time. The subversive day Pete Downing arrived with a sleeping bag filled with pot from Tangiers. He unrolled it on the floor. The dope was two inches deep along the entire length of the bag, enough to keep our heads alight for months, if not years. Having put back enough for the Cambridgistas' requirements for the next few months, Pete, for some reason lost in the smog of dope smoke, decamped to Oxford where he decided to hide the plastic-wrapped sleeping bag cache in a tree somewhere in the countryside outside that city.

Nigel and Jenny were sharing a house with him. One day a guy showed up who was, it turned out, Pete's partner in the dope smuggling. He demanded to see his cache, so Pete drove him into the countryside. Pete's report to Nigel of what happened next was surreal and chilling. They couldn't find the tree. After hours of looking, the partner got rather upset.

"I ran him over." Pete said it in such a way that we didn't dare ask him why or what happened to the guy. I think I believed him and had no intention of asking him to elaborate. It was too scary. Foreshadowings of future criminality.

Soon came the day we knew we must take our Dadaist vision out to the people. Our new confidence found its strongest expression in the poems we were writing and in our love for jazz as the ideal music of immediacy. I approached Dick Heckstall-Smith and Art Theman who had both said they were interested in experimenting with a mixture of jazz and poems. They brought in Bamber Gascoigne's brother Brian on vibes and Chris Bateson on trumpet.

After a few tryouts, we felt we had enough fluency in this new medium to put on a public concert. The small room of the Guildhall was hired and posters printed. We called it *Roodmoodments*. We developed a precise schedule for the concert: six minutes for this jazz-poem, fourteen for the tape-collage, eight for Nigel's piece, fifteen for the band to blow. We looked forward to the evening with some trepidation, but mostly a sense of excitement that this would be some kind of watershed in the performing arts.

The only precedence that we knew about was *Red Bird,* a record by Christopher Logue. It was flat, unexciting with little interaction between the poet and the musicians.

Dick Heckstall-Smith with John Mayall on piano.

Scotty, the Vespa and Nigel.

We would get beyond that by using poetry as jazz and vice versa. What a revolution we were unleashing: three poets and a jazz quintet blurring the boundaries between music, poem and performance! In 1963 it was unprecedented.

But while we planned and fretted over the concert, my love life was taking several twists and turns. The greater my confidence in my role as subversive poet, as cultural revolutionary, the worse I treated Anita. I would let her come and stay a couple of nights, and emphasis there on the 'let', then would get fed up with her stupidity, always after we'd made love, and make out that I couldn't get on with my important work with her sitting around, looking bored.

"Look, I won't make a noise, promise. I'll just sit here in the corner and read a book. You won't know I'm here." Anita would say, but I couldn't accept it. She couldn't possibly want to read a book, and I would tell her to go, again. A few days later I'd get randy and lonely. I would buy her some black lingerie and persuade her to come back for a night or two, but the whole charade would only repeat itself.

Despite demanding complete loyalty from Anita, I was not averse to playing the field. The witheringly beautiful and dazzlingly clever Marina Warner, on her way to becoming a television intellectual and author, was then the girlfriend of Brian Gascoigne, the vibes player for *Roodmoodments*. He threw a smart party for her seventeenth birthday in Kings. I gate crashed and – a great coup – monopolised her for the majority of the evening. She inspired an all-demanding love.

So, I thought, did I with her. But she was hard to get on the phone for the next week and I had no way of confirming it. When I did manage to talk to her and persuade her to come up to the Hang Chow, it had all begun to fizzle. She shunned my clumsy advances. The lid was finally blown when she invited me home to meet mummy and daddy. She had won an exhibition to Oxford at seventeen, and was not playing the same game as me. She saw no need to leave home, to claim premature independence, and any romance with her would have to be conducted with the usual weapons of theatre, restaurants, maybe dances – that whole thing – somewhere a committed revolutionary couldn't go.

I don't know how much Anita knew of this episode, but she was getting increasingly disillusioned with the way I treated her. She started to go out with other dudes, which made me insanely jealous. I would chase round all the Saturday night parties on my bicycle searching for her, but without much luck.

Until there she was, smooching with Scotty, a GI well known on the social scene. They saw me and they looked back at each other as though they'd prepared a stratagem for just this eventuality. They didn't stop dancing. It was intolerable; she even had the nerve to wear her high-heeled boots for the guy. I went up to them as soon as the music stopped.

"Anita, can I have a word with you?"

"Don't mind me," said Scotty not shifting an inch, his arms still round her waist, her arms still on his shoulders.

"Anita," I persisted, "will you come out into the kitchen so I can talk to you. I need to talk to you." I looked as soulful and hard done by as I could. It had always worked before.

"Can't you see, I'm with Scotty. Why don't you piss off?" I couldn't believe it: that old panic was returning; someone I'd been taking for granted was telling me to go away.

"But Anita, I…" The music started up again and they started to jive, forcing me to the side of the room. He almost jived as well as I did. I went out into the kitchen and got drunk. Whatever our relationship had been was over, although I couldn't bring myself to admit it for some weeks.

Roodmoodments finally came round. To be stoned was to be more sensitive to all the movements of such an event, to the nuances of the music and the audience, and so we got stoned, far too stoned, before

we went to the Guildhall. One of the reasons for the precise schedule was that it shouldn't have mattered how stoned we were, we would
just follow the plan and everything would come off all right. But
when we got to the hall and found, to our amazement, that some two
hundred people had paid their four and sixes to get in, the negative
side of the marijuana high started to operate. The sight of all those
people looking up at us on the stage and expecting great things was
terrifying.

Only about ten minutes late, we started according to our plan.
The band played a standard to warm up the audience and then Johnny
was on. He was good, his poem blended well with the rhythm section, while Art Theman added a blues-wailing counterpoint on top.
The audience applauded.

Nigel was next: a piece that used the two tenor saxes alone as they
built up a dialogue with his almost conversational nonsense poem.
After about two lines, I thought I heard voices from the audience,
but couldn't make it out. He went on and the saxes went on. There
was a shout of "rubbish" and some of the chairs were shuffled noisily about. He managed to finish the piece. Some of the audience
applauded, but there were people booing as well. We went into a
huddle on the stage, signalling the band to hold their fire.

"It's Pete Jenner and his cronies, isn't it?" I asked Nigel in a desperate whisper. Pete Jenner, who was the *Floyd*'s first manager and is
now something big in pop.

"Yes, I'm afraid so. Christ, what a thing to do."

"Yeah well, we can't do that slow quiet thing next. They're bound
to boo that. Let's go straight into the tape collage."

"They won't like that any better."

"Maybe not, but at least it'll give us time to think how we're going
to handle this."

So we went on, in hardly audible whispers, with our backs turned
to the audience, as we tried to divert the flood of panic that threatened to engulf us. We put the tape on, but it didn't help. The audience got more restive with shouts of "When's it going to start?" and
"Call this modern art?"

Our panic slowly got the better of us. We spent more time whis-
pering, hoping that some miracle would restore the audience into
our control. The carefully worked out schedule was forgotten and
after a few more loudly heckled poems with the band, we gave up.

The band salvaged what time was left with what was probably a
very good jam session, while we crept back to the Hang Chow, our

spirits broken. All our ebullience was gone and a cloud of doubt settled over all three of us. It was the break-up of a fiery, prolific period, the entry into another slough.

But the reviews were better than our memories. The one in *Varsity* had some kind things to say:

> *Deliberate informality was a successful characteristic from the opening poem, a piece of humorous gibberish entitled "Sewers", with the rich chorus of "rats, rats, rats, rats". The attempt to arrive at a few truths of our personality via this self-conscious nonsense was well launched by Pryor. "Sad Words" brought him into contact at last with his audience through the conclusion: "Man, I'm off my head with an automatic grumble."*
> *The performers' great enthusiasm, noises, and half-acted sequences were infectious. Pryor came nearest to a successful merging of jazz and poetry with "Tomorrow", including a lovely muted jazz introduction, and "Lord, Lord", asking effective questions to a rapid staccato drumming.*

But we were laid low. The reviews missed the point. I suppose I imagined that most people felt like I did: ghostlike, unconnected. Getting through was heroic. My earlier lack had become an anger: if how I felt was how it really was for everyone, then why did they all pretend to be so small minded, so grey, so flabby?

This puncturing of the balloon of our performing bravura was, in hindsight, a tragedy – the end of the innocence of our poetry, the end of the poetry of our gilded youth. The nihilism of Beckett and Dada would take the upper hand from this moment.

Fifty-five years previously, in 1909, Rupert Brooke had been in Grantchester urging his friends (including my grandparents, Gwen and Jacques) to adopt a simple life of poetry. He wrote:

> *The idea, the splendour of this escape back into youth, fascinated us. We imagined a number of young people, splendidly young together vowing to live such an idea, parting to do their 'work in the world' for a time and then, twenty years later, meeting on some windy road, one prearranged spring morning, reborn to find and make a new world together, vanishing from the knowledge of men and things they knew before, resurgent in sun and rain...*

They made a solemn pact to meet for breakfast at Basel station on 1 May 1933 when they would all be double their current ages. Rupert wrote to Jacques:

The great essential thing is the Organized Chance of Living Again instead of becoming a greying literary hack, mumbling along in some London suburb... middle aged, tied with more and more ties, busier and busier, fussier and fussier... the world will fade to us, fade, grow tasteless, habitual, dull.

But by 1933 Rupert and Jacques would be dead, and another of their group insane.

We'll be children [of] seventy-years, instead of seven. We'll live Romance, not talk of it. We'll show the grey unbelieving age, we'll teach the whole damn World, that there's a better Heaven than the pale serene Anglican windless harmonium-buzzing Eternity of the Christians, a Heaven in Time, now and for ever, ending for each, staying for all, a Heaven of Laughter and Bodies and Flowers and Love and People and Sun and Wind, in the only place we know or care for, ON EARTH.

I am not going to be a resident fellow of Kings, nor a lecturer in Leeds, I am going to be a Bloody POET.

3 Morning Glory in Paris

My first trips abroad, with the family to France, to run up mountains in Norway with my cousins and to be 'exchanged' with an Italian boy in Venice, were not really abroad. I transferred all my head's home apparatus with me and could just as well have been in a strange part of England as a foreign country. Now I had a degree of independence. I had a monthly allowance and a bank account. I could seriously consider going abroad at my own behest.

There was only one place to go: that city of mind-explorers, Paris, which was made even more attractive by the fact that a nephew of my grandfather, Jacques Raverat, would let me live in one of his two studios for nothing.

So off I went on the great adventure with my belongings wrapped up in a suitcase, the lonely boat across, the strange train and then la Gare du Nord with no more than vague memories of O level French. The cafés on the street, the berets, garlic and shoulder shrugs; the plane trees growing through grills, les clochards, the buses with lavatory chains on the platform at the back. Essence of Paris.

My cousin was good to his word and after a few days in their smart flat, he drove me out to the studio in Montparnasse. It was on the ground floor, built against a wall in the garden of a typical Parisian, Baron Haussmann tenement. It had a glass roof and no furniture. He helped me find a mattress and some blankets and then left me to it. I got some orange boxes for a table and book shelves and it was complete. A cold, draughty, writer's garret in Paris (even if it was on the ground floor). In the adjoining studio was an ageing sculptor who had spent his life making bas-reliefs from which coins and medals were struck.

Now I could venture out into creative Paris in the cafes in the Latin Quarter and Montparnasse that were the haunts of the expatriate community, huddling together in mutual support. They weren't difficult to find: duffel coats, jeans and beards, mostly Americans. Our purpose was the same: to be *working artists*.

But something under the polite surface was about to break through. The police with their machine guns, the ubiquitous black marias, the bourgeois so obvious. De Gaulle had just come out of retirement

and Parisians were edgy. The war in Algeria was not going well.

One afternoon the cafe I was sitting in was raided by the police. With my dark features I must have been taken for an Algerian. Despite waving my English passport, I was bundled into a black maria with several others. I was now truly oppressed.

It was monstrous; it was stimulating. We were driven to a police station the other side of Paris and put in a cage. We were kept there for a good three hours, before any of the pigs took notice of us. When they heard my English voice and took a proper look at my passport, they let me go, with no word of apology or explanation. I now had serious kudos.

Bruce, from Hartford Connecticut, with a fresh earnest, ducking and diving intellect was at the leading edge of the next wave of beatnickery. His lean face sported a painter's goatee beard. He had an expensive Leica camera and was a good photographer (the pictures of me in Paris are his). He spoke fluent French and had a lovely Algerian girlfriend called Leila, who spoke little English. She was in constant dread of being picked up by the police and sent back to her homeland, where she faced almost certain death. I never discovered quite why. Bruce had met William Burroughs, to whom he referred constantly in his conversation.

"William says it's all cut-up anyway, this writing, the process of internal editing;" or "Bill says the thought police actually exist". To keep my end up, I developed my respect for Samuel Beckett's work into an equal fetish. Strange that we should thrive on two equally sharp visions of despair, that our hope as writers lay in two such hopeless outlooks.

And yet not so strange. The worlds of Beckett and Burroughs are reductions, essences of pointlessness that caught the world as we found it, but somehow left the individual in tact, allowed him to exist in his stupid, absurd dreams and routines. Strangely, the absurdity was stimulating and held promise that we might get things right, righter.

Jazz was in there too. Coltrane, Mingus and a wonderfully weird new man, Ornette Coleman, who did 'free improvisation' or what he called 'harmolodics', on a *plastic* alto. One of my favourite haunts was a bar called the Blue Note, which had a shelf as long as the bar, crammed with many metres of jazz albums, amongst them the latest Coltrane and even some Cecil Taylor, whose music I was able to unleash on Bruce.

We were able to see Mingus in the flesh, when, in April, he gave two concerts in Paris at Salle Wagram. We sat very near the front. It was maybe Mingus's greatest band, his sextet with Eric Dolphy (on alto, bass clarinet and flute), tenor-saxophonist Clifford Jordan, trumpeter Johnny Coles, pianist Jaki Byard and drummer Danny Richmond. Johnny Coles took ill between the two gigs and Mingus made much of it, placing Coles' trumpet on his empty stool and every now and then picking up his bass and pointing it at the stool. Dolphy died soon afterwards in Berlin.

The minute Sheena, an English art student studying in Paris, and I set eyes on each other there was a sparkling and a twinkling and an eyeing-up. She came back to my pad that same day. She was lithe, with short auburn hair and an independent mind. This exciting girl on the threshold of finding creativity for herself was my brown-eyed beauty of the low lands. I had to tell her how much I loved her two or three times a day to make this hip young chick my woman. She'd come and stay on my mattress every now and then. But I couldn't stand it if she got too close.

What began to complicate my knots with Sheena, and later exploded them and much else besides was a flower, or rather, its seeds. Bruce had heard that the seeds of Morning Glory, a strain of convolvulus, contained LSD 6, a crude form of the LSD 25 that Timothy Leary was just beginning to unleash. Three quarters of the contents of the kind of packet you could then buy from seed merchants was about the right dose. The trouble was that you had to chew the oily seeds, about twice the size of a grape pip, into a pulp for the active ingredients to be released in the stomach. This produced powerful waves of nausea that you had to fight your way through before the trip proper could begin.

Bruce had decided that the best way to ameliorate the nausea, which could last up to half an hour, was to launch out into the metro where the multiplicity of sensory inputs would drown out the urge to puke. We chewed our seeds at nine one evening. The night, with

Slaving over a hot Parisian bidet

its emptiness, was better for tripping. As soon as we could bear to walk, we set off down the street. Colours. The pavement.

Itself, the pavement, but also the cracks.

Or rather the joins between the textures of solidity, and the foot clomps over it, smashes down. The air, dusky-air, feel it on your exposed eyeballs, the colours; look
at that man, he's walking, he doesn't know through or on what. density.
Into the earth, his earth, nowhere to lay his head, man to travel his city, into the earth, down
the steps into the metro, the descent is so decorated, the wrought-iron balustrade
to the underskirts of the city.
The climb down; the climbdown.

"Listen to the Seven," says Bruce. "The seven clicks, the seven dots. The secret is in *how* you listen, whether you hear, whether you are taken up."

Automatic the barrier. The way to pass is closed when a train. The trick. The trick, says Bruce, is to wait till you hear the rumble, wait the wrong side, then at the first whoosh of air, rush. It's being in tune with machines.

Training to Montmartre, to sex. The left hand path, by indulgence, the senses. Incoherent knowledge that this is magic, or Magick as Crowley had travelled. To be part of earth, to partake in earth, to eat earth, to be lost. To believe the illusion completely, oh Maya.

The Seven: metro motor clicking over. Doors shut, train starts. Click, click and Bruce says, "there, you hear it: Number One." The motor, the electric motor speeds, switching gear clicks. We get to Number Four and I hear it. What? The elevation in the listening for the Seven. I don't hear the elevation, but the elevation is in the hearing. More colours, I hear them.
and faces, skulls, blues and reds, skulls, atavistic.

Parisians on their way to or from and I see their skulls. They are no more people, they are their history.

Libido now realisable, or is it the name, the language that excites.

Anticipation anyway. With it, we climb up out up from and into the bowels of the night, into the fire, the neon, the market of bodies, the dealing in mythologies and arousals.

We go to a really French strip show: the art of signs and given conventions. We pay to get in.

RED
PLUSH
VELVET

is what pours in through the holes in the front of our eyeballs. Stunned, I mean, man, pulverised by redness, passion. You sit at a table, little round table, order a drink, a coke, can't manage alcohol as well. Music starts. Sur le Pont d'Avignon jazzed-up spreads into the velvet fittings. The curtains spread back and there.

And there a blonde woman? No, a blonde lady? A girl, well: seductress and yet she won't, is unreachable we must be passive in our seats. SHE, anyway, SHE wears a very short dress with little petticoats, like little girls (don't) wear at parties, pink and white gingham, bows in her hair, sucks her thumb, holds a doll and dances, hip-bumps, coquettishly. But she is woman, her breasts, her legs, her high heels, the signs to which we pavlov. The doll is not a little girl's doll, but a man-ikin. She fondles it, plays it, sucks it, rubs it on her frills. Then the image, the little-girl-woman starts to take off, to strip her sign-clothes with stroking, self-caressing as though you, we, the men, as though we could do it that well.

'This is the pleasure you like to think you can give to the woman you like to think you can have': the signs she talks with in her language of make-you-believe, or, anyway make-you-forget this is all a sham, a fake, but, but, but we are aroused. Her breasts she fondles, she does it for us. Curtain. Daze. We already have the idea, the force towards completion. What would it be like, when you've paid for it?

We stagger back to the open night to put the question to the test. Forty Francs, a grubby hotel and I discover. We have reached a state so high (so low) that all sensory experience is orgasm, therefore no orgasm possible. I warn Bruce before he wastes any money.

"D'you see how it's all about being amused? Distracted? So that we can avoid the larger questions, the pain."

"Yes," replies Bruce, "but isn't the larger question just that: a way of avoiding what is not a question. We may realise that amusements, what is called 'entertainment' and 'pleasure', are a way of avoiding the pain of the big question. But isn't that pain the result of the mind thinking it can solve everything, in other words, of there being a 'question' at all?"

"You have it." I had just crossed five paving stones in three strides. "All we can do is count the number of different ways we can suck the limited number of stones we have to suck."

"Yes," says Bruce with great emphasis. "We suck our mind's stones to give us comfort, but if we can stop being I, stop having a specific identity that needs comfort, then the sky is literally the limit. D'you read me?" This time my left foot landed right on a crack between two paving stones.

"But," I grabbed his arm. We both agreed with what had not been said. "But, if we can understand each other without saying anything, like we just did then," I pointed to the position of my left foot, "well, we must, to some degree, have interchangeable identities: I, you and me, or, you, I and you."

Now late in the night, not a soul as we approach the dawn grey that is expressed with a bowl of onion soup in Les Halles as the vegetable market finishes its night's work. It is a slow progress. We stop every two yards or so to share the latest revelation. Bleary, but envisioned eyes, colours breaking down to grey, people unaware of the seething whirlpools of light and texture they walk through and on, go to work, fulfil their part in what is called the daily round and round and round.

Mid-morning I get back to my mattress, exhausted, but not able to sleep, the light now disturbs me, the ancient sculptor is hacking away at his bas-reliefs next door, what hope have I, have we? I envy Bruce his warm bed with Leila. At lunch time I go to Sheena's room and ask her to drop whatever she's doing and come back with me to give me warmth, both inside and out. She does, she is interested in the trip, she lies on the mattress with me. But…

How to describe, to convey the depths of insight to someone who hasn't been there. She is compliant, pliant and has affection, even respect for me, but what good is it, she is so tied to the trappings of her identity. I thought. Trappings, I thought.

"Don't you see, you've got to be able to rise above what you are, what makes you Sheena, to be able to see how it really is? We saw it last night, Bruce and I. We rose above what makes us Bruce and William and were able to see."

"That's fantastic," I turned away, "No, I mean it, it really does sound as though the two of you did have some amazing insights. Why on earth don't you write about it? You keep on about being a writer, but I haven't seen you write anything."

"Interesting insights, indeed! It was far more than that; far, far more. But yes, I will write something. Why don't you go and sit over there." She went, and after much hesitation I started what was to be the natural successor to the novels of Samuel Beckett. So I thought, I thought. The trappings, anyway.

Her ego at it again and for what gain, thinks she, she wants to put that first gem of back-going sense or nonsense back to the old way of the can where all is smelly or rosy (you can't have both).

I said I loved her tra la la soon that got left behind cos now I am simply watching her like some offensive acquaintance or something thinks she love means to be forgiven…this flow of words from inside the evil old spirit that goes on and on talking to the wind.

So it ran for another three pages.

I took it with me when I went that evening to meet up with Bruce. He found it a revelation, the new writing, as I did what he had to show me. We confirmed each other in our sense of being at the edge, the furthest reach of the mind. Everything else became subservient to the lucidity of our shared madness, our vision. If those around us could not understand what we were so excited about, it was their fault, not ours.

We fell into the habit of chewing Morning Glory seeds every four or five days. We could maintain our visionary drive without having to bother with the painful task of relating what we knew and saw with the lumpen, so-called everyday, world.

The lucidity of our shared madness was born of protest, kindled by anger, and kept fresh by fear. For it was madness. We could not communicate the urgency of our visions. But it was also not madness. We were in full control of our actions, however strange they were. We coped with normality.

There was the strange visit Bruce and I made to Daevid Allen, an Australian guitarist who was king of the Parisian teaheads and was to found the seminal acid rock group *Gong* a couple of years later. His flat was in a very ordinary back street in Les Halles, above a Chinese laundry. I pulled on the string. Nothing happened. On stepping back into the road we could see that the string ran all the way up to the fifth floor, where it was fixed to a bell on a coil of sprung iron. I pulled again and again. There were lights on and had to be someone in. Eventually a little window opened.

"Yeah, yeah. Qui est? Who's there, man? What d'ya want?"

"It's Bruce and William."

"Who, man?"

"Bruce and William."

"Never heard of them, hang on, man." He turned back into the room and re-emerged. "Sorry man, here's the key." A small parachute sailed down towards us with the key attached.

It was a long way up to the fifth floor launching pad, a flat of three rooms made into one long one, with kitchen and bathroom to one side. The walls were lined with bunks furnished with Arabian cushions for the proper languishing of kif smokers – a purpose-built pothead's den.

We stood blinking. Daevid nodded us to sit, his hands taken up in rolling an enormous six-paper joint. Music seemed to be coming from the walls, Moroccan desert music. Daevid's lady, Gilli Smyth glided, she glode round the people with sweet cakes and, given the material, I could roll one myself, another joint and slowly become part of the room.

"Well, I hope they do damn well come over and drop in on Paris, them parachutes man, they're fantastic." Someone said.

"But the OAS are even more right wing than this present lot, and there'd be blood, man, a whole lot of blood." Someone else answered. Daevid was fiddling with some gadget behind him.

"Be blood, man. A whole lot of blood. Be blood, man. A whole lot of blood. Be blood, man." He must have a tape loop going.

"For Christ's sake man!" The first guy was annoyed.

"Sake man, sake man, sake man."

"Yeah?" asked Daevid.

"We can't talk at all with you mucking about with those tapes."

"Thought you enjoyed them," said Daevid without much interest. "It's the way we listen, or don't listen. Our ears are so involved in detecting meaning that we can't listen."

"To what? Or do I mean, to which?" I felt emboldened, slowly transmogrified. The web of sound, of doped smoke, of what I could see. It was all synchronous, the drips of rain on the window, the dervish loud speakers in this fifth floor collection of stoned impressions, above a Chinese laundry.

"Willyum," said Daevid, "this microphone knows no boundaries. Up here, everything can be heard. When we float, are loose, we can sense the flux. Don't worry about it. That's what gums up the works. Man, don't you see how getting past the separation is the thing. Nothing is *either* inside your head *or* outside it; everything is both."

"Everything is both. That I like, yeah, everything is both," Bruce was talking for the first time. "You mean like everything is dependent on everything else. Truth lies in… wow, how about that: 'truth lies in' like there is as much truth in any one thing as there is in anything else. It's the arbitrary editing that our minds do to whatever's happening that makes some things seem more significant than others." This was turning into one of Bruce's big numbers.

I was getting confused. I was so stoned and this talk of truth had me puzzled, no, worried. I had no idea what it was, or rather, what was, what was true, but Bruce and the others seemed to share a burning insight as to its nature. For me, it was certainly true that I loved Sheena, but it was equally true that I didn't care for her at all. It was true that I was a genius, but it was also true that I didn't know the first thing about writing. I drifted away into the bad lands of paranoia and self-doubt. I didn't say any more that evening and left early and on my own, to go back to my garret to ponder these questions.

But I did seem to be onto something special. My words were writings that came from vision, not sight, but direct contact with an understanding that baffled me. The only alternative was that it was complete rubbish, which was unthinkable.

I had to have a word, a concept, a label I could apply to what I was doing. The only one available that fully caught the sense in which I was breaking unknown ground, but was not appreciated by my contemporaries, was *genius*.

It didn't happen all at once. I had to keep testing the idea on Bruce and anyone else that came my way. Bruce thought he probably agreed, but that it was a bit odd that I should worry quite so much about *what* I was, and not just get on with the work in hand. Sheena, on the other hand, was obviously one of those contemporaries who just couldn't understand, and had to resort to humouring me.

"OK, you're a genius. What difference does it make?" She asked wearily.

"Well, if I'm the genius I think I am, a successor to Beckett, then it's only fair that people should know. I mean, if you knew that you were another Picasso or something, you'd want people to know. The point is: I know what I am, you only have to read what I've written."

"But I have. I think it's boring gobbledegook."

"But that's exactly what I've been saying. You can't appreciate it; it's way ahead of its time, it's a work of genius."

"Whatever you say William. Why don't you shut up and come to bed?"

"I will, I will, but I've got some thinking to do first."

The next day I had made up my mind. I must go back to Cambridge as soon as possible. I had a duty to tell my friends and parents of my recent discoveries. They really ought to know that their friend and son was a genius.

I managed to get my soaring mind home to Cambridge via train and ferry, clutching my precious writings, my proof. My poor parents, my patient friends!

The extreme limit of wisdom, that's what the public calls madness. (Jean Cocteau)

My mother damned my vision with faint acknowledgement, saying, "Yes dear, I'm sure you're a genius," and my father, having read my few pages, said he didn't understand it, but was sure it was interesting. They were incapable: they could not rise to the challenge that a deranged son posed. If we don't talk about it, it will go away.

After a few days, my father said he had something for me and took me into his study. There on the desk was a brand new portable typewriter.

"Present for you," was all he said, and no more was needed. A brave and generous way of telling me to go off and prove it? Or gesture parenting? A few days later I returned to Paris, so that I could get down to the real thing: being a genius with my Olympia portable typewriter in its zip-up carry case.

But Paris had changed. My previous visionary state had evaporated and, what was far worse, Sheena would have nothing to do with me. At her *pension*, her girlfriend said she was out and wouldn't be back till the next day. I went on my way to the Café Americaine unsuspecting. A seething sea of unknowing fear and need, I sat at one of the pavement tables to have a coffee with an Austrian acquaintance.

Then I saw her. She was with her friend, the girl who had told me Sheena was away for the day. I ran after them as they disappeared round the corner. I couldn't see them in the next street, so I ran to the next corner. They were just about to turn into a large gateway. Sheena turned and looked with her large brown eyes straight into mine. But she wouldn't even stop to talk to me. I imagined that her friend had some hold over her, maybe even a gun in her back and that her look had been to reassure herself that help was at hand.

They were now walking quickly along what turned out to be a large tunnel. It was obvious that Sheena's girlfriend was a bad lot. She'd lied to me, but I couldn't make out why she should want to kidnap the one I loved. For I found that I loved and pined for Sheena very deeply. Maybe it was just some kind of game, something that involved this strange tunnel. Then, as I came round a sharp corner, there she was, hands on hips, a look of defiance on her face, her short auburn hair somehow glowing.

"Hello William. What are you doing here?"

"I'm trying to talk to you. I wanted to tell you that I'm back. I wanted you to come over to my place this evening. I thought we might go to the moon or something." I looked hopefully up at her, for she was very tall.

"Good God, don't you know? I can't waste my time going to the moon with you. I'm a member of The Place now and spend most of my time there. That's where I'm going now, meeting Bruce and Leila in half an hour. But it's no good you following. They never let non-members in, never."

"You mean this tunnel is the entrance to whatever you call it, to the Place?" I was very puzzled. She was tall and beautiful.

"Where did you think it went? You'd better get out. They can be nasty to non-members. You just don't belong here, William,

you just don't belong." I snapped out of my reverie in time to hear just those last words. I didn't know what she'd been talking about, but it was all too clear that our relationship was finished, that she didn't want any more to do with me.

I rode the Metro back and forth, round and round, staring at the floor. The clicking of the motors did nothing for me, but at least I had the feeling I was doing something. I could blank out the worst part of the grief and desperation that had me by the guts. What am I going to do? Can't help it if I'm a genius. Oh God, what *am* I going to do?

Some time later I heard that there was to be a blues concert with Sonny Terry at the Sorbonne, and figured that she'd be sure to go. She loved that kind of music. I reasoned that she couldn't very well not let me sit with her.

But I was wrong. There she was with a lively group of friends, but they ignored me. All I could do was sit at the back and pretend I had no idea they would be there and that I too was there because I loved the blues. I did. I wept. I was alone. They were a group of noisily happy people.

The black dog of a hole, a gnawing, pulsating lack, an absence of purpose or sense, dominated my solar plexus, always pulling my attention down to pointlessness.

Bruce, whom I saw every now and then, was concerned about my state. I had become a zombie, and when, after three weeks, I showed no sign of snapping out of it, he gently persuaded me that the best thing I could do was go back home to Cambridge and try to forget.

I went home, with nothing written on my new typewriter, a broken poet. I had very little to offer in the way of explanation, such was the darkness.

As an experience, madness is terrific…and in its lava I still find most of the things I write about. (Virginia Woolf)

Back in Chaucer Road, I moped around, always a tight sinking in my guts, a mantra of 'Sheena, Sheena, Sheena' in my mind. The typewriter case gathered dust, unopened. I was back in the bosom of my family, but ducking to Dave's or Storm's for a spliff whenever possible.

My A level results had come through and I had good grades, qualifying me to sit the entrance exam to Trinity. I did little revision. It was hard to take the exam seriously when I knew I'd be taking it in my father's rooms in college, and would be invigilated by one of his colleagues.

When the time came my mind was still with Sheena. I'd forgotten much of the work and I failed, not disastrously. What was to be done? William must come up to Cambridge, that went without saying. He's obviously bright enough, just finds it hard to apply himself at the moment. And so I was let in by the back door, suspended and pulled by strings. My father stuck his neck out and there was a row with another don, whose son the strings did not pull. Daddy would recount how Sir Charles Forte had sent him a case of vintage port when he had turned down his son, Rocco. The elliptical ways of gentlemen.

It was now late spring in Cambridge. I was to start at Trinity that October and had time to spare, as had Dave and Storm, before they went their various ways to Art College and the like. Someone came up with the idea of going to Greece in a cheap old banger. It needn't cost more than a hundred quid which, when split four ways, was not a lot. I said I'd go along, partly because I had nothing better to do, but also because I thought I remembered Sheena saying that she intended to be in Greece that summer. Storm, the only one of us with a licence, was left to find a suitable car.

Pete Downing had made one of his discoveries. For only one and sixpence, less than the price of a front row seat in the Regal, one could buy a small hexagonal blue-glass bottle filled with a diarrhoea and stomach medicine. This was Boots', the chemists, own brand of what is more widely known as Dr Collis Browne's Chlorodyne, an anodyne dating from Victorian times, when it was introduced as a safe replacement for laudanum. The main interest of this foul-smelling, dark brown goo for us was that it contained an appreciable amount of opium. Pete had also discovered how to nullify the effects of the emetic (the stuff that allows them to call it 'safe'): just boil the contents with a spoonful of sugar.

One afternoon when all the family were out, Pete, Andrew, Nigel and Dave came round, bringing three bottles of the stuff. We emptied them into a small battered saucepan that my mother wouldn't miss, added some sugar and boiled the resultant mixture. As soon as it had stopped effervescing, Pete declared it to be ready. We let it cool and divided it among five cups. It tasted disgusting, but we managed to get it down without vomiting.

None of us had had opium or any of its derivatives before and didn't know what to expect. We sat round waiting. Nothing happened. A blanket of nothing, a fuzzy wrapping of mental cotton wool. We felt nothing, no sensation and yet a buzz, a humming and, with that, a release and disinterested amusement. Our minds could follow themselves, go where and how they wished with no emotional complication, no pain. I was no longer the shell, the tormented genius that had lost the love of his life and could not engage with his friends. Now I could BE. Now I was free from the hole in my belly. Now my intelligence could do what it was supposed to do.

This was a key moment in the making of my addiction. For Andrew, Nigel, Dave and Pete it was no more than a stoned experience.

After some time marvelling at how we became so nicely contained, we were moved to go out into the garden and try out our new stone-like mode amongst the trees and bushes. The greatest delight came from simply standing around as though playing the children's game 'statues'. It was a wonder to be able to be so very immobile, to allow nature to grow around us, the wind to blow in our faces. Maybe it was the experience of permanence that only a rock would feel. For me, it was wonderful to be able to revel in just being, no more, just being. To simply BE, with no nagging doubt, fear or conflict. This stuff was instant wholeness in a bottle.

Around 1300 BC, in the capital city of Thebes, Egyptians begin cultivation of opium thebaicum. The Phoenicians and Minoans trade it into Greece, Carthage, and Europe.

Storm had found a battered old Humber Hawk, the kind VIPs used in English films of the early fifties, and we bought it for fifty pounds. Two weeks later we set off for Greece with our travellers' cheques and a few belongings. Dave was authentically in search of inspiration from the classical sights; Storm the jet set on Mykonos, while I was chasing my ghost and hoping to meet up with some of the people I'd known in Paris, the hip people. By the time we reached Zagreb, only one of the car's doors would open and the engine sounded utterly miserable, but we decided we should drive it to a standstill, preferably in Greece. I had an address in Athens.

I recognised my contacts as soon as they opened the door, not that I'd met them before, but as fellow travellers along the drugged path of cultural anarchy and revolution. They told me that an English girl called Sheena, they couldn't remember her last name, but the description matched, had been in Athens just three weeks earlier. She had gone on to the island of Hydra, where, I was told, it was definitely all happening. I was delirious with the anticipation of a reconciliation. A few joints of their excellent Moroccan kif helped me into the first state of elation I'd experienced in many months. Two days later I was on Hydra.

It is a small island, all rock rising sharply from the sea. It didn't take long, sitting around the quayside cafes, to meet up with members of the flourishing community of expatriate American writers and artists. The guy I met hadn't heard of any English girl called Sheena, but suggested I go up to Harold Norse's house at the top end of town, where a group of people from Paris were staying.

I climbed up the hundreds of steps diffidently, not at all sure how a stray English beat would be greeted. I needn't have worried. Coolness reigned in the rambling whitewashed house on top of the hill, no questions were asked, it was just accepted that I was there and that was it. That I had put in my time in Paris and knew some of the right people, helped, but I found the complete non-reaction to my arrival disconcerting. An indication that I was not as cool as my hosts.

Although it was only midday, I worried about where I would sleep that night. I couldn't bear to go back to the sordid pension I'd been in the previous night and my funds wouldn't stretch to a proper hotel.

"Is there anywhere I can sleep, you know, any old corner will do?" I asked the bronzed American clutching an expensive-looking twelve-string guitar.

"Sure man. Hey, have you tried this kif? Theo brought it over from Beirut last week. His father's in the embassy there, man. It's a gas, means he can ride round in a car with CD plates and the local fuzz can't touch him."

"Thanks." I took a few drags on the proffered joint. "Hey, that's nice. I know there was something I was going to ask, but," I started to giggle, "but I'm not sure if I've already asked it. That's the trouble with questions: the answers seem to matter."

"Man, I dunno if you asked a question or not." I thought there was a note of irritation in his voice. He was tall and muscular with a Clint Eastwood kind of rugged. He played an Indian sounding blues for a while. He took some deep drags from the joint and narrowed his eyes even further at the classically beautiful view – we were on the roof of the house. After what could have been half an hour, he spoke, "Did you say your name was Bill, Bill Pryor?"

"I didn't but it is, well, it's William actually, my friends call me William. Who are you?"

"Me? Oh I'm Sam, Sam Brinkoff." He offered me his hand and I shook it. "They call you William, do they?" He had me worried, I thought he might leap on me, saying something like, 'I've been waiting to catch up with you, you dirty rat', but he just finished the joint and started playing again. After a long, slow Route 66, he turned to look at me.

"There was someone here talking about you, a coupla weeks back. A chick named Sheena. Mean anything to you?"

I reacted in silence. She had been there and had talked about me. What had she said? Did she long to get back with me? Did she have a new boyfriend? But before I could get completely lost in this obsessive speculation, Sam cut in.

"Bit of a drag that chick."

"Why?" He had taken me by surprise and I had to play it by ear.

"Well; Bill, she kept on and on putting you down for taking Morning Glory seeds. Said you started to act a little crazy. And then a whole lot of that little girl stuff, you know, 'he never took me out on dates' and all that yappy sort of stuff. You're well rid of her, man. You don't seem crazy to me."

"That's good," I replied nervously, trying to live up to the image I thought he had of me, a fearless and hip drug explorer. "Why don't you play some more, what you did just then was far out, man."

"I will, I will, just as soon as I roll us a joint of this stuff." He produced a block of what looked like very dark hash. "You know what this is? No? It's hash and opium mixed. It's from Turkey. Should blow your mind, really blow your mind."

It did. Two or three joints of it hit me like the Chlorodyne had, but with a dark overtone of hash. Sam played his guitar like a sitar making blues and the slinky melancholy slunk for hours, for a long time, for a time, for our time and the feeling that it was my world, this world, returned. The obsession about Sheena was broken. I was acceptable in this hip company. I could laugh.

"That question, man," I said after a few hours, "that question."

"What question?"

"The one I couldn't remember if I'd asked it or not. Now I can see that I don't need to ask it, that is if I haven't already asked it. You see, I was going to ask if there was anywhere I could sleep. Well, you don't need somewhere to sleep, if you're already asleep, do you?"

"I guess not."

"What I mean is: you've already got somewhere if you're asleep, haven't you?" I found this line of banality immensely satisfying and fell asleep with it.

330 BC: Alexander the Great introduces opium to the people of Persia and India.

4 MORAL SCIENCES AND TOTAL ART

A tall, thin nineteen year old beatnik, I got back to Cambridge some-how, liberated from Sheena, stoned a good deal, feeling a part of the international hippie conspiracy, but also lonely, isolated and begin-ning to be aware that something was working on me that I didn't understand.

October soon came round and time for me to start out as a real live undergraduate. A grad, the life form us locals tended to despise. The porters nodded to me when I went through Great Gate. A clean-ing lady came to clean up every morning and called me "sir". I was given rooms in Whewell's Court, not a hundred yards and only a decade or so, from the room where Wittgenstein gave his last lec-tures. I liked being an undergraduate.

I had decided to read philosophy, or as it was then rather strangely called at Cambridge, *Moral Sciences*. I hoped it might be about the exploration of the big questions: identity, purpose and meaning. It wasn't. It never occurred to me to read English Literature, that it could have any relevance to my pretensions as writer. Somehow the two occupied different universes; academics had no interest in what was or could be written in the moment, only in what was safely dead.

The hip, local social scene revolving around Storm and Nigel contin-ued unabated – the company of freshmen was pallid by comparison. On the whole they were childish, loudmouthed and, above all, unhip. The centre of my universe was usually elsewhere, round at Storm's for instance, but with half a bottle of Chlorodyne this restlessness was quickly overcome. I could stay in my rooms to work, or even to write a poem. I could go to Storm's at my own behest, not that of feeling left out.

Andrew, who inhabited different edges of the same social scene and who was also something of a social deviant, was also reading Moral Sciences. We were avant garde together. We went to Professor John Wisdom's lectures together.

If it was only his unkempt beard and six foot three frame, Andrew would be imposing, but add his Ferrari mind and you have someone who is likely to have a powerful effect. "When I wake up in the morning, it just starts," he once complained to me. No wonder he went on to become a professional philosopher, but, at that time, he was an absurdist, who created concrete poetry and hung out with his school friend, Roger Waters.

At the Criterion, stoned, no doubt.

The note from Sam arrived in my second term, forwarded from Chaucer Road. He was just back from Hydra with some goodies I might be interested in. Could he come and visit me, bringing some of that hash and opium stuff. It would be quite something to be visited by a hip, twelve-string guitar playing American.

"Hi William," he said as he came in the door. "How's it going?"

"Oh fine, fine," I replied nervously, having no idea where we were heading. "Hey, come in and sit down, man."

I rolled a hash and opium joint. It had the same power that I remembered. I put on Eric Dolphy's *Out to Lunch*: his bass clarinet laying down a spiky, gruff commentary. We appreciated each other's company in increasingly stoned silence.

"Bill, what do you feel about H, you know, heroin?" He blurted out as though he'd been working out a way to ask. All I could think was that I am not 'Bill'; I am William.

I had always said that anyone who touches the stuff must be mad. Well, I thought I had said it. Anyway, I, for one, had no intention of getting hooked. He was only asking out of something to say, wasn't he?

1527: Opium reintroduced into European medical literature by Paracelsus as laudanum, made up as black pills or Stones of Immortality.

"I really don't know. I mean, it must be an awful drag to get hooked, to need the stuff every day. I think that people who get hooked only have themselves to blame. Such an idiotic thing to do."

"Don't know so much, takes weeks to get hooked." I should have known; he is a junky. "Yeah, you've got to use it everyday for weeks before it gets you hooked. Look, I'm asking, because I happen to have some here. Would you like to try a real small fix? Can't hurt you. No way is it going to get you hooked."

"Well.... I don't know," I prevaricated. The phial he'd just put on the table had his name on the pharmacist's label. How come he'd written that he was just back from Greece, when he'd obviously been back long enough to get himself registered. Why had he lied to me? But, on the other hand, did it matter? He had it all there on my table: the tiny pills of heroin, the syringe in its box and some needles in their foil. Just one tiny dose couldn't turn me into a raving addict, not just like that, not one minute fix. And I would know what it was like. I would be able to tell people how dangerous it was.

"Well, OK then, just as an experiment, but only a small one, a really small one." His face took on a serious purpose as he went to the sink in the bedroom and brought back a glass of water.

"Yeah, just a really tiny one. How do you, well, go about it?" The anticipation became granular in the endings of my nerves, not unlike that before sex.

"What you do is this," Sam launched into what was obviously a ritual.

"You put the amount of H you want into this glass phial," he produced it from his pocket and put half one of the little pills into it.

"That should be right for you. I need much more than that to give me a buzz, half a grain, but that should do you nicely for your first fix. Then you half-fill the syringe with water, like this, and squirt it, so, into the phial. Shake it a little, and if it doesn't want to dissolve like that, you heat it up a little."

He passed it over the flame of his cigarette lighter a few times and the water boiled, dissolving the remains of the pill. There was now a clear, colourless liquid in the phial.

"Right, roll up your sleeve. Yeah, that's it, and now you tie your belt round, no, not there, hang on, let me. Hold this."

He handed me the syringe into which he had by now sucked the contents of the phial and showed me how to wrap the belt round my arm, just above the elbow, keeping it tight against my knee. My veins quickly swelled up. He took the syringe from me and pressed the sharp point of the needle, the shiny, tapered, metal point, against one of the veins and slowly pierced the skin.

At first, the vein retreated, but with an almost audible click, such was our concentration, it soon penetrated the wall of the vein. All four of our eyes were focused on the tiny spot where the metal shaft of the needle entered my arm. I held my lower lip behind my teeth, he screwed up his brow in concentration.

"That's it. We've got it. Let go the belt. Wish I had veins like this." I lifted my arm from my knee to release the belt. He pulled the plunger a short way out of the syringe. A cloud of crimson swelled up into the colourless liquid.

"Here, you do it. Much better you do it." I pushed the plunger halfway and not more than twenty seconds later there was a flash, the taste so much in my root, my basis, my matrix that it could have been my bones that were buzzing. I played with it: pushing and pulling the plunger to watch the crimson liquid rush to mix with the heroin essence. It was a good five minutes before I'd emptied the syringe.

1606: Ships chartered by Elizabeth I are instructed to purchase the finest Indian opium and transport it back to England.

I sat back, oblivious of the blood on my arm, oblivious of anything unpleasant, that anything *could* be unpleasant. It was that same wrapped up feeling that I'd got from Chlorodyne, but much cleaner, much more fundamental. It came through and in my blood. Sam flushed out the syringe to clean it and repeated the whole ritual for himself, but this time with three whole pills, six times the dose I'd had. Just as he extracted the needle from his arm, I realised that I felt sick and went over to the sink. I opened my mouth and vomit came out, as though the process was nothing to do with me. I wiped my mouth.

"I've just been sick, apparently." Talk seemed pointless, now that I tried it. Sam was staring at the curtains, the pupils of his eyes were tiny full stops. Slowly, he seemed to realise that I'd said something and turned towards me.

"Yeah, that's not unusual the first few times," he said in a slurred voice. "Your body takes some time to adjust to a drug this powerful, this pure." I vomited a few more times that evening, but it didn't matter, it really didn't matter. I was floating, suspended from the world. My body and its functions very distant. Before long I developed another symptom common to those under the effect of junk, an incessant itch just beneath the skin as though my blood were the agent, but that didn't matter either. I was borne up from an unloving world on welcoming, fluid dreams that I could control. Eric Dolphy sounded round, furry and sinuous.

Everything one does in life, even love, occurs in an express train racing toward death. To smoke opium is to get out of the train while it is still moving. It is to concern oneself with something other than life or death. (Jean Cocteau)

Sam stayed the night on my sofa. I emerged the next morning to make some coffee, interrupting him as he had his first fix of the day. It didn't help my fragile state of mind, into which, now the previous night's fix had worn off, a nagging fear was making itself felt. It was a fear that maybe I had embarked down a very dangerous road. I knew that my first fix of heroin had been the most *consoling* experience of my life. It was not that I was feeling any physical craving, just that I was scared at what junk might be doing, what it was revealing, in my mind. Before Sam left to catch a train back to London, I tried to voice some of my apprehensions. His reply was to haunt me.

"It's your body, William. Nobody's got the right to tell you what you can or can't do with it, especially with the mess they've got the world into. If it gives you pleasure, if it allows you to do things you wouldn't otherwise be able to do, then it's OK. You're not harming anyone else. You can do what you like with your own body."

1680: English apothecary, **Thomas Sydenham**, introduces Sydenham's Laudanum, a compound of opium, sherry wine and herbs and precursor of Dr Collis Browne's Chlorodyne.

In 1964, the recreational use of soft drugs was only just becoming a widespread phenomenon. Acid was still legal. There were few addicts in the UK and most of those were therapeutic, had became addicted due to prolonged use of morphine in its proper role as pain killer, in hospital or in war. Opiate addiction was a medical, not a sociopathic condition. Opium, usually in the form of laudanum, had been quite legal for the Victorians and remained so into the first part of the twentieth century. Freud and many other eminent Victorians used cocaine as a legitimate tool of their trade.

After the war, the emergence of black market morphine and increasing numbers of therapeutic addicts started to change the picture. But the government persisted in its enlightened approach to addiction as set down in the various Dangerous Drugs Acts. Addicts were still regarded as victims, in need of the State's benevolence. It was recognised that he could not manage without a regular supply of his drug, and it was felt the best way to keep a potentially dangerous (as far as the state was concerned) situation under control was to get the addict to come to the state or its agent for that supply.

Hence the system arose whereby the addict could go to any doctor for his drugs, as long as he was registered with the Home Office. In 1964 there were well under a thousand such registered addicts, and very little, if any, black market heroin, other than that sold by registered addicts.

And somewhere along the line the blues walked in. The blues walked in, man. The beginning of the slow movement, the blues, the addiction. Where did it come from? I ask. Complicated, I reply, avoiding the answering. Yes, complicated. To say it was to do with my emotionally starved, middle class upbringing is true, but it is also true that all sorts get hooked: rich and poor, star and nonentity, aristocrat and peasant – emotional constriction is prevalent everywhere.

To become an addict, the experience of the drug must answer some urgent need, must soften some searing pain, must provide a way out from some inner disaster. Opium and then heroin gave me relief from the pain and confusion of my upbringing. I could escape the anger. I could know my creativity. As the habit establishes itself, the pain of the addiction, the withdrawal symptoms, overcome and subsume the pain the drug is answering. It becomes a self-fulfilling prediction: you make the pain of the family conscious; so you act it out; so you are dismissed for being self-obsessed and not caring a shit for anyone but yourself; so you make more of the family's pain conscious by becoming the pain of the family and the community.

I was often asked: "Why do you do it? You are so intelligent. You have such a nice family. You are so gifted. Why *do* you do it?"

"Because we need me to, you and I. Because the scream has to be screamed. We can't go on and on and on pretending. There is a tear in the fabric and it cannot be patched. I don't know who I am, but I do know I must scream!"

The Darwin, Pryor, Cambridge, Bloomsbury middle class vice had squeezed me of meaning, of joy, of liking myself, of even knowing what or who I was. It started in my pram. My mother left me to cry. I don't suppose I was often taken to her breast in love, more in nervousness. She had been ignored by her father, the passionate French painter dying of MS. The man child was a threat.

Some pieces for the incomplete puzzle: When small, Peter Hickson, my playmate from next door was given the name 'Horrible Hicko' behind his back. My parents had to let me know where we held such people, the son of an ex-mayor of Cambridge who was, most definitely, not PLU (people like us), but of the *nouveaux riches*. Hicko was different in some subtle, indefinable, but important way. No it wasn't indefinable, it was very clear: he wasn't as good as us because his family used *serviettes*, sat on a *settee* in the *lounge*, had no *taste*, and, worst of all, had slight, but noticeable local accents. Hicko was my best friend, but I learnt, subtly, to despise him.

Such were the late fifties in enlightened Cambridge that Mr Butters, the headmaster at my prep school, was regarded as a charming eccentric. One of his quirks was a keenness that his boys should be 'regular' and, to this end, he installed a system of light signals in a main corridor to show which of the many lavatory cubicles some distance away were occupied. If his lights indicated they were being too infrequently used, he would give us a solemn address about the splendours of regularity in all our habits and functions. Anthony Stern now tells me that, after I left, Mr Butters was forced to resign after improprieties with smaller boys came to light!

It was at this school that I learnt to use my body to get my own way. I would develop the most awful stomach ache on the two days of the week that we were meant to play the dreaded game of football. My mother would write a note asking for me to be excused. I was taken to see the doctor. Such was my need that I preferred to let my parents and the doctor think there was something wrong with me, rather than be made to play the messy, muddy game.

In the art department, Miss Burke, a replica of jowled Margaret Rutherford in the St Trinian's movies with her tweed skirts and brogues, stalked round our easels in search of blackheads. When she spotted one, she would pounce. The embarrassed owner would be told to stand still while she squeezed it out between her thumbnails. We just accepted it as something that art teachers did. No more strange than many other grownup habits.

In the trees around the tennis courts, gangs held sway. Or rather, *the* gang, Simpson's gang, acting out their Tarzan and Dan Dare fantasies, while those unfortunates not allowed to belong pretended they didn't care. I was amazed to discover that Simpson's rejects were known as 'Pryor's Gang'. Ant was not in Simpson's gang. Nor was he in Pryor's Gang. I didn't understand why I couldn't join Simpson's or why Ant wouldn't be in my gang.

1793: The British East India Company establishes a monopoly on the opium trade.

Nothing too traumatic, but it was all adding to the weight of not fitting my skin. Then came a serious trauma. One afternoon, I was wheeling my bike over the footbridge across the small river on my way home from seeing Ant. There was a man. He was standing on the bridge. He wore a mud-coloured mac. He started talking to me. Being the nice, well-brought up boy that I was, I stopped and answered his questions. He suggested that it would be a nice thing to do if he opened my fly buttons. It felt no more strange than Miss Burke squeezing my blackheads. I don't suppose I answered him, but acquiesced. He seemed a nice man. He found my penis. He sucked it.

I rushed home, more bewildered than assaulted. I told my mother that a man had done something to me. Eventually mummy and daddy wheedled the whole story out of me and my father went ballistic. Red in the face. Outraged. He phoned the police. He organised search parties. He was going to lynch the man, but they never found him. No more was said. I was left to deal with it as best I could.

Not only did I get myself assaulted (yes, I quickly learnt it was, somehow, my fault) but I couldn't manage the Divinity paper of the Common Entrance. They thought sending me to board at the prep school, all of two miles from home, might do the trick. But I was even more miserable and perplexed. Sent away for failing to learn something they, good Darwinians all, found ludicrous. Do as I say, not as I do.

That didn't work, so I had to be sent to Aspatria in Cumberland. I was learning how deep was the fissure between feeling and getting on. Send your eleven year old son three hundred miles away from home to learn something you don't believe in so that you can spend a great deal of money giving him an 'education' you don't really believe in, not really. An absurd barbarity completed at Eton!

How completely and utterly and totally ridiculous it is: that I am somehow superior to you if I am born in a certain kind of family. And even more absurd that you should pay through the nose to establish your superiority through your children's 'education'! The curious subtleties of distinguishing which families are superior to which. And that learning these subtleties and the signs and semblances that mark out these differences should occupy an emotionally important part of middle class education. The final absurdity is that the whole British private education system should be founded on the premise that this privilege has to be protected.

Eton is a closed society, a world unto itself, and over its five hundred years of introspective existence there has developed a well defined and often most peculiar system of mores, rules and language.

One was led to believe that the ability to wade convincingly through this morass equips a chap to be a leader of men. What you won on the playing fields of Eton is no battle, it's the whole English disease, it sticks right to you, permeates all your social attitudes, whether you ride it or it rides you.

The (I suppose) unconscious purpose of the extraordinary tailcoat uniform, still worn to this day, is to emphasise the superiority and difference you have gained just by being at one of the most expensive schools in Christendom.

The wilful and absurd snubbing of the modern world that is Eton, and thus the upper middle class, is best exemplified in the Wall Game. Played by two teams of pugilists dressed in tattered suits of padding that are handed down from generation to generation, only those who have won favour in the eyes of the leading sportsmen of the day get to play it. They form a sort of rugby scrum, except that it's called a 'bully', pressed hard against an ancient fifteen-foot high wall.

As far as the spectator goes, that's about it. The bully hardly moves except to dig itself further into the mud, while the ball is thrown in and kicked out with determined regularity. It is a game Samuel Beckett might have invented. When I was there, a goal hadn't been scored for years. There could never be any away matches, for the obvious reason that the game isn't played anywhere else. The absurd is so deep in the British middle-class heart.

> 1800: The British Levant Company [almost certainly run by Old Etonians] purchases nearly half of all of the opium coming out of Smyrna, Turkey strictly for importation to Europe and the United States.

My housemaster, Peter Hazell's unorthodox quaker beliefs made him unpopular. By reading from C.S. Lewis at prayers, he was disturbing the accepted pattern of things. Nearly everyone got confirmed when they were about fourteen. It meant one could get out of the house after lock-up once a week for special classes and, when the big day came, one got presents and a slap-up meal from 'one's people' (Eton speak for 'your family') as well as an extra holiday from school. I don't really know why, but I refused to go through with this charade. This was the first sign to the chaps in the house that Pryor was, what shall we say, weird.

One evening I heard the heavy, steel-rimmed tread of Hazell as he approached my room at the end of the corridor. What was it this time? Had he found out about the jazz records? No, and instead of ripping into me about some unsporting deed or other, he congratulated me, he actually approved of my standing up for my principles. I was gobsmacked because I hadn't been aware of having any up till then. From then on I counted principles as one of my greatest assets, something to counteract team spirit, wetness and elbow grease.

Yes, I am saying that the dishonesty, hypocrisy, absurdity and decrepitude of the emotional life encouraged at Eton causes immense damage. The weight of that damage, the energy spent healing that destruction, far, far outweighs any good that is to be found in the system. It taught that warped and utterly dysfunctional family relations are good. It encouraged a ridiculous, but destructive self-aggrandisement that has no place in the twenty-first century.

Without anyone to feed it, the cuckoo died.

5 It's All Happening

Nineteen years old, coming to the end of my first year at Cambridge, I found myself going up to London to visit Sam. He lived off the King's Road with Tania, a chubby Sloany English actress, who was 'resting' all the time I knew her. Their small flat did not accord with the image of the junky as someone who lives in utmost squalor. It was what might be called cosy.

Sam offered me a fix soon after I arrived, and this time I was able to perform the whole ritual myself, and was only slightly sick as I drifted away into the familiar sea of warm security. Tania didn't use heroin herself, but seemed able to tolerate our doing so without much revulsion.

On my third trip to see Sam, he judged it right to take me to meet Alexander Trocchi, poet, author of *Cain's Book* and mentor of a group of junky intellectuals. He was a Scots version of William Burroughs, in that the use of heroin and cocaine was integral to his writing and ideas.

> 1803: Friedrich Sertuerner of Paderborn, Germany, discovers the active ingredient of opium by dissolving it in acid then neutralizing it with ammonia. The result: Principium Somniferum or morphine. Physicians believe that opium had finally been perfected and tamed. Morphine is lauded as "God's own medicine" for its reliablity, long-lasting effects and safety.

He lived in a decaying, Notting Hill house with a large kitchen that served as the nerve-centre for the group. On the table were glasses of water in which syringes were suspended by cardboard holders; round it, a group of intense faces. They welcomed me coolly. Trocchi's face was a skull with little flesh on it, the talk of Sigma Project. After Sam had introduced me and explained my circumstances, one of the group, Marcus, a rodent-like Australian in a leather jacket, gave me four pills of H and a spare syringe. I had my fix in full view (such a surgical procedure with blood and needles would seem to demand at least curtains, but that wouldn't be cool).

Marcus said that I could get my supply from him until I decided to find myself a sympathetic doctor. I was still dithering, agonising as to whether I was hooked. His assumption that I needed a regular supply and his apparent readiness to give it to me left me with little doubt.

Around the kitchen table we fixed and we conspired and we plotted the cultural revolution. The winter palace of the art establishment was to be stormed. We of the underground were tunnelling

The Bolsheviks, a woodcut by my grandmother, Gwen Raverat

beneath them to subvert the system and bring it crashing down. Trocchi's Sigma Project, was a cocaine and heroin induced conspiracy to bypass capitalist control of the spread of information by the printed word.

Frequent additions to the *Sigma Folio* would tell subscribers everything they needed to know, whether it be radical politics, drugs information, jazz reviews or poetry. The thousands, if not millions, who were to make the Beatles, the Stones, Bob Dylan and Allen Ginsberg famous, would all subscribe and be galvanised by the same undistorted information, the same truth. Trouble was, it was to turn out, the culturally oppressed masses weren't hugely interested. Most didn't even know they were oppressed! And, like other revolutions, the Sigma Project was bereft of love. Hence its snobbery and brutality.

I was swept into Trocchi's rationale that held straight society's disapproval of hard drug use in contempt. It was my body, wasn't it? In his *Cain's Book,* Trocchi wrote:

> *The eyelids droop, the blood is aware of itself, a slow phosphorescence in all the fabric of the flesh and nerve and bone; it is that the organism has a sense of being intact and unbrittle, and above all inviolable. For the attitude born of this sense of inviolability some Americans have used the word 'cool'.*

I was going up to London as often as I could to score from Marcus, and it wasn't long before he felt it necessary to start charging me ten shillings a grain. (That's 50 pence for 65 milligrams. On the street today the same amount of unadulterated heroin would cost at least £100.) Marcus, Sam, Trocchi and friends were all registered addicts and got their supplies free of any charge through the National Health Service.

Through all this upheaval and the beginnings of addiction, I still managed to do some work, some philosophy, although it was difficult. I loved the idea of Descartes at the fireside, rejecting all that he knew at that moment because it might be illusion, until he was left with just one certainty: that he was thinking and that this was the only satisfactory proof of his existence: *cogito ergo sum.*

I could apply this to my situation and stretch it a bit further. If my thinking was the only proof of my existence and the quality of that thinking is the only measure of my worth, as the academic environment of Cambridge led me to believe, then the use of heroin and cocaine to facilitate clear and innovatory thought must be justified. The emotional conflicts that went unresolved and thus grew because of that use were of little significance beside this brave new life of the mind.

What was left out of the writings I did then, was always left out, is the heroin cause of the needle effect high, the evil white horse, and the pain, loneliness, fear, loathing and gaping hole right through the middle of my life, well, existence. So the rationale needed to be developed, the war manifesto. The user's being repels non-users simply because he *is* a user. There is a self-contained, self-observing obsession that is impenetrable, so it was all the more extraordinary that I should still be out there with Nigel and Ant.

1827 E. Merck & Company of Darmstadt, Germany, begins commercial manufacturing of morphine.

But the drive and passion saw us beginning to practice what we preached; we were beginning to happen (verb: to put on a happening).

Nigel and I had forgotten the worst ravages of being heckled at *Roodmoodments*. Happenings were what we did: we happened, we evolved, we improvised from scripts, we encouraged our spectators to influence what we did next. More live, indeterminate art than theatre, but a performance where anything could happen. The purpose a purely Dadaistic one: to disrupt and discombobulate, to carry the audience to another discontinuous understanding. Yes, that messianic tendency to change people, to wake them up.

John Cage had done one in 1952 at Black Mountain College, with paintings by Robert Rauschenberg, a ballet by Merce Cunningham, a poem by Charles Olsen and the music of David Tudor in a single space. Allan Kaprow developed the idea in New York in 1959 with *18 Happenings in 6 Parts* in the Reuben Gallery. And in 1960 Jean-Jacques Lebel, disciple of Antonin Artaud, presented the *Enterrement d'une Chose* (Burial of a Thing) in Venice.

I don't know how much of this we knew then – probably most of it, but ill-digested. The idea fitted perfectly with our wish to be re-volting in public, to hit the bourgeoisie where it hurt, to undermine the comfortable Cambridge view of art.

Ant Stern, by this time pulled into St Johns by his father's strings as I had been into Trinity, heard that we were putting on the Happening and came along, determined to undermine our underminings. When he got home that night he wrote the following excerpts as part of his unpublished novel *Cambridge Blues*:

> *Tonight William and Nigel have a Dada Happening.*
> *"We want to make people realize how absurd life is."*
> *"Surely they know that already?"*
> *"Not all of them – the stupid ones don't know it."*
> *An ambivalent attitude to us and the Happening, but he was taking notice, entering the spirit of the thing.*
> *We all agree that happenings are a load of rubbish. Even so there are a number of reasons why we will go along. Firstly to see William making a fool of himself, secondly to see the hecklers make a fool of William. Thirdly to make fools of ourselves. My god this sounds as if I were with it all along. But in fact I'm not.*

Others have told me that they were scared of me at the time. My drug induced strength of opinion was, I suppose, scary. I would not reveal any vulnerability.

> *William and Nigel have, in order to communicate 'total art' to the acquies-*
> *cent, awestruck denizens of this our noble city, installed a considerable amount*

of household junk: children's toys from Woolworths: of special interest to all students of Zen is a plastic stengun, which fires sparks when its trigger is pulled to the accompaniment of a stream of high pitched, staccato clicking sounds. On the front of the piano is chalked the following pregnant message for mankind: "There are no answers."

Nigel and I then began to recite a play, a sketch I had written, set in the year 2000 in which a deaf mute and a young writer discuss a play that the deaf mute has written. The play the characters are discussing (difficult for the deaf mute) is the play they are acting, set, as I said, in the year 2000. As though the play were swallowing itself alive. Nigel plays the deaf mute, me the writer. We repeat the play a few times. Anthony accuses me of saying:

"The trolls should get what's happening after about the third time round. It's very bop you know."
But the trolls alas, boorish and irreverent as ever, have begun to hoot. William replies with a brilliant gesture, to wit: firing his stengun into the unarmed defenceless audience, with reckless and flagrant disregard for the Geneva Convention.
Shouts of "Go home Dada," "William Pryor for King," "Fraudulent liars resign".

We get both record players going: one playing Varese, the other a raga, both turned up full. As Ant wrote:

The alienation of modernism receives its supreme and apocalyptical exposition. It goes on for a considerable time. Pieces of newspaper have been distributed among the audience, who are requested to read aloud, as loud as possible in fact. Nigel has rubbed out the previous message on the piano and has written: 'Words are merely symbols' in chalk.
Cries of "phoneys resign" and "exhibitionist morons go home" are uttered even more vehemently, when William begins to break pieces of crockery on the floor with a mallet. Nigel reads a cut-up poem, a negro plays on the bongos. It's Jeff who is brilliant. The audience appears to be not only 'participating' but taking over the whole proceedings. A rival Happening is going on in one corner where two people are staging a mock fistfight, burning large sheets of newspaper on the floor and performing a ritual dance around the bonfire. Extinguished with a dash a beer.
I notice William eyeing me rather sternly. I know he expects me to perform some meaningful everyday act. If I don't come to his aid, I shall never be able to look him in the eye again.
In a few minutes I have found what I want: a bicycle with a tool kit. Knock the plaster off the walls going upstairs with it. I dismantle it: wheels, chain, tyres,

inner tube, handle bars, saddle, nuts and bolts all over the floor like marbles. Bits of bicycle everywhere when I have finished. I decide to leave for good before anyone tries to make me put it together. I leave William with his poems and dismembered bicycle. Somebody will be walking home tonight, but one has to make sacrifices....

He who understands baboon [will] *do more towards metaphysics than Locke.*
(Charles Darwin)*

As I got towards the end of my first year at Trinity I was fixing nearly every day, and this meant going to London at least once a week. I would go to Nigel and Jenny's place in Cromwell Road after scoring from Marcus or Sam. Nigel was then at the London School of Film Technique and had become one of the luminaries of the psychedelic movement that had sprung up in London in the wake of Timothy Leary. Donavon, Jagger, Syd Barrett were visitors to the flat. There were frequent group trips to other awarenesses. Nigel kept an eye-drop bottle full of LSD in the fridge and would put a couple of drops on your tongue just for the asking.

In the large, airless hall someone had built a platform, a false ceiling with enough headroom above it to serve as a small, even more airless room where I would sleep when I stayed the night. It was in this unworldly and dark space that I first experienced true withdrawal symptoms. I had used more H than usual the day before, and as it began to wear off that night, I found I couldn't get back to sleep. I had woken up soaked in sweat, with sharp pains in my arms and legs, and an insatiable craving that drove all other thoughts from my mind.

1837: Elizabeth Barrett Browning falls under the spell of morphine. She writes *Poetical Paragraphs*.

Then, as soon as the hour was reasonable, the desperate bus journey to see Marcus, to get that fix to put it right, but not finding him till mid-morning, and he not being able to spare any, you understand?, none to spare, why don't you try Sam?, and just enough for a taxi, and thank God, there he is through the window and he opens the door and yes, he gives me a fix. As time went by, more and more

---

*Notebook M (16 August 1838) in P. H. Barrett *et al.* (eds.) *Charles Darwin's Notebooks 1836–1844* (1987)

of my days would be spent in such one-pointed endeavour.

In between trips and fixes and joints one day, Nigel told me that Johnny Johnson, the American we'd shared with above the Hang Chow, the committed beat teahead and poet, had jumped out of a third floor window in a suicide attempt, and was now severely crippled. I couldn't bring myself to go and see him. Some time later, I heard that he'd finally made it. He had dragged his half-paralysed body to an even higher window when no one was looking and thrown himself out. He was dead. I closed my mind.

With easy access to Nigel's bottle, filled with pharmaceutical LSD straight and legally from the Sandoz labs in Switzerland, it was inevitable that I should go on a few trips with Nigel and his fellow Psychonauts. Often fear and paranoia would get the upper hand, dictating the direction of my internal wanderings. The breakthrough and enlightenment that I'd known on Morning Glory seeds wasn't there.

Though once we found a strange power. We crossed Cromwell Road in the middle of a trip and walked, one after the other, the wrong way up the taxi exit from what was then called the West London Air Terminal. It was a helix with no pavement and only room for the taxis, taking them down a floor to the street. The helix was so tight they couldn't possibly see us coming. But we had the power to stop them even entering the ramp while we walked slowly up it. We didn't meet one.

On another occasion I was coming down from a trip started the previous evening, when a man who introduced himself as Billy Bolitho swept into the flat. He had something of Oscar Wilde about him with his cape and aristocratic manner. He was in fact the right honourable William Bolitho, son of some obscure Anglo-Irish Marquis. He opened the smart leather briefcase he was carrying, to reveal that it had within it a section, handmade from the same leather as the case, each of whose little pockets contained a large glass ampoule.

"Fancy some methedrine, old chap?" I wasn't sure what it was and mumbled a noncommittal answer. He broke open an ampoule and sucked half the contents into a syringe he produced from the depths of his briefcase. Before I could protest, he had stuck the needle right through my shirt into my arm and pushed the plunger.

Methedrine is pure amphetamine, and it gave me an immediate rush, putting my mind on a gear I didn't know existed. I couldn't stop talking. My hypercharged brain thought it understood the whole historical process and needed to talk it out. It didn't matter whether anyone was interested. Billy had one himself and then asked me if I'd like to go with him to pick up a new supply of amps.

"Been on this stuff for years, you know. Only registered methedrine addict in England. Damned Jerries invented the stuff to keep their fighter pilots awake. Quite harmless! Does make you a bit thirsty, but that's nothing. Do the work of two people, of course, less need for sleep. Been on it for years, since just after the damned war." And so he went on and on until we reached his Chelsea flat. There were two men waiting for him, playing darts with syringes. Billy unsealed one of the boxes of ampoules that I'd been with him to collect and threw a couple to his friends. Everyone fixed, everyone talked. He gave me some amps to take with me when I left.

> 1843: Dr. Alexander Wood of Edinburgh discovers a new technique of administering morphine: injection with a syringe. He finds the effects on his patients instantaneous and three times more potent than that of orally administered morphine.

6 MARGARETA AND WHOLLY COMMUNION

Early 1965: I was just 20, a fully-fledged junky, smackhead, horsehound, fixing in toilets with impunity. My secret life kept me inside my head, always defending my space, keeping people out.

Nigel wanted me to be best man at his wedding, so I must have been able to keep the drugged and the everyday apart to some extent. At the registry office and family reception in Cambridge, the contrast couldn't have been stronger between the generations. Parents hadn't fully emerged from the fifties, but us young things! Mini skirts were so new and so shocking. Jenny was the height of fashion in her futurist, very short Courreges suit, while the groom stole the show with his Chelsea boots, long coiffured hair, velvet suit and flounced shirt.

Eventually, duty was done and the young things escaped to London and Cromwell Road for the real rave-up that went on all night. The whole of psychedelic London was there, man.

Through the crowd I couldn't help but notice her: a statuesque blonde, with sparkling eyes, honey-golden hair and a face alive with expression. I had to meet her, but dare not believe I would be of any interest. She was surrounded by a group of admiring London hipsters, all older than me. As I ran through a hundred different permutations of the opening gambit in my head, I would lose sight of her and go into a panic.

The solution as to the best opening gambit was, of course, to go to the loo and have a small fix of heroin and cocaine. Then I wouldn't need a gambit. I ran down the stairs as soon as I'd got the precious fluid into my vein, but she was nowhere to be seen. No one I asked knew where the blonde had gone, nor who she was. I rushed out into the street in the hope that I'd catch sight of her.

She was still in view, ambling along with two fans, deep in conversation. I chased after them and attached myself to the back of the group, the outsider trying to insinuate himself into the grownups conversation. I mean, she was so much Marlene Dietrich, Marilyn Monroe, the blond sophisticate. But I stuck with them as they walked towards Fulham. And it happened, the hipsters drifted away and we were left alone.

There was an intense, but embarrassed interest between us; nei-ther of us quite sure it was happening. She invited me back to her flat, her name was Margareta. She was Swedish, with a subtle and sexy lilt to her womanly voice. She was a mature 25.

And within hours we fell in love: simple as that and quick as that. A passionate discovery that there could be and was another human being so attractive, so much in tune with the same aspects. She was a RADA-trained actress, separated from her actor husband. I stayed with her for two enchanted days, quite suspended from the world. My addiction, which I did nothing to hide from her, was not unat-tractive. In fact there was a certain perverse glamour to it, especially since I gave off the aura of being in control of it, of using heroin for my own revolutionary and romantic purposes.

I now had two strong reasons to go up to London at least once a week, a double addiction, for our relationship soon became both obsessive and possessive. She was five years my senior and I was jealous of her colourful, lively life in London. I wanted to know where she'd been, who she'd talked to, who she thought about. To begin with, Margareta was able to regard my jealous lover stuff with amused tolerance, to put it down to my relative youth. It was a sign of my need to take her into myself.

She was the epitome of my romantic longings: independent, at-tractive, mature and intelligent and I wanted these qualities of hers to rub off on me through our symbiosis. It was a Tristan and Isolde love. She was my mind's, as well as my body's passion.

Slowly and surely, our inexhaustible lust for each other, kept cool with heroin, opened a door, and what lay behind was dark. It was mainly my door, but her yearnings played a part.

Before long, Margareta decided to move from her Fulham flat, with its painful associations of a broken marriage and a husband over the road with his girlfriend. She knew a young doctor whose surgery and home were in Sydney Street, Chelsea. He agreed to let her his attic. It so happened that he was one of the few 'junky doc-tors', licensed to 'treat' addicts by issuing them with prescriptions for whatever quantity of heroin and cocaine they could persuade him they needed. He believed he was helping them get their habits under control. His rationale was that he would only take on new patients he believed really wanted to get off.

If we both went to his surgery, and Margareta went in to see him first to plead my case, we felt he could hardly refuse to give me a scrip. We were right. Without even asking to look at my arms for proof that I was using, he wrote a scrip there and then for one and a half grains of heroin a day (nine pills or jacks). It was for seven days. My supply would have to be collected every day from the chemist.

His one condition was that he would only prescribe heroin until the end of the academic year, at which time I would have to go into a hospital for a cure. It was a small price to pay for a regular supply of free heroin for the next six weeks. He even relented on my having to collect my supply daily when I pointed out that I'd have to come up from Cambridge, and gave me scrips to last three days at a time.

To go into a chemist, hand over a piece of paper and be given a phial containing four and a half grains of heroin, twenty-seven jacks was extraordinary. I was beginning to admit that I was hooked, not that there was anything wrong with me, but simply that I belonged to a select group of social dissidents.

With the help of the occasional cocaine and amphetamine that I bought from fellow drug-users, I managed to complete most of my work and to everybody's surprise, not least my own, I got a 2.1 in my Part One exam at the end of the summer term. I could look forward to three months of well-earned recreation.

True to his word, Margareta's doctor friend refused to give me any more scrips now that the academic year had ended and I had to look round for an alternative source of supply. I had no intention of going to hospital for a cure, which in those days consisted of doing a cold turkey with little sedation and then occupational therapy and talking to a psychiatrist once or twice a month. I went to Sam for advice.

"No problem, man," he said blithely. "I'll take you to see Lady Frankau.* She'll look after you. She likes students." This sounded both ominous and weird: *Lady* Frankau? Who *likes students?* He told me that she was the wife of a consultant surgeon who treated junkies privately, i.e. outside the National Health Service. I was relieved to hear that she was also a fully qualified doctor.

*Jazz star's diaries reveal society doctor who kept him high

He was a hot American trumpet player, full of drop-dead cool, "the James Dean of jazz". She was a white-haired, elderly London doctor. Heroin brought them together.

Chet Baker and Isabella Frankau, even by the standards of the crazy circles they moved in, were an odd alliance. While Baker was jamming around the Algerian quarter of Paris in cellars reeking of sweat and Gauloises, Lady Frankau would spend weekends at Ickleton Grange, her Essex country home near Saffron Walden, preparing Sunday lunch for her husband Sir Claude, a consulting surgeon at St George's Hospital. Back in London during the week she would prescribe to a Bohemian circle of poets, writers, actors and jazzmen. Baker's addiction to heroin and cocaine is well known, but that his trusted supplier was Isabella at her elegant consulting rooms at 32 Wimpole Street, is only now revealed with the publication of Baker's lost diaries. [continued over]

Sam and I went to her surgery the next morning. Most of the others in her sumptuous Wimpole Street waiting room were Canadians. She was in her seventies and frail, though with the firm manner of an intelligent aristocrat. After establishing that I was an undergraduate at Cambridge, that I'd been addicted for several months and that I needed a regular supply, she didn't hesitate to give me a prescription for the two grains a day for which I asked.

Her theory seemed to be that she would give addicts what they needed (i.e. what they asked for) so that she could establish the extent of the addiction and then keep them to this dose to stabilise their situation. This usually included enough so there was some to sell. There was rarely any talk of cures and her patients had few complaints about such a system. Anyway, whatever the reasons, she seemed only too pleased to be able to help an otherwise respectable student who unfortunately found himself addicted.

[cont.] Her role in his addiction arose from her fame among North American users. Lady Frankau specialised in treating addiction, first alcohol, then heroin. Only 12 doctors were allowed to prescribe the drug in the fifties, all with private practices in London. In the United States and Canada, prescribing heroin was banned, so when Lady Frankau went on a lecture tour, outlining her sympathetic treatment of addicts, a fan club of admiring users followed her back across the Atlantic for "treatment". Lots of it. Her manner was brusque, but trusting and straightforward. "She was a doctor pure and simple," says Joan Frankau, her daughter in law. "She laid down the law and managed to wean quite a few off heroin and there was no such thing as methadone in those days." Mrs Frankau said that unlike some of her more unscrupulous colleagues who made a brisk trade out of prescriptions, she genuinely cared for those who saw her. Addicts who visited her surgery recall that she was uninterested in making money from her work and would often let patients off the consultation fee if they were short of money. Baker wasn't in that category but paid her a visit in 1962 while filming *The Stolen Hours* with Susan Hayward. Lady Frankau, he wrote, ". . . was about 75 years old . . . and very businesslike. She simply asked my name, my address and how much cocaine and heroin I wanted per day". For the equivalent of £1.80 she wrote him a "script" - prescription - for cocaine which would have cost him £312 in New York, and another for 10g of heroin. "After that first day my scripts were all for 20g each and I was off and running," he wrote. After he finished filming and his work permit expired, Lady Frankau lied, claiming he was too sick to travel, to allow him to stay in England, he said. Baker was eventually arrested on drug charges. After a month in jail he was deported with his wife and baby son to France, where he began singing and playing at the Le Chat Qui Peche. In the diaries he describes how he and other musicians, including Stan Getz and Anita O'Day, hung out at Chez Ali in the Algerian quarter: "I sent a couple of people to see Lady Frankau. They all came back with heroin and coke." Lady Frankau's life spanned an era of changing attitudes towards drug use. When she was a young girl Harrods sold laudanum, but towards the end of her career it was heroin that had become more widespread and the system of allowing private doctors to prescribe began to be seen as part of the problem. In 1967, the year Lady Frankau died, the right to prescribe heroin liberally was restricted to psychiatrists working in drying-out clinics, and a chapter in the of British drug treatment was closed. (*Sunday Telegraph*, February 28th, 1999)

That summer had the kind of intensity of involvement that easily tricks the memory into thinking it was good. The selective retention of certain facts over the rest of the context and mood has led me, in the more recent past, to boast of things that happened.

There was the time I was staying with Margareta in her attic. Dressed only in a lacy peignoir, she makes coffee. The sun is shining through the skylight. I sit on the edge of the bed, a grimy necktie loosely draped round my left arm. I watch the colourless fluid in the syringe turn scarlet as I draw up blood. Suddenly I shut my eyes, screw up my face in satisfaction. I have pushed the plunger home. Margareta butters some toast.

"That looked like it felt good. You want some toast? I'll make some if you do." Margareta asks me.

"No thanks." She takes her coffee back to bed to read the part she's trying to learn. I thumb through the records by the Dansette, my eyes hardly open.

"What are you doing today?" I ask.

"Apart from learning this part I've got to go and see someone at the Beeb about a part in Mrs Dale's Diary."

"I suppose that means you'll be going for a meal with him, or is that none of my business, like the bloke you had drinks with yesterday?"

"Yes, that's right, none of your business." She throws the script down on the bed in disgust and starts to get dressed. "I might as well go and see him early if you're just going to sit around fixing and asking stupid questions." She puts on a blue flowered summer dress, makes her hair into a golden ponytail and applies lipstick.

"Margareta? I'm sorry. I didn't mean to be possessive really. It's just that..." The doorbell rings. "I love you so much. Who's that? You expecting anyone?"

"Probably one of your junky friends. Go and answer it, will you? I've got to finish getting ready."

It was the police, who had reason to believe that there were drugs secreted on the premises. They had a search warrant. I had a few pills of heroin in a phial in my jacket pocket. They were illegal, because they were not from my scrip but had been bought from Marcus. They searched diligently, but found nothing. They then asked me to turn out my pockets. Panic. But the man held the phial up to the light, rattled it and gave it back to me without a word. They left.

The day we fooled the police. The day the drug squad couldn't recognise heroin.

Then there was *Wholly Communion*. A confused celebration of the spirit of hipness at the Royal Albert Hall, to which some six thousand came. The biggest poetry reading ever to take place in England, before or since. Trocchi was the prime mover and we got it organised in a very short time. Ant was Peter Whitehead's cameraman for the making of the documentary of the same name.

I imagine – clear memory is one of the first casualties of sustained heroin and cocaine use – it happened something like this: I arrived at Trocchi's house to find it a hive of verbal activity, bees of wisdom buzzing everywhere. John Esam, Jill and Dan Richter, Marcus and Trocchi were all round the table. There were syringes on the table and a phial of coke. I took a seat by the Aga. I had dark glasses on, as junkies did.

Marcus, had just scored a few grains of coke and we were all speeding away, talking about poetry readings in general. How they were staid and boring affairs, how poetry is life and readings are just readings and the need we all felt to transcend that, to bring the performance of poems, the living of them into a central position not just in our lives but the lives of many.

"Of course we could always hire the Albert Hall," said someone, I think it was John.

"Yeah wouldn't it be great. We could get Ginsberg, Corso and Ferlinghetti to pull the crowds; they're in Paris right now, you know," someone else said. It was a nice fantasy to play with up there on coke and it went on getting more improbable.

"But why don't we?" said Alex. Then everyone got excited when they realised there was nothing to stop us. We *could* damn well hire the Albert Hall, no less. It would be the beginning of the new, when the established codes of living would be overthrown as redundant, when the poem would rule our lives, or rather, our lives would be a poem.

Ginsberg said it better. The poem *Who Be Kind To* that he read that night catches that feeling of revolution and protest, later published in *Wholly Communion*, the book of the event:

> *Be kind to yourself, because the bliss of your own kindness will flood the police tomorrow,*
> *be kind to your neighbour, who weeps solid tears on the television sofa –*
> *he had no other home, and hears nothing but the hard voice of telephones*

Not great poetry, but powerful oratory to six thousand converted packed into one place at one time. It was mood and mind altering chemicals that kept the whole thing afloat, that were the background energy that was itself subsumed under the symbol of revolt, just as some of that revolt, as Trocchi says, was subsumed under the symbol of juvenile delinquency.

Margareta developed this idea about going to Sweden. A month in her family's country cabin with only the pine trees and the sea to talk to would surely allow me to get clear of heroin. It was to be a last ditch attempt to get me off with love and affection before it was too late. I agreed to it with some trepidation, but swept along by her confidence, I began to see that life *could* be much better without the constant need for a chemical to keep me straight.

Margareta had gone to Sweden ahead of me and would meet me off the boat. I boarded the Danish boat and was introducing myself to the man I was to share a cabin with when there was loud knocking on the door. It was the ship's purser, accompanied by two bulky men in the usual drab raincoats.

"Mr Pryor? These two gentlemen would like a word with you."

"Excuse me, sir," he turned to my cabin companion, "would you be so good as to step outside for a few minutes, so that these gentlemen can talk?" He did. 'Gentlemen' indeed! I knew what they were and could guess why they had come onto the boat to talk to me. I'd seen one of them standing behind the immigration officer who'd stamped my passport. They must have found my name on some list of registered addicts. But knowing that I was clean, carrying no drugs at all, didn't stop my heart thumping.

They searched meticulously through all my belongings, refusing to give any explanation of their action. They registered no disappointment when they didn't find anything and apologised politely for any inconvenience they might have caused as they left. When my cabin-friend returned, I adopted a pose of blustering and wounded innocence (which I more than half believed). Otherwise he might think I was some kind of filthy drug pusher.

Margareta met me on the quay in Gothenberg and took me to her parents' flat. A sweet old couple. They had no English and I had no Swedish; so we had to smile a lot. It wouldn't do for me to sleep with her, just ten yards away from their bedroom, even though this was Sweden, and anyway her bed was too small. So I was put up on the divan in the sitting room. I couldn't sleep. I chewed the sheets. I groaned. I tossed violently. I chewed the sheets again. A fitful doze brought relief around dawn, and then the mockery of the dawn cho-

Margareta and I in the Swedish countryside.

rus when turmoil is all there is! 'We're wonderfully happy, thank you very much,' the birds say, 'Pity about your misery.'

The days were one long pretence that gnarled anguish wasn't gnawing its way through the holes in my arms. Whenever Margareta and I were alone together, in her tiny bedroom or out in the streets, I could drop the charade and reveal my monumental self pity. Wasn't there anything I could get from a chemist's shop that would help? Didn't she know any drug-users in Gothenberg who could provide something, heroin, morphine, opium, something to dull the pain. But no, long walks were the only medicine. Keep the mind occupied.

At the end of the week, Margareta's father took us by car and ferry into the country, to the island on which they had their typically Swedish country cabin. It was some distance down a gravel road, four miles from the nearest shop. Pine woods offering chanterelles, swimming in the little coves and inlets, the cabin itself, a weatherboard structure with three rooms looking out over a fast running stream, the plentiful autumn sun. There were old peasant-farmer friends of Margareta whom we could visit, and her company, a beautiful and intelligent woman. All this, and I could not let go of suffering, even though the pain in my arms and legs was much better and I was beginning to get some sleep.

The obsession was such that I wrote a desperate letter to Sam, asking him to send me a grain of heroin in a hollowed-out paperback. Every day the postman brought nothing and I would reset all my expectations onto his next delivery. No heroin ever did arrive.

After two weeks I began to feel fit, but daren't admit it to myself. I would go off on long walks in the woods by myself, and on two occasions came back with several pounds of chanterelles. Margareta and I cleaned and cooked them in cream. They were delicious. But I could take it no more. I had to get back to Cambridge, the sooner the better, although I conned myself that it wouldn't be straight back to junk. The next academic year wasn't far off.

I got the boat back to London a week later. Margareta was to stay a few more weeks. I made straight for Sam's. At first he was reluctant to turn me on. I'd been off the stuff for several weeks, hadn't I? But his resistance soon crumbled. Blessed relief. It was a homecoming, a return to the wondrous cotton-wool kingdom where nothing hurt and all was safe.

> 1895: Heinrich Dreser working for The Bayer Company of Elberfeld, Germany, finds that diluting morphine with acetyls produces a drug without the common morphine side effects. Bayer begins production of diacetyl-morphine and coins the name 'heroin', because it was what Victorian pharmacists called an 'heroic' drug; one that effected dramatic change, quickly.

Once again I had the problem of finding a regular supply. Sam was prepared to help for a few days only, but after that I'd have to go elsewhere. After some agonising, I decided I could approach Lady Frankau, if I stressed that it was a temporary measure. I rang her from home, where I was staying until term started. She wasn't in, but her secretary-companion said that, since it was an emergency, she would prevail on her mistress to meet me in her car at the end of Chaucer Road that evening on her way into Cambridge from her country house in Essex.

I was waiting at the appointed time, apprehensive and cold, not knowing what to expect. A black Bentley purred to a halt beside me. The uniformed chauffeur jumped out, opened the rear door and gestured me to get in. There was her ladyship with a fox-fur round her shoulders. I got in next to her.

"You really can't wait? You have to have something right now?"

"Yes, I've only had one fix today. I need some badly."

"But what happened to that cure you went to Sweden for?"

"I had to come back to do some work for next term," I lied.

"And what do you think you need?" She'd already got her prescription pad out and was looking for a pen.

"Two grains a day."

"All right then, I'll give you a week's supply at two grains a day, but…" She looked up from writing the prescription.

"Yes?"

"You must find a doctor in Cambridge who is prepared to help you. It's obviously too disruptive to your studies for you to keep coming to see me in London. When you've found one, tell him to telephone me. You know, to confirm that you've been getting heroin on prescription."

I couldn't argue with that. It had never crossed my mind to get a local doctor to give me my prescriptions.

"OK, I'll do that. Thanks so much for your help."

And she was off down the road in her chauffeur-driven Bentley. I ran home with my scrip, grabbed my bike, and peddled furiously off to the only chemist in Cambridge that stocked heroin, who was due to shut in a few minutes. He gave me my phial with its twelve little pills. I got a couple of syringes and rushed home to fix.

I used the downstairs loo because any drops of blood wouldn't show up too much on the red floor tiles. I don't think I was suspected at that time, just that my behaviour was a bit odd that I would spend half an hour in the loo and that I would rush out of the house at chemist-opening time in the morning without any explanations as to where I was going.

The only doctor I could think of approaching in Cambridge was the young partner of the family GP, with whom I'd already had some dealings and whom I found to be compassionate and therefore manipulable.

I went to his surgery and told him, quite simply, that I was an addict in need of supplies and had come to him for help. I told him that I was registered and that he was welcome to give Lady Frankau a ring to confirm what I told him. He was taken aback and confessed to not having dealt with an addict before. He asked me to return that evening, to give him time to consult his colleagues as to the legal situation and make other enquiries. When I went back, he said that he could help me and would give me a separate prescription for each day and that he would need to see me once a week.

I was nicely set up for the coming term. The chemist was only two hundred yards from my new digs in Jesus Lane.

7 MELODIOUS THUNK

Autumn 1965 and I was twenty years old, a junky registered with the Home Office, and starting my second year at Cambridge University. So far, the welfare state and my moneyed middle-class cocoon had cossetted me from the extremes of degradation and depravity that are usually associated with junkies. My parents knew nothing about my habit, although I must have been a constant source of anxiety through my wild behaviour and surly reluctance to communicate with them or anyone else of their generation. But that's what scapegoats are supposed to do.

Though sometimes there were twinkles crossing the divide. I was listening to my new Monk* album at home in the vacation and my father came into the room.

"Is that Melodious Thunk?" he asked impishly.

"Yes," I replied, "Isn't he great?"

With digs away from College, I would have more freedom to come and go as I pleased. My rooms were on the ground floor, facing directly on to Jesus Lane and within two minutes of the College. The landlady was amiable enough in the way that student landladies have.

I would wake early, at about six, when the restless, nagging aches of withdrawal would surface through whatever sleep I'd been lucky to get that night. If I had managed to be sensible, I would have a couple of jacks left over for the morning, to get me straight. I would then gouge hungrily in my arm with a needle until I found a vein. Then the drawing up of blood, to watch it flower in the colourless heroin solution. The titillating foreplay to the act that had become the meaning of my life: to push home the plunger and embrace my bloodstream with its liquid comforter. All needs were channelled into one. Using the algebra of that need, we get: H (a constant) + W (the withdrawal variable) = B (Burrough's Constant, Bliss).

Frequently, though, I didn't manage to save any H for the morn-

---

* Thelonious Monk's name, appearance (he liked funny hats) and personality (an occasionally uncommunicative introvert) helped to brand him as some kind of nut. Fortunately Alfred Lion of *Blue Note* believed in him and recorded Monk extensively during 1947-48 and 1951-52.

ing and then I experienced the full torment of hell's objective time as I waited for each second to pass until the chemist opened at nine o'clock. The pain of that separation from my substance chiefly made itself known through sharp, throbbing aches in my arms, at the many points where my blood found union with its opiate. Often my first fix after such a wait was abnormally large, to make up for the hours of suffering, and it would send me into a fitful sleep. And as scar tissue built up on my veins, they became lumpy and hard. I was developing tracks, the telltale sign of heroin addiction.

My bicycle would be one of a heap leaning against the railings outside my digs. Grabbing it and getting to Professor Wisdom's lectures on time at nine was a challenge, whatever the state of my drug input.

Professor Wisdom was at the cutting edge, continuing and expanding Ludwig Wittgenstein's linguistic philosophy. He would arrive for his lectures on his bicycle (sometimes a horse), wearing riding breeches, the white hair surrounding his bald patch forming little wings. Without any preliminaries, he would wade straight into the actual doing of philosophy.

He preferred to go straight to the puzzlement of a problem and thrash it out from there, showing how the oddness lay in the language we used to talk about the problem, not anywhere else. His lectures were improvisations. We had no idea of the direction a lecture would take before he started, or of the conclusions, if any, it would reach. Andrew was always a welcome co-conspirator at these improvisations.

This focus on language as formative force has resonated somewhere in my mind ever since.

In the early 1900's the philanthropic Saint James Society in the US mounts a campaign to supply free samples of heroin through the mail to morphine addicts who are trying give up their habits.

Nigel was now into his last year at the London School of Film Technique and had embarked on his final project, the making of a sixteen millimetre silent film, to last from fifteen to twenty minutes. The school provided a Bolex camera, as much film stock as he might need, and editing facilities.

"What is it? What is the plot?" Nigel's silver lame boots twinkled as he spoke. We were sitting in my room in Jesus Lane, drinking tea.

"Could it be," I ventured, "could it be a progress through absurdity?"

"Yeah, possibly. What do you mean?"

"I mean," making it up as I went along, "that, in the film, we see someone being pulled through the absurdity of life."

"No sorry, still don't get it." Nor did I really. But that wasn't going to stop me.

"How about a tramp? You know, big rough overcoat," I got up and went to the back of the door, "like this one and Doc Martins." I ambled back to my University digs armchair, "and he's – yes, this is it – got a rope tied round his middle that pulls him – we never see who does the pulling – to his karma."

"What on earth is 'karma'?" Nigel hadn't come to see Trungpa Rimpoche. This was 1965 and the word hadn't spread far and wide yet.

"Literally, the law of cause and effect, but also destiny. As you sow, so shall you reap. What's going to happen to you is unavoidable. It is your karma. It is written."

"Eenteresting," said Nigel with a mock Jungian accent. "So we have a tramp and he's pulled by a rope through whatever towards his karma? Eenteresting. It could be both the inside and the outside. We could have him looking at himself as a tramp being pulled through… What's he called, this tramp?"

"I thought it was a silent movie," said I.

"Yes but he still needs a name." I looked out of the window. "How about Jesus Lane. Get it? Mr Lane, Mr Jesus Lane."

"Ah," said Nigel. "The film could be called *A Day in the Eye of Jesus Lane*." He looked pleased.

"Fantastic. *A Day in the Eye of Jesus Lane*." It rolled off the mind's tongue very nicely. "Can I play the tramp?"

"Of course, dear boy."

We had a sketch of a shooting script. The first few shots would be – now that we knew what the film was called, and that it was all about a day in the eye of a tramp called Jesus Lane – set in the street they named after him.

My first moment as a film star arrived. It took all morning to get it right, the light, the everything. Margareta, being an actress, had come down to watch and participate. The opening shot was a close up of my eyes. As they open and look about themselves, the camera zooms out to show me lying on my bed with a blanket up to my nose.

The shot continues with me slowly pulling back the blanket to reveal that I'm wearing my Crombie and dirty boots, with the rope tied round my waist. The rope starts to pull me up.

And so it went on: every scene challenging cinematic conventions and daring the audience to make sense of it. Nigel edited it to move very fast and the overall effect was one of confused anarchy. It keeps looking as though it's going to have meaning, but never does.

It was a film that arose from Dada, Becket, Burroughs and underground filmmakers like Brakhage and Kenneth Anger. Plot and continuity were of minor importance; it was more relevant to give the audience dislocation and shock. We only had a vague idea about symbolism and then usually in retrospect. The rope, for instance, could be seen as the noose of convention and habit that pulls man through the bewildering scenes of life. Or as a piece of rope, come to that.

There's a scene near the end of the film where I open a door in Nigel's Cromwell Road flat to find the room full of people smoking grass, and I am waved away, I am excluded from the sacrament, the door is shut in my face. When Nigel came to complete the film the following summer, I was ensconced in a psychiatric hospital and the tramp figure was made to transmute into one that looked remarkably like Andrew.

One of the tragedies of old age is that no one can find a print of the film anywhere! It is gone.

Margareta was still the love of my life, even though we were seeing less of each other. She was getting more parts and had less time to come to Cambridge and I no longer needed to go to London for my heroin. But our increased propensity to stormy and sometimes violent quarrels also kept us apart. I needed her to belong to me and to accept my addiction, not as a tolerable weakness, but as the necessary condition of a revolutionary and sensitive artist/poet/philosopher. Before long all my demands on her had crystallised into a single obsession: that she divorce her husband and marry me, that way we could live out our destinies together in a blaze of glory.

> 1902: In various medical journals, physicians discuss the side effects of using heroin as a morphine step-down cure. Several physicians argue that their patients suffered from heroin withdrawal symptoms equal to those of morphine addiction.

Margareta didn't see things my way at all. She didn't even feel it particularly urgent that she divorce her husband, even though he was living with another woman. They had a mutually acceptable agreement whereby they lived apart and respected each other's privacy. She saw no need to go any further. I couldn't accept this. I wrote letters and poems to her. My one physical need was being matched by a single mental obsession: that her unwillingness to marry me, our inability to be at peace with one another was entirely due to her not appreciating the enormity and urgency of the situation.

Something of the genius syndrome remained. Surely, this, my lover, this ideal woman, can recognise how imperative it is that such genius and vision, as is mine, have the partner that destiny has allotted them. Such a love, that rises far beyond the common coupling of ordinary mortals, must surely be made right and lasting with the contract of marriage? But she would not see it that way, and could not. I was trying to trap her, to swallow her up. My demands oppressed her like a leach trying to suck her lifeblood into my obsessive syringe.

And so we quarrelled, we fought, we inflicted our inner conflicts on each other.

Margareta finally agreed to come down to talk the whole thing over one last time.

On Cambridge's bleak, windswept station platform, there she was, every inch the blond goddess of beauty and svelte sexuality. We ran to each other's arms; kissed and nuzzled necks. On the bus into town, we looked long into each other's eyes. There was expectation, anticipation and a warmth from being together again.

Once in my room, I helped her off with her coat; already a greater intimacy. Her soft, tight, ribbed blue jumper with enormous soft collar had the fragrance of Swedish summers and her shape of desire.

"How's your work going, William?" She sat next to me in front of the gas fire, the sort that sputtered its heat up the white coruscations. I had bought some crumpets to spear on the toasting fork with which every undergraduate room was equipped.

"OK I suppose. I've done next week's essay, so I wouldn't have to worry about it while you're here. You are going to stay the weekend?"

"I don't see why not." She looked away. "Yes, I'd love that."

"That's good." I went over to the kettle to make coffee. "Did you get my last two letters?" I asked as nonchalantly as possible.

"Yes, thank you. D'you think the landlady heard me come in?"

"I doubt it. Anyway we're doing nothing wrong, you've just come round for coffee, that's all. What did you think? Of what I said in my letters?" I needed her to respond, though I knew full well where it would lead. Each time I thought it would be different.

"Oh that's good," she pointed to the dove of peace made from pine shavings that she'd given me. "I like the way you've hung it from that light." She paused, pecked me on the lips and gave me a soulful look. "William, can't we just enjoy being together. You know, go out for a meal, go to the cinema and come back here to bed. Can't we?"

"Yes, my love, of course we can." I gave her a hug. "Look, I'll put on a record while I have a fix. You could read this if you want, and then we'll go out." I thrust one of my new poems about the idyllic nature of our love into her hand and went over to lock the door. I wasn't going to creep off to the lavatory to do it. I wasn't going to hide what and how I was.

As I got a hit and pulled the blood back into the syringe, I noticed through the corner of my eye that Margareta was watching me with an expression of resignation. I concentrated on the relief, the wave of security that washed through me as I pressed with my thumb. I left the syringe sticking in my arm while I reached for a tissue. I pulled out some more blood to flush out the remaining heroin solution. I repeated this twice more. I was puzzled, in a remote sort of way, why I was making such a palaver of this particular fix.

"Feel better?" Margareta asked when I'd finished, "can we go out and eat now?"

"Sure." But I made no move, just sat with that thickness of vision, wondering at her beauty. "You didn't say what you thought about my letters. You must have thought something."

"Of course I did. But, William," she turned to look softly at me, "please, please let's not talk about all that now. You remember what happened when you came up to London. Let's just be happy together." I wiped the last spot of blood from my arm and pulled down my sleeve. I took the record off.

"But Margareta, it's vital. I want you to marry me. I really do. It could be so beautiful. Don't you want to be with me as much as possible?"

"Yes William… No, William." She was getting distraught. "Look: I don't want to talk about it, OK? There's no point. Nothing's changed. Let's talk about something else, or better still, go out for that meal."

"I don't want to talk about it either, really, but you did say you would! I don't know if you really love me. I don't know if you see what I do of the possibilities. Often I think I don't want to go on, it's tearing me apart, all this not knowing. Surely, if you love me, then you would want to be with me all the time. I don't think you really love me. I think you think I'm some sort of interesting diversion from your boring life in London. No, I don't mean that. It's just that

I don't know where I stand any more."

"William, how many times do I have to tell you? You know that I love you. I wouldn't be here if I didn't." She straightened her skirt. "Can't we go and have something to eat now? I'm starving."

"Sorry, yes I know you love me," I said, oblivious of her plea as I paced back and forth. "But I also think you want to hurt me. You know how important it is to me and yet you refuse to even talk about it. Please tell me, after what I put in those letters, why, why don't you want to marry me?" An instinct for tragedy drove me on.

"OK William, if that's what you want, you bastard." The sudden change in her voice and manner jolted my heart. Her bottom lip quivered. Once again, I'd driven her into a despair not unlike my own. A rising, hysterical frustration.

"I don't want to marry you," she suppressed a scream. "I don't intend to marry you, even if I were free to, which I'm not. You have no respect for my feelings. You expect me to do exactly what you want. It's…"

"Don't be so emotional," I cut her off. "Just because I can see things you can't; just because I know what a good marriage we'd have. I think you think Roy will come back to you and that's why you don't want to divorce him. You're just stringing me along as some kind of insurance in case your plans don't work out." Even as I said it, I knew I didn't mean it.

"Why, you…" She lunged towards me and caught me on the side of the head. "You are so self-centred. You are so… so self-obsessed." She lashed out with her foot. I was getting frightened. Her fury gave her great strength. I took my belt out of my trousers. To defend myself, I thought, and made a trial sweep with it.

That was the limit for Margareta, that was it. She tore down the dove of peace from the lampshade and started to tear it to pieces. That my love should, for no apparent reason, become an agent of fury and destruction. What had I done to deserve this?

"Please, no Margareta, don't." I was crying now, imploring her to stop. The dove was in pieces and she was tearing up a photo of herself that she'd given me. "Please, please, don't do this to me. I didn't mean any harm. Why is it so wrong to want to marry you?"

"Oh William," there was a hint of compassion in her voice. "You're so sad, so pathetic. Your junk, your tears, your pleading, your whining." She picked up her coat and overnight bag. "For God's sake don't follow me, William. I'm going and want to be left alone."

"Don't go, please don't go." I clutched at her arm. "I won't talk about all that any more I promise. Please don't go."

"You're so childish. You really don't know *what* you want, do you?" She wrenched herself free. "No, William, I'm going and don't try to stop me." I sat down and buried my head in my arms on the table. Margareta came up to me and very lightly stroked my hair.

"I'm sorry it had to be like this. I'll write to you. Maybe we can straighten it out." With that she went.

I had an extra large fix and dozed my way through the rest of that evening.

Margareta did write, and three weeks later I went to stay with her for a weekend. We didn't row. The need we had for each other, physical and emotional, was such that we were able to reach a short-lived tacit agreement not to talk about certain things.

I was trying to get to grips with an essay about the differences between inductive and deductive reasoning, when there was a knock on my door. It was Sam. I hadn't expected him and wasn't all that glad to see him. His presence could well jeopardise the secrecy of my addiction. Up till then, I assumed that no one in College knew anything about it, and with Sam around, anything could happen. But he pushed my fears into the background when he said he'd brought me some cocaine.

What little I'd had of the stuff had been a revelation. It sent you into such elated realms of *knowing,* such a seeming crystal clarity. It opened the top of your head and let cosmic winds blow there. We fixed good fixes. We celebrated our being together in the hidden, the occult club of junkiedom; we listened to Albert Ayler, the newest, the hippest, who played his tenor saxophone as though it were the universe squealing. Sam's phial of heroin got knocked over, which was a drag, but we picked up all the jacks we could find and soon forgot about it. Sam went after first fix the next day, and I went to a lecture and then on to the library to read up some more for my essay.

Waiting for me when I got back that evening there was a note asking me to go and see my tutor. I couldn't think what it was about.

"It's your body, William. Nobody's got the right to tell you what you can or can't do with it, especially with the mess they've got the world into. If it gives you pleasure, if it allows you to do things you wouldn't otherwise be able to do, then it's OK. You're not harming anyone else. You can do what you like with your own body."

Could I?

One's Tutor at Cambridge is *in loco parentis* and thus responsible for one's 'moral and academic welfare'. I had no idea what mine could want to see me about. No, I hoped beyond hope that he didn't want to see me about junk and suppressed the possibility.

My tutor was Harry Williams, a friend and colleague of my father's and a radical priest. Radical in that he practised and preached a low church approach that involved, for instance, his going on retreat at regular intervals. He had chubby red cheeks and a bonhomie that transcended the usual priestliness.

In a famous sermon he had said, "Most people's wilderness is inside them, not outside. It's a wilderness of being alone that we try to relieve by chatter, or heroin, or religion, or sex – or possibly a combination of all four." Actually he said, "gin", his tipple, not "heroin". My father kept telling me what a good fellow Harry was. I couldn't hear him. I thought he meant that he approved of him, not that Harry was a good man, a truly good man. He is one of the people of my youth I would like to meet now, now that I could appreciate him.

I knocked on his door in Great Court. This collision was poignant: the grungy modernity that was me with the carefully nurtured and immensely wealthy tradition exemplified in the 16th century splendour of Great Court. Especially since it was Harry, the very best of the compassionate liberalism that Cambridge generated, trying to reach out to me. But we could find no contact. There was no bridge between us.

"Ah, William. Do come in and sit down." I did. "I'll come straight to the point. Your landlady found these in her hoover yesterday after she'd done your room, and, quite rightly, brought them to me." He unwrapped a piece of letter-paper to reveal two jacks of heroin. How on earth did she know to look through the dirt in her vacuum cleaner? How did she know that they weren't saccharine pills? Harry must have sensed the direction my thoughts were taking.

"It's all right William, I know they are heroin and have had a word with your doctor. He's told me what he can about your problem, and we're resolved to do everything in our power to help you. We have no intention of sending you down. Naturally I had to tell your father, and, although he half-suspected something of the kind was going on, he was deeply shocked." He paused to let what he had said sink in.

"Your work, I'm told, while being far from satisfactory, is not beyond redemption and we feel, your father and I, that the best thing to do is to keep you under the strict control of the doctor until you can be got into a hospital somewhere for a cure. Should he come up with a place before the end of the academic year, then, not to worry, we can give you a leave of absence for as long as it takes to get you better.

"Obviously, the college would not like any of this too widely known and we'll need an undertaking from you that you will co-operate. What do you think?" My head was still full of anger at the landlady for being so downright intrusive into my affairs. If she'd looked through the dirt in her hoover, then what else wasn't she capable of? But Harry wanted an answer and it was obvious that I had no option but to go along with his plans and feign gratitude for his understanding.

"I don't know… Oh, yes, I suppose… Does this strict control mean that he'll cut my supplies down? How long would I have to be in hospital? Was my father very upset?"

"Yes, he was. More that you couldn't bring yourself to ask for help before things got to this stage, than anything else, but I suggest you go and have a talk with him. It's the least you can do. I'm afraid I can't answer the other questions. You'll have to talk to the doctor about them," Harry gathered his forces to make one last attempt at bridging the gap.

"Now, William, the important thing, as far as I'm concerned, is that we'll do everything we can to help you through your present difficulty, but we can't do a thing without your co-operation. I'm told that you stand little chance of living till the end of the decade, let alone being able to finish your course at university, if you carry on the way you have been in the last few months. You do realise how urgent it is that you be cured, don't you? Especially in your case, someone of such obvious intelligence from a happy and loving family background. I know you can beat this thing if you try and if you let us help."

By this time, the message had sunk in. I was in a corner, but at least I was to go on getting my supplies until they got me into hospital.

"Yes, I'm sorry, I didn't quite see how bad things were. Yes, you have my co-operation as long as my present supply isn't reduced. I really am grateful for the understanding you've shown."

"Good, good! It's the least I could do, considering the awful situation you're in. Now, you will go and see your parents, won't you?" I said I would and hurried back to my room. Not once did he try to foist any Christianity on me.

I locked the door and had a half-grain fix with the last of the coke that Sam had left me. It brought me comfort. It relieved me of the sense of impending doom, that everyone was closing in on me. When the initial impact of the fix had worn off, I set off on my bike to see my parents. I had to convince them that, despite appearances, there wasn't all that much to worry about. My habit was under the control of the doctor whom they knew and respected; I could get off it easily enough if I wanted to. Hadn't I gone nearly four weeks in Sweden without anything?

The tragedy of the inevitable scapegoat unfolded further. They all knew I was a junky now: the college, my parents, my sisters, my friends. The memes and the genes and the chemistry were all pointing in the same direction: to great suffering all round as I careered towards an early and sordid death. I had been chosen to be the focus of the absurdity and suffering feedback loop.

Hadn't I had the best education, the happiest and most secure home life? Well, no, actually, however it looked on the surface. And yet, here was their son, a junky, just like one reads about in the papers. Why, William, why? Other people's sons didn't become junkies. Quite so. Other people's parents didn't, oh I don't know, didn't have some unconscious need for their sons to be addicts.

I found them in the kitchen. On the square stools with red vinyl tops, on the foot-square black and white tiled floor, under the clothes dryer, pulled up on its pulleys. The childhood ordinary met the adult despair. I had made ball runs in the sand pit just outside the window. When complete the whole family had to watch and predict which, of several holes at the bottom of the sand mountain, the tennis ball would appear from. They never got it right. The hole the ball would emerge from was always disguised as something else.

A grownup junky, we talked in the clash of childhood and dystopia.

My mother with her hair in a bun, dressed in browns and reds, distraught, stroking the tiny hairs between her eyebrows with the little finger of her right hand, as she did when upset.

"I just can't understand how you ever got involved in this sort of thing. We couldn't help knowing what you felt about marijuana, but you always said it was harmless and how it was only idiots who went on to harder drugs. You're not an idiot. Why couldn't you tell us about it?" My mother, just managing to keep back the tears. My father just sat there, glum.

"I suppose you were injecting yourself, those times you spent such ages in the loo. And I suppose you were rushing off to get your wretched heroin those mornings you pushed off without any breakfast, looking so pale." She said 'heroin' with the distaste she would reserve for words like 'condom' or 'prostitute'.

"That's right," was all I could manage.

"Look, William," my father surfaced through his gloom. "I hope you realise what Harry is doing for you. Most people would have been flung out for far less, but he thinks you are worth helping, God knows why. You must do whatever he and the doctor ask you to do, and then we'll get you into a hospital and, before you know it, you'll be as right as rain and can go on and get your degree." He paused, we all paused, not looking at each other. He didn't believe it. A barely contained hysteria.

"What happened? How *could* you do such a *stupid* thing as get yourself addicted? The marijuana I can just about understand, but for an intelligent chap like you to take heroin..." My father was starting to express his profound bewilderment. *Stupid* was the operative word here.

How could I begin to tell them of the revolution of which my addiction was a part? Sigma project would make no sense to them. How could I tell them that their cultural and social milieu was nothing but a bourgeois artefact? And yet, and yet, how I secretly wished I lived in the comfort of that bourgeois certainty. But this was war and I was deep in enemy territory.

There was Eton. They couldn't deny that it had been inhumane and blind to send me there, barbarous to keep me there and perverse to think I had in any way failed the system. I held them responsible for the wounds I had endured. If my newly discovered addiction was to be seen as sickness, then I would hold them responsible. What I couldn't handle was their love and care. The guilt, the anger, the shame.

"It was Eton," I grunted after a while.

"What was? What *has* Eton got to do with it?" asked my father indignantly. Eton had been good for him.

"I was so miserable there. I still have nightmares about the place. They were all *so* stupid, the system was so stupid. It has nothing to do with the real world, how it really is."

"I still don't see the connection. You're not saying that you got addicted because you were miserable at Eton, are you?"

"Oh God." I threw up my hands in frustration. "Yes, yes, yes, but not the way you think. The misery you made me go through at Eton because you're so tied to the class-system it perpetuates, that misery left such a deep mark on me inside that I..." I searched for the right words. "I had to find *some* way of breaking through all that."

I hesitated. They didn't want to hear this. How could they?

"Go on," said my father trying very hard to understand.

"Well, there is a way, a way that breaks through people's blindness as to their condition, their social conditioning. If it involves the use of heroin, yes, and cocaine, then that's all right. It's only my body, my life that I'm affecting and surely I'm free to do what I like with my own body." My mother and father were left wide-eyed at the violence of my utterance. We fiddled with our coffee cups.

"But," my mother came in defiantly, tearfully, "it's not true. You do affect other people by taking that stuff. What about us? And your sisters? Have you thought what I'm going to say to my friends: 'my son's a heroin addict, you know'? Anyway, I think you would have been miserable at whatever school you went to. You wouldn't have wanted to go to Impington Village College, would you?"

"I don't know so much." The thought had just crept into my head that it was over three hours since my last fix. I needed another.

"William," my father said in a placatory tone. "Whatever the merits or otherwise of your going to Eton, you *are* hurting other people with your heroin. Mummy hasn't been able to sleep or eat properly ever since we found out. You haven't said anything about the idea of going to some hospital for a cure. Are you willing to go?"

"Yes, yes, I'll go." Anything to keep them off my back. I got up to leave. He put his arm round my shoulder. Not something he had done more than five times in my whole life.

"William, it's all right. We don't want to fight you. Maybe it was wrong to send you to Eton, but what matters now is that we get you well again, off that vile stuff."

I shrugged his arm off my shoulder and left. It wasn't vile stuff; it was my life.

I'll die young, but it's like kissing God. (Lenny Bruce)

8 'Pataphysics* and the Asylum

Dada had become so important – fur-lined tea cups, signed urinals and all – that I found myself announcing to all and sundry that I was the founder of the Cambridge Neo 'Pataphysical Society. Alfred Jarry, who 'invented' the superscience of 'pataphysics, intended that apostrophe before the P, though why is lost in the mists of Dada.

The sign of the Society was a large round enamel lapel badge I wore, showing a painted spiral. This badge *was* the Society. People would ask, "What's that?" and I would say, "It's the badge of the Cambridge Neo 'Pataphysical Society." And they would say, "Oh," thinking that I meant that it showed I was a member, that it was a *sign* of membership. They would have been wrong, of course. The badge *was* the Society and I was proud to wear the Society on my lapel. And that would be that. I never detected any other members.

Andrew was in sympathy with this tendency and, together with Nigel, we decided to implement the Sigma Project and happen some more. The most successful one, the most disorientating to the audience happened in the cellar of the University Debating Society's building, known as the Union. Every Thursday there was a student hop there and Andrew persuaded the rock group to let us stage an unannounced event during their break and to let us use their microphones.

For weeks beforehand we had been preparing a tape on the very modern stereo Sony reel-to-reel tape recorder that my father had given me for my birthday. It had speakers in the lid, which could be detached and put in opposing corners of the room. Using loops of tape of various length on another cheap mono tape recorder, we would record stuff from the Sony on to a loop that would keep re-

---

* 'Pataphysics is the science of the realm beyond metaphysics; or 'Pataphysics lies as far beyond metaphysics as metaphysics lies beyond physics – in one direction or another. Now, metaphysics is a word which can mean exactly what one wants it to mean, whence its continuing popularity. To Aristotle it meant merely the field of speculation he took up after physics. The pataphysician beholds the entire created universe, and all others with it, and sees that they are neither good nor bad but pataphysical. Rene Daumal, writing in the twentieth century, said that he proposed to do for metaphysics what Jules Verne had done for physics. 'Pataphysics, then, entering the great beyond, in whatever direction it may lie, offers us a voyage of discovery and adventure into what Jarry called 'ethernity'. That, of course, is where we all live. (From Superliminal Note by Roger Shattuck in *Evergreen Review*, vol.4, no.13, 1960)

peating itself while we recorded more electronic music by Varese from the record player and our reading poems backwards. This way we made a random multi-track, multi-variance, multi-sense sound track for our happening. In spirit, not unlike the musical experiments Terry Riley had begun in New York, but not really very musical. We called it *Multiverse.**

"But what does it mean?"

"But what's the point?"

None whatsoever. None! The lack of point is the meaning!

Such was my heroin-inspired razor-sharp certainty of the right-on-ness of our happening, that I persuaded Nigel that he should have a fix before the gig. Forgive me!

As the band got into their last number, we infiltrated the merrily dancing throng. The group went off for a drink. I started emptying

An archive picture of me, Andrew and Nigel in simultaneous poetic uprising

---

* The tape of Multiverse came to light as I edited this book, after hiding in various cupboards for 37 years. I rushed to the Web to find someone who might transfer it to a CD. I phoned the local name I found and was invited round. Amidst squalor untidied for decades in a drab semi, I was greeted by a grey-haired man in a sensible, ankle-length woollen skirt. Body language told me I was not meant to notice. We fought our way through piles of 78's to the machines. While he transferred my tape, he chatted away about rescuing recordings of Lord Haw Haw that were used to send the traitor to the gallows. "Would you mind," he asked, "if I sent a copy of this to the National Sound Archive?" Not taking him too seriously, I said no, I wouldn't mind. As I left, he mentioned that he also did dress making. Half an hour after my return home, I got a call from the head of the National Sound Archive (part of the British Library) to say how pleased they were to be offered the recording.

a sack of leaves onto the heads of the dancers; Nigel wrote poems on the blackboard that Andrew would rub out before anyone could read them. Our 'pataphysical music was playing through the group's amplifier; Andrew read a newspaper backwards; I stood on a chair in the middle of the floor trying, but always failing, to read a poem; more leaves were emptied; and so on and on for twenty minutes. To our surprise, the Thursday night ravers took it in their stride. If this was avant-garde art, and the word went round that it was, then it wasn't so bad. Absolute rubbish of course, but quite good fun, not unlike the sort of thing one got up to on rag day.

Reality is a crutch for people who can't handle drugs. (George Bernard Shaw)

Around this time my sister Lucy, who was finishing her time at the Quaker Friends School in Saffron Walden, was being courted by Julian Hough. Whenever our paths crossed I was struck by the compelling strangeness of this guy, couldn't put my finger on it though. Later on it showed itself. He became the wild man of street theatre, founding the *National Theatre of Brent*, a wonderfully 'pataphysical company that would perform the entire works of Shakespeare with two actors in half an hour. 'Pataphysical because, in his play *Pere Ubu*, Alfred Jarry has the entire French army played by one actor.

Julian achieved quite some fame and was actually on the telly once or twice, with the *National Theatre of Brent* and, most oddly, when he played a guards officer in one episode of *The Sweeney*. He was also in the movies: as Fourth Peasant in Terry Gilliam's 1977 *Jabberwocky*; the vicar in a 1978 horror movie with Alan Bates, *The Shout*; a reporter in Stephen Frears' first proper movie in 1979, *Bloody Kids*; and finally, Bertrand Tavenier's *Le Mort en Direct* in 1980. A film career.

But, when his girlfriend rejected him, it was as if a switch had been flicked and he went mad. He was kicked out of his own company. And then his creative genius went into reverse, something clicked and he became an alcoholic hobo. He would somehow manage to bump into you in Tottenham Court Road and suggest in a compelling, red-nosed and blurred way that it would be a good idea if you contribute £5 to his cause. He would call round and ring the front door bell at midnight wanting a sofa to sleep on and a sandwich. He had no home and refused all attempts to get him settled.

1965-1970: US involvement in Vietnam is blamed for the surge in illegal heroin smuggled into the States. To aid US allies, the CIA sets up a charter airline, Air America, to transport raw opium from Burma and Laos. The number of heroin addicts in the US reaches an estimated 750,000.

The looming hospital cure hung over me like a sentence of deportation. In 1965 there was hardly any provision for the treatment of addiction in the whole of Britain, no one knew how to handle it. My doctor was beginning to despair of finding a hospital that offered some hope of effecting a cure. All the Cambridge area could offer was sedation in the local loony bin. So it was with some relief that he heard about a new unit specifically for the treatment of heroin addiction that had just opened in Surrey.

He made contact, and to his relief and my despair, they said they would take me even though I was not within their catchment area. I was told that it was a purpose-built unit in the grounds of a large mental hospital and that I would need to be there for at least three months. Harry arranged for a leave of absence from the University. I was to go there during the Easter vacation, and stay as long as they told me to. I wouldn't be missing any exams, since the second part of the Moral Sciences Tripos was a two-year course. I was told I could even have my own room in the unit, so that I could study.

A few days before I was due at Cane Hill Hospital, Coulsden, I packed up a large number of books, all the records I couldn't do without, my new stereo tape recorder, my clothes and typewriter, and set off to collect a good store of sympathy from first my parents, and then Margareta. Since they were my last days of freedom as a practising junky, I scored extra from Sam and managed to spend my time with Margareta in a constant state of dismembered, speeding highness. She not only tolerated this final fling, but was full of compassion for the torments to which I was so bravely about to subject myself. When it came time to catch the train to Coulsden, I must have looked every inch the weird hippie drug addict. My feet were black because of open sandals and no baths, my hair long and matted, my eyes hard and wild.

As the taxi drove into the grounds of the hospital, I began to worry. I had been conned! This was no modern drug rehab unit – it was a Victorian lunatic asylum.* The sweeping drive through institutional parkland lead to the utter hugeness and hidden hell of the place. The taxi-driver clearly thought I was just another nutter, but one with half a car-full of possessions. I was tired, my last fix was beginning to wear off, and when the man at the reception office told me to follow him down an interminable corridor, hope drained from me. I struggled to keep up with him as I carried my two large suitcases and heavy tape recorder

---

* Cane Hill Lunatic Asylum was built in 1883 on the edge of Coulsden, Surrey, to incarcerate the insane and feeble-minded of Greater London.

down the brown and puce-green corridor, past frequent heavy doors that looked difficult to open without a key.

After a mile's walk, he stopped outside a door that looked no different from any of the others we'd passed. He chose a large iron key from his ring and unlocked the door.

"New arrival for you," he said to the man inside, and left, locking the door behind him.

"You Pryor?" asked the man, who I took to be a nurse. He had the presence of a railway porter, a hospital functionary, a prison officer. His bunch of keys was enormous and he had biros in the top pocket of his jacket. But he didn't seem unkind.

"Yes. This is the addiction unit, I suppose?"

"That's right. If you leave all that stuff here. I'll have to go through it later. You can pop into that cubicle for me and get undressed. The doctor'll be along in a minute to check you over. Throw your clothes out, then I can go through them."

"What d'you mean: 'go through' my clothes?"

"Oh just to make sure you haven't brought anything in that you shouldn't." I felt like a numbered beast for the slaughter, a Jew for the gas oven. Before I went into the cubicle, I noticed two or three rough looking men hovering at the far end of the passage, fellow patients I supposed. I undressed and pushed my clothes under the curtain. The man removed them. The cubicle was much too tall. It was just part of the ward that had been clumsily partitioned off. As I waited for the doctor to appear, sitting naked on the couch, I realised that the row of doors I'd noticed along one side of the ward, each with its curious brass door knob and peep-hole, were the doors of cells. I'd been waiting for an age, I was cold. I yelled out for the nurse. Five minutes later he put his head round the curtain.

"What's all the fuss about, then?"

"I'm sorry, but I'm getting cold and I need a fix. I thought you operated a gradual withdrawal scheme here."

"We do, but the duty doctor's got to see you first. Those feet," he pointed, "are a disgrace. How can you live like that? You see what heroin does to you, takes away all pride in your appearance." Then suddenly, taking us both by surprise, in swept the duty doctor. He was Indian and very soon made it clear that he had little time for addicts. They didn't do addicts in India, well not middle class ones.

"Lie on your front. I'm going to examine your rectum."

"Why, for God's sake?" I was in shock, couldn't believe this reception, but numbly complied.

"Addicts have been known to smuggle drugs in the anus." He

prodded with little consideration for the pain he caused.

"Now I will be examining your arms." As he did, he tut tutted. "Your GP is saying in this letter that you were having the two and the one half grains a day, is this right please?"

"Yes, and I haven't had a fix since two this afternoon. Can I please have something soon?" I pleaded.

"When we're ready, then you'll be getting something." He turned to the nurse. "This patient is filthy. I don't know how they can be living like this. Give him one half of a grain when he is bathing." He hurried away.

The nurse steered me to the bathroom, turned on the institutional bath taps in the institutional bath, surrounded by cracked white tiles. He came back ten agonising minutes later with a stainless-steel kidney dish. Before I knew what he was doing, he'd stuck the syringe it contained into my shoulder and injected my allocation of heroin into the muscle. I hardly felt it.

"Don't we get to mainline here? You know, actually in the vein? I couldn't feel that at all." I complained.

"You want to enjoy your injections? You're here, in case you didn't know, to be cured of your addiction, not to carry on the way you did outside."

When I emerged from the bath, he showed me to the room that was to be mine. It was indeed a cell. There was no door knob on the inside, the catch had been jammed so that the door couldn't be shut properly, the window was high up in the wall and had bars over it, and there was only a standard issue bed and locker as furniture. My possessions were stacked on the floor. I kicked the door shut, sat on the bed and sobbed.

Sobbed down to the bottom of my soul. I may have been a scapegoat once, but now I was nothing but a junky, caught up in the machine of consequences. There was no hope.

This was certainly no progressive drug rehabilitation unit, but simply a redecorated ward of a huge Victorian lunatic asylum village that had been given a coat of paint and a fancy name. One of my new colleagues, if that's the word, lost no time in telling me that upstairs was a locked loony ward and every now and then you could hear beds being thrown about.

The next morning I was woken by the nurse (though that word gives altogether the wrong impression; warder might be better) so that he could give me my morning fix and told that breakfast would be in half an hour. Time enough to meet my fellow patients. They were all under thirty. Paul, with combed, Brylcreamed hair and a surgical boot with callipers, was the first to show any sign of friend-liness. His gushing bonhomie contrasted with the prevailing air of latent aggression and tattooed arms.

"What were you on?" He asked.

"Three grains," I lied.

"Did you use downers? I was on downers, any kind of barbs I could get my hands on. Along with two grains of H a day. Who was your doctor? I was with Petro." He talked enthusiastically, swapping campaign badges with a fellow foot soldier.

"Well, various. I ended up with an ordinary GP in Cambridge, but before that I was with Dr Grey and then Lady Frankau. But tell me, what happens here? Are we allowed out at all? How long do I get H for? What's this Dr Becket like?" The questions came tumbling out. I was particularly curious about Dr Becket, the doctor who had set up the unit.

"Oh, he's all right, he sticks up for us against the hospital admin-istration. You know that the unit was his idea and he had to fight them for it? Yes, he's OK. He even turns a blind eye to the smoking of dope, as long as we keep it well hidden from the rest of the hos-pital." At that point, one of the two nurses on duty came into the day room where we were sitting and said that Dr Dale Becket had ar-rived and would like to see me. Paul gave me the thumbs-up sign as I followed the nurse.

"William? William Pryor? Do sit down." I sat facing him across a desk in one of the cells that had been converted into an office. Pete, the nurse who had fetched me, hovered by the window. That he should share a surname with the most profound writer to come out of Eu-rope in the 20th century, already disposed me to like him. A kindly bank manager, a clipped schoolteacher who wants you to be enthusi-astic, Dr Becket had gold-rimmed spectacles and a crisp white coat.

"Look, I've only just been told about the way you were treated on your admission last night and all I can say is that I'm sorry." I didn't know what he was talking about, but he inspired confidence.

"You see, I've left strict instructions that new admissions to the unit must be told to arrive only when I'm on duty, otherwise we run the risk that the duty doctor will be one of those at this hospital who strongly disapprove of what they would call the special treatment of addicts. Dr Patel who saw you last night is one of those, and, unluck-ily, the nurse was a relief who is not known for his sympathy towards addicts either. So, I must apologise if your reception wasn't very pleasant, but there seems to have been a breakdown in our commu-nications. Now, let's see," he consulted my notes. Pete winked at me in encouragement.

"Ah yes, your doctor in Cambridge was prescribing two and a half grains of heroin a day and you have been registered as an addict with the home office for about eighteen months, is that right?"

"That's about it," I replied.

"And you've been given two injections since you arrived, both of half a grain, one last night and one this morning?"

"Yes."

"Right, now I'll explain how we do things here. Your injections will be reduced by one-sixth of a grain a day, overall. In other words, to-morrow you'll get one and a third grains in three fixes and so on. You don't think that's too rapid do you? No? Good. That'll mean we'll have you right off at the end of next week, when you can come into our twice-weekly group meeting. If you find the withdrawal too painful, we can consider giving you very small quantities of physeptone to help, but I must stress that the longer you drag it out, the longer it's going to take to get you cured. As for the best way to use your time: I'm told you've brought your university books with you and I suggest you make good use of them. Apart from that, patients are expected to keep the unit clean and tidy. There's a ping-pong table in the main block. The C of E vicar calls by twice a week. There's television, and there's Peter here to talk to. Have you any questions?"

"Yes, what happens at these group meetings?"

"Well," Dr Becket exchanged a knowing grin with Pete, "that's rather difficult to say. In a sense they are a kind of parliament for the unit, in that you are free to criticise anyone else and comment on their progress or lack of it. Also, within certain limits, the treatment policy is deter-mined by these meetings. The idea is to involve you, the patient, as much as possible, in the day-to-day running of the unit, to enhance your sense of motivation to get clear from heroin. But I should point out that the unit has only been open for three months now and it is developing all the time. The important thing here is that you decide to get rid of your habit. We help, but you do the work. OK?" He paused, threw a grin at me and shuffled his papers.

"Now I'd like to ask you some questions; just so I know more about you and am better able to help. Could you tell me about your father? Is he strict? Are you close to him? How does he get on with your mother? All that sort of thing." So this was a Freudian approach.

I emerged from my first game of psychiatry after half an hour and went into the day room. Most of the other patients were there, and had obviously been primed by Paul as to my credentials as a junky. We talked about doctors, pills, the merits of different highs, the size of our habits and the overdoses we'd had. No one men-

tioned anything about the cure we were there for. After lunch of
steamed meat pies, gravy, floppy chips, with rice pudding afterwards,
served from a battered metal trolley that had come nearly a mile
from the kitchens, Paul took me to one side.

"How much bread you got?" He whispered.

"Why? What's it got to do with you?"

"Well, it's like this, if Ken can get enough bread together he's going up
the Dilly tonight, you know, to score. It'll cost about five bob a jack by the
time he's paid his train fare and had some for himself. You want some?"

"But how the hell does he get out of here without being noticed?"

"That's no problem. You know those big windows in the day room,
well, we've got a screwdriver and can take off the blocks that stop
them being opened more than a few inches. D'you want some and, if
so, how much?"

"I've only got a couple of quid on me, the rest's in the office; give
him that." I handed him two pound notes, but he pushed it back.

"No, *you* give it him. He's the tall bloke with tattoos on his hands."
Ken took my money with hardly a word. I didn't feel I could trust
him, but it was worth a try. Anything to relieve the depression the
so-called addiction unit was causing me.

Ken disappeared straight after supper, saying he'd be back around
midnight. Meanwhile Paul took me on a tour of the ward. He showed
me how the syringe needed for the illicit heroin was hidden in a
lavatory cistern; he got the night nurse to unlock the end door in the
row of what were called side-rooms.

As soon as we saw inside it was obvious why it was kept locked. It
was a padded cell. It had the usual high ceiling, while the walls and
floor were lined with leatherette upholstery in the plump, buttoned-
down style of a gentleman's club ottoman sofa. There was no window.
Where the floor met the walls, there was a drainage channel. The inside of the door was upholstered and, with it shut, there was nothing
to be heard or seen, just the soft walls and floor to be felt. Sensory
deprivation, most effective, all to prevent the patient harming himself!

Ken appeared outside the window at eleven thirty and was let in. He
said he'd only been able to score three grains in all, but he was so
obviously stoned out of his mind that I didn't believe it. Still, I got half
a grain for my money and had to be grateful for that. There was then
a long wait while everybody else used the syringe.* I had to go last
because I'd had my official fixes while the others hadn't had anything
since they'd been weaned off. The ritual took place in one of the lava-

---

*AIDS was still but a future nightmare.

tory cubicles with someone keeping watch outside and someone else playing cards with the night nurse to keep him occupied.

So, in my first day in the addiction unit I had learned a great deal about surviving as a practising junky and made no progress towards the 'cure'. I realised that a good many of the men in the unit were there simply to keep some doctor, social worker or probation officer happy. They had no intention of giving up heroin for any longer than they could possibly help it. Like them, I was not *real* without it.

The time for my last official injection of heroin came all too soon. So important was it, that I spent all of two hours persuading the nurse to let me inject myself, right into the vein. But it soon wore off and I was left with the dreadful prospect of no consolation from heroin in my blood. Later I extracted some money from the office and persuaded Ken to go out that night and score.

The group meetings were disorganised. Because Dr Becket allowed them to be so informal, the patients were able to bog them down with discussion of washing-up rotas and meal times and avoid any consideration of more internal matters. Eventually he issued an appeal. Would every member of the group put forward a proposal as to how the treatment could be improved. We were given two days to think about it in which time I was able to come up with an idea I thought pretty novel.

At the next meeting, I said: "Dr Becket, I think you're aware people are getting out of here and going up to London to score, yes?" I was rather cocky, although the hostile looks I got made me more cautious.

"Yes. In fact I'm having a staff meeting later today to discuss just that."

"Well, my idea is that these relapses be made official. Instead of going behind your back to fix and setting our treatment back each time, why not make it official." Ripples of amazement ran round the group.

"What I mean is this: when a patient is brought off heroin initially, he has to go for one day without anything. On the second day, he is *offered* a fix of one jack, one sixth of a grain, but has the choice as to whether he has it."

People were putting up their hands to say something, they were clearly in awe. But I wouldn't be stopped.

"If he doesn't take that one, he must go two whole days without anything before he is made the same offer; then three whole days, and so on."

"Very interesting," said Dr Becket. Still I wouldn't stop.

"The idea is that each time he has to make a choice between the temporary relief one fix will give and the inevitable withdrawal symptoms that would result on the one hand, and going without that fix *out of choice* on the other. I'm sure that most of us would take the first few fixes, but there must come a point when the prospect of having to go through those withdrawal symptoms yet another time will outweigh the temporary relief of a fix of one jack. What do you think?"

He liked it, they all liked it, and, to my satisfaction, the scheme was adopted as official policy with one proviso: that anyone caught using illicit heroin would be asked to leave the unit immediately. I wanted it called the Pryor Withdrawal Method. Part of me really did want to get off.

But I soon realised that I'd been hoist with my own petard. The use of illicit H would now be much more difficult to conceal, if only because there was to be a daily arm-inspection to enforce the new scheme and, to make matters worse, my official relapses were only one pill, one solitary jack, and the wait between them doubled each time.

My ingenuity had backfired. I began to take the idea of a cure seriously. An Everest of impending guilt said to me that I couldn't afford to be thrown out of the unit since it would jeopardise my place at Trinity and there was no telling what it would do to my parents. So maybe I was riding my petard after all.

Just as I predicted, I took the first three fixes that were offered, and, sure enough, the withdrawal pains that followed made the high seem of doubtful worth. I had got through my four-day wait. The craving began to wear off, but perhaps only in anticipation of the fix to come. The nurse called me into the office.

"Do you want it then?"

"I think so, oh, I don't know." I was trying to get him to make the decision for me.

"Go on with you, you're as right as rain. You don't need it." But what did he know of my need. I'd come through four whole days on the lure of the fix I was now entitled to, why should I refuse it? On the other hand, I *could* refuse it.

"You know how bad you'll feel tomorrow, Bill, and then you'll have a long wait before you have another chance to make the right decision." I wavered, then shut my eyes and jumped.

"All right, you win. I won't have it." I started for the door.

"Hang on, Bill. You do understand that you can't come back later on today and say you've changed your mind. You've decided not to have a fix today, and that's it. Well done." I'd actually refused a fix of heroin.

After six weeks without a fix, I began to emerge from the hungry ghost of unreality that is withdrawal and found I was quite healthy, physically anyway. I was allowed to wander around the hospital and its grounds quite freely. On an impulse I rang Nigel. He knew I was in hospital but didn't know where. He asked if he could come and visit me. We arranged that he'd come the following week, in a lull in the shooting of *A Day in the Igh of Jesus Lane*.

Despite my newfound health, the craving remained. It may have been all in the mind, but whenever I felt low, the aches and restlessness would start up again. Remembering what he'd said about physeptone, I decided to talk to Dr Becket.

"It's inevitable that you go on feeling like that for some time. You've given your body, and, more particularly, your brain, quite a hammering in the last two years and it takes quite a time for them to recover. Still, I am surprised that it should be bothering you quite so much after, what is it, six weeks? I think what we'll do is give you a small dose of physeptone linctus everyday. That should calm you down considerably. I think we could also speed up the psychoanalysis. We've got to get to the root of your addiction. I'll see you twice a week from now on, all right?"

Then Nigel brought his blotting paper and we had our apparition of demented music.

I had to get out. Nigel's visit had been too sharp a reminder that so much was happening out there. The best way was to play Dr Beckett's game. He would then be on my side. Anyway, he needed a 'cure' more than I needed his sanction. I couldn't risk my place at university and was reluctant to wound my parents any further.

Doctors, family and friends needed me to be well, and this was something I had to go along with, but a deeper me felt there was no possibility at all of my ever being able to do without heroin, that this sobriety was for their convenience and peace of mind alone. My addiction was a deeper truth than the possibility of a contented drug free existence. I was born to suffer it. Born to suffer?

Of course it all looked a bit different the next day and I was as confused as any of the other patients, queuing up for my daily dose of physeptone linctus. But something of that defiance remained. They shall not control my thoughts, they shall not erase my individuality. I was learning fast. I showed a surprising keenness to get to the roots of the problem whenever Dr Becket was around; not only *my* roots but, increasingly, those of the other patients as well.

A week or so after Nigel's visit, my parents came to see me. I'd tried to dissuade them. Their middle class sensibility would be embarrassing in front of my fellow addicts who, in turn, would shock my parents. But they came, bearing a basket of fresh fruit. It was awful, straight out of Dickens. The gentlefolk doing their good works among the deranged and feeble-minded in the asylum and discovering that their long lost son was amongst them. We went to the only cafe near the hospital as soon as we could, a dainty teashop. Sitting on the Windsor chairs, facing scones and a pot of tea, suburban housewives chatting and staring.

"I never thought I'd see you in a place, well, like that," said my mother with some difficulty. I knew what she meant. I had become something alien, something from the furthest slum. What had she done wrong, for her son to turn out like this, to end up in a, well, a lunatic asylum?

"Do they feed you properly? How are you getting on, you know, with the treatment? I hope you're co-operating."

"No, the food is disgusting, but I'll survive. Dr Becket thinks I'm coming along very well. I should be out in a few weeks." I didn't quite have the nerve to say that I'd be cured, even though that was how, in fact, I would be labelled.

By mutual agreement Margareta did not come to visit me. I didn't want her to see me in those surroundings and we both felt that it might give our troubled relationship a chance to heal if we didn't see each other. Maybe we were too frightened. Maybe I didn't want to reveal my one source of beauty to my fellow thugs.

The running of the unit became more and more chaotic as Dr Becket tried to enforce his new ruling that anyone caught, or known to be taking illicit heroin would be automatically ejected. It had been open for nearly six months and he had no cures to show for it. Pressures from the hospital management were changing his attitude. It would now count as a cure if a patient were to leave taking physeptone, even if this was in a liquid, injectable form to satisfy the need to stick needles into one's body. I determined to present myself as a prime candidate for the role of first cured patient. It wasn't difficult. All I had to do was say the right things and show willing.

Two and a half months after I'd arrived, I was discharged with the doctor's approval as a cured heroin addict. He gave me a prescription for several boxes of physeptone ampoules and a box of disposable syringes; this so that I wouldn't feel tempted to score any heroin just for the sake of sticking a needle in my arm. I had appointments to see him at his outpatient clinic.

9 Jamaica, Holes & Coltrane

As soon as I got to London, I rang Sam. I needed a real fix. Tania answered. I thought I heard a stifled sob when I said who it was. With no explanation, she asked urgently if she could meet me in a cafe near their flat. I couldn't refuse, and hurried off to the nearest public toilet to fix a couple of my physeptone ampoules. Her dark glasses said she'd been crying.

"Oh William, I'm so glad you came. It's Sam." She stifled a sob. I was beginning to suspect the worst.

"What on earth is the problem?" I asked with a catch in my voice and put my hand over hers on the café table.

"He'd been using an awful lot, a grain of H with half of coke in each fix. When you went into hospital, you, of all people, who had only been registered such a short time, he felt really bad." She was fighting back the sobs.

"Go on, please."

"Well, he wanted so much to get off and your going in for a cure just made that worse. Then suddenly one day he got this idea of doing a cold turkey in his father's place in Illinois. Mad really."

"Yeah," I commiserated, "it doesn't work for many people."

"Anyway, his father sent him the air fare and off he went. He said I could follow in two or three weeks, when he was over the worst. He thought that by going there, where it would be impossible to get hold of anything, he'd be able to do it." Finally the sobs burst through. I got up and went round to her side of the table and held her.

"I thought he could do it. He was so determined." She took a sip of coffee. I looked sympathetic and sat down again.

"He phoned me when he got there and made it sound cool. Then nothing. A week later I got a letter from his father." She convulsed in sobs again. I patted and dabbed.

"It must have been awful. There's no need to go on," I had guessed where we were going.

"No, I want to. Sam had arrived and had been fine for the first two days: quiet and untalkative, but fine. That's when he phoned me. Then he must have started to feel the withdrawal, because he started to drive round all the local doctors asking them for something, morphine, opium, physeptone, anything that would relieve his withdrawal symptoms." She paused for a sob and put her head in her hands. Then gathered herself again.

"He was in small town America. They all refused to help. Wouldn't even give him an aspirin. On his fourth night home, Sam borrowed his father's shotgun to go out after rabbits, or so he said. He shot himself right through the head out in the fields behind the house. There was a dead rabbit by his feet." She stared at me, now too desolate to cry. She took my hands in hers and looked steadfastly at me.

"William, I'm so glad you're cured. For God's sake, stay off it whatever you do. That's what Sam would want. Please, William, promise me you'll stay off H for the rest of your life." I looked down at the empty coffee cups and fiddled with the sugar bowl.

"Sure, don't worry. Now I must be going, I've got to get back to Cambridge." I left her sitting there. Didn't see her ever again.

I went straight to the Dilly junkydrome, the twenty-four hour Boots chemists in Piccadilly. I'd only been there for quarter of an hour when a scaghead I recognised from Lady Frankau's waiting room emerged. I adhered to him, with pointless sidelong glances, as he scuttled towards the public toilets. He agreed to sell me two grains for four pounds, but I'd have to go with him to fix.

Furtively we sidled, one after the other so as not to let the assembled pissers think we were queer or anything, into a cubicle. Bolting the door and placing my sweating back against it, I gave him one of my disposable syringes as he sat on the toilet. He pulled the chain and drew up water from the resultant flush. He shook the syringe until the jacks dissolved. He strapped his belt round his arm. There were bruises, scars and scabs all the way from above his elbow down to his wrist and then on the back of his hand.

"I'll try this one," he pointed to a fresh looking scab, "got a hit there yesterday." He slithered the diagonal sharpness of the needle into a scab. Blood trickled down his arm, thick, dark crimson. He pushed it further in, drew it out again, changed the angle, pushed it further in.

"The bastard. The vein's nearly gone." He persisted for a full five minutes, but no blood appeared in the syringe. He couldn't get a hit. His veins had nearly all gone, become so callused with scar tissue as to be impenetrable with even the sharpest needle.

"I'll have to go in on the back of me hand." He tied the belt round his wrist and slapped the back of his hand a few times. No veins were visible. He winced as he pushed the needle in at a point about an inch from his wrist. The pain caused him to utter a continuous low moan, as he manoeuvred the point of the needle beneath the skin of his hand.

"Got it," he whispered with grim satisfaction. A tiny strand of blood rose into the syringe as he pulled back the plunger.

"Shit," he cursed more grimly, "lost it." The blood had stopped coming. The needle must have slipped out of the vein as quickly as it had gone in.

"Have you got another needle you can let us have, man? This'll be blocked by now. The blood will've clotted." He pulled the needle out of his hand. I handed him a new one in its plastic sheath. He took the old one off the syringe. There was a gelatinous glob of redness hanging from it, the clotted blood. He re-armed the syringe with the new needle, transferred the belt to his right arm and started again.

This ritual of degradation went on for a full fifteen minutes before he got his hit and, with a great sigh, was able to push the longed-for liquid playfully into his vein. Had it not been for the fact that he seemed to demand my presence as part of the price for the two grains that he now handed over, I would not have stayed. Well, as long as I had the two grains.

An inner voice said this blood bath was the *inevitable* result of ten or more years of heroin addiction. A few weeks down the Dilly and I too would have the scabs and tracks of this narcotist!

He stood up to allow me to sit on the lavatory seat to fix. I put three jacks into a syringe and sucked up water from the rim of the lavatory bowl as he'd done. I injected the steel of the needle through my skin into my vein. The blessed mingling of blood and opiate. The rapid crossing of the blood-brain barrier as the high, the rush, the buzz, the relief. I flushed the heroin in and out, billowing pretty crimson clouds, as I savoured the consolation of the buzz. I wiped my arm with a sheet of Bronco* lavatory paper made damp with spittle.

My next port of call was a much-delayed visit to Margareta in Chelsea. I didn't have to tell her that the cure had been a farce, she only needed to look at my face. But she was as radiantly beautiful as ever.

"Darling," she said as she hugged me. We embraced and I smelt the intoxicating scent of her hair and neck as I nuzzled. She was

---

* Bronco lavatory paper is a signifier of the primitive conveniences we had to endure in the sixties. It was much like tracing paper, shiny on one side and rough on the other – hardly suited to its task.

slim, tall, shapely, blond, intelligent, Swedish and sensual. What more could a man want?

"How has it been? What have they been doing to you?" she asked.

"It was grim really. I'm glad you didn't visit, though I missed you dreadfully, but you would have found it depressing." We sat at her dining table, gazing fondly. "What's been happening for you?"

"Not a lot. Mrs Dale's Diary finished two weeks ago and I haven't had anything since then. Will you stay the night," she put her hand on my arm, "or do you have to rush off back to Cambridge."

I stayed. We went to bed and stayed there. Cane Hill had worn me down, had ground any obsessiveness about her out of me. I was able to enjoy her company.

"You know I'm seeing Marcus every now and then, don't you?" Even this didn't phase me. We were both free to lead our own lives. Maybe this is how we should have been all along. Not making claims on each other.

My parents were glad to see me, the prodigal son returned, and I was careful to say nothing that would disabuse them of the idea that I was now cured. My boxes of ampoules lay hidden in my suitcase.

"Come and have a nice cup of tea in the kitchen when you're unpacked," said my mother. I carried my case up the back stairs to my room. The memory-matrix was there and reassuring. I opened my case and carefully placed my legal and legitimate ampoules in my sock drawer. I went downstairs for that cup of tea. They were both waiting.

"There," said my father, "I must say, you do look better."

"Yes, better," said my mother distractedly. I stared at my teacup, not believing them.

"I will have to take physeptone for the foreseeable future. You know that don't you?" I looked up to check we were all playing the same game. They were. "It's nothing to worry about. It's medicine."

"So, you're going to behave from now, are you William?" asked my mother pointlessly, not expecting an answer.

"I have something to tell you that might cheer you up," said my father.

"What's that?" I grunted.

"The University of the West Indies has asked me to invigilate their biology exams. I said I would do so on one condition: that they pay for Sophie and two children to go with me," he smiled at me.

"How amazing," I summoned up some enthusiasm. "Are you including me in that?"

"Well yes, we thought it would be an excellent way for you to get your health back before your final year. Mummy and I fly out in two weeks and you can come over when you like. I am going to Guyana, after the exams, to see the rainforest, but you can stay on in Jamaica right up to September if you like." They both turned to me expecting an enthusiastic response.

"Fantastic," I replied.

I could stop over in New York on the way and Jamaica was the land of plentiful ganja. The only problem was to secure a supply of physeptone.

I explained the situation to Dr Becket when I kept my appointment with him two weeks later and, to my relief, he agreed to let me have a large supply of physeptone in pill form, to be swallowed like aspirin. He dated the prescription for two hundred 5-milligram tablets so that I couldn't cash it until the day of departure and gave me a supply of ampoules to last me till then.

My parents had gone on ahead to Jamaica, leaving me to see my tutors about the essays I'd done in hospital and follow them ten days later. Flying all that way alone, in the latest VC10 jet, thoroughly accorded with all my grandiose pretensions. I was convivial with all and sundry, in a cool way of course, and drank rather too much. I didn't let on that my mother was going to meet me off the plane at Montego Bay. Hipsters don't have mothers.

They'd installed themselves in a large bungalow near Oche Rios. My father had already finished his invigilating and had gone off to spend two weeks in what he called the last real rain forest in the world in Guyana, where he could marvel at the exotic insect life. I needed to find somewhere cheap to live.

An expatriate teacher, who had known my sister Emily when they both worked in Bolivia, said she had a friend who had a zinc cabin. He said I could use it for as long as I liked free of charge. It was on the beach in a village called Long Bay, halfway between Kingston and Montego Bay. I accepted the offer on the spot and he gave me the key.

As soon as I'd seen my family off at the airport, giving my mother copious reassurances that I'd be a good boy, I went out to the University Campus to find my father's friend Dr Farquar. I persuaded him that I should have a prescription for as much physeptone as I asked for. It had been some time since he'd been in general practice and he had no experience of addiction. This was my insurance policy, even though there was still another two weeks supply left in the bottle I'd reclaimed from my mother. The pharmacist at the largest chemist in Kingston was rather surprised at the prescription, but after a long search was able to find some of the precious pills. I also got four disposable syringes 'for my diabetes'.

I was now free to get in the Jamaican groove. I went to the bus station to catch the Kingston Flyer that would take me along the north coast to Long Bay. In common with most Jamaican buses the Flyer was custom-built and richly decorated with Rastafarian emblems and slogans. It was driven at terrifying, but exhilarating speeds down the pot-holed roads, paying little attention to the chickens, donkeys, pedestrians, cartloads of bananas and sugarcane that cluttered the way. I was let off the bus outside the Long Bay Post Office and General Stores at one end of the village. I'd been told to ask there for directions to the cabin.

It was not unlike a saloon in a western, set back from the road, shaded by an enormous avocado tree and opposite what appeared to be the village refuse tip. It was a dilapidated wooden structure with a long bar at one end and a much smaller General Stores and Post Office at the other. The most striking piece of furniture was a gleaming jukebox that was pounding out a bluebeat record when I walked in.

A few young men, leaning on the bar, were lazily expressing the downbeat with slow hip movements. I set my case down by the door. They all stared. A white man was obviously something of a novelty, especially one getting off the Flyer. I moseyed up to the bar and asked the bar tender for a white rum. I asked him where the zinc cabin was and he replied, with some deference, that his boy would show me and carry my bags. The 'boy' was about nineteen and called Alban Mcqueenie.

Long Bay gets its name from the simple fact that the village straggles the coast road for the length of a long bay which is one long beach of blond sand, fringed by cocoanut palms. Apart from the General Stores, the only other notable buildings were the hotel, all concrete arches and sun-loungers, the fundamentalist chapel, and the MacPhersons' compound. This last was a breeze-block and cement rendered monstrosity of a house that was surrounded by a high concrete wall that stretched right from the road, some two hundred yards down to high-water mark.

The cabin was on the far side of this fortress, just sitting there amongst the palms, built apparently straight on the sand. It was painted white to reflect some of the sun's heat, and was constructed entirely of corrugated zinc. It was not unlike those green corrugated village cricket pavilions back home.

Alban hovered while I undid the padlock. A wave of hot, foul air rushed at me when I opened the door. There was a small kitchen with a cold tap and a bottled gas burner, a makeshift shower and a main room that held a doubtful bed. All the internal partitions were of zinc. The floor was the sand of the beach. I unlocked the shutters that served as windows and, having told Alban I would see him later at the General Stores, I shut the door. This will do very nicely, I thought, a place any self-respecting beatnik would be proud of.

I unpacked the bottles of pills and the syringes I'd got in King-ston and stuffed a wad of cotton wool in the largest of these. I ground up two of the pills and poured the powder on top of the wad. All I had to do then, according to the theory I'd learnt at Cane Hill, was force a measured quantity of water through the plug of powder and cotton wool and I would have a solution of physeptone that I could inject into a vein. The first time it came through as a milky fluid that I didn't dare inject; it might give me another of the fevers I'd had from using unsterile water, a form of septicaemia. I had to push it through twice more before it came at all clear and I felt it was rea-sonably safe to fix.

Through hanging around at the Stores, drinking rum with Alban and friends, Mr Williams, the proprietor, invited me to play domi-noes in the back room with the local bigwigs: the police sergeant, himself, and the head waiter from the hotel.

There was usually an audience for these games. I was the source of much amusement because I found dominoes, at the speed they played it, a very taxing game. For a start I couldn't hold all my domi-noes in one hand the way they did, and their habit of banging each piece down with great gusto confused me.

I'm sure the police sergeant knew that I was a druggy and yet he took great pride in telling me what the Jamaican police were doing to control the rampant ganja harvest and its consumption. My white-ness must have overcome what scruples he might have had about divulging such information.

Alban was delighted to know I was a rude boy, that I smoked the holy weed, and said I should come along to hear the local calypso band playing at the hotel. The bass player had a plot of ganja up in the bush. Meanwhile he rolled a joint or two and good it was to sit under the palms and watch the sea and the stars, getting quietly stoned.

When we got to the hotel that Saturday, the band was in full swing: guitar, banjo and home-made bass throbbing out traditional calypsos for the rich Americans. Manny, the bass player, told me how it was fine to be paid for playing this music, with its more or less improvised lyrics, but it wasn't the real thing at all. That was now the province of the Rastafarian ska bands from Trenchtown, Kingston. I was puzzled. How could electric bands be playing the real thing?

"Bicarz mun, dem singin bout all dis badness wi livin wid; all de shit dese pollytishuns kip pushin on we."

Manny invited me to go with him up to his plot in the hills and would arrange a horse for me. There were no roads and it was too far to walk. Next day he was outside the cabin with two mangy horses; no saddles or other such nonsense, but it was the kind of hardship I could weave into a nice story later for my credentials as an international hipster.

We reached his plot in the early afternoon, after a leisurely ascent through first the smallholdings of plantain, sugarcane, and coconut palms, and then the bush proper. A well-trodden jungle of small trees and lush undergrowth. It was in a small clearing well away from the track we'd come up. Manny pointed out that the surrounding trees were taller than most and gave excellent cover from any police helicopter that might fly over. In the middle of the clearing was a plot, twenty feet by fifteen, of ganja; my first sight of the stuff actually growing. Like large droopy nettles, the plants stood about five feet tall. I was puzzled that Manny wasn't more concerned that Rastas from the camp we'd passed lower down the trail didn't come and steal what they needed from his plot.

"Mun, dem Rasta, dey say dis de holy weed. Why dey gwine to mek botherayshun, mun. Dem rude boys. Mi not gwine worry bout dem."

He cut down a couple of plants; we smoked his chillum; cut up the rest and wrapped it in a copy of the Daily Gleaner; watered the plot from a nearby stream and set off on the trail back home.

The owner of the cabin came over from Kingston to do some scuba diving, making me feel uptight, despite lending me his spare set of diving gear. He brought his mind with him: the whole enchilada I hoped I had moved on from. But then he said something that was, unwittingly, to make his squareness worthwhile. We were walking away from the General Stores.

"It's amazing! I've been here nearly two years, and yet you seem to know more about Jamaica and Jamaicans after only, what is it, two months. They seem to accept you as one of them."

There I was in the closest simulacrum to paradise that I'd come across, and I'd spend hours in the unbearable heat of my tin hut, fiddling with cotton wool, powdered pills of physeptone and syringes! I had already had a few sweating fevers as a result of dirty fixes and yet I persisted in sticking needles into my arms, even though I could keep myself straight perfectly well by just swallowing the pills. The few needles I had were starting to get very blunt and I would spend hours trying to sharpen them with emery boards bought at the General Stores.

I was ashamed of my private activities. I didn't want the people of Long Bay to know what I got up to, to know that I was a junky. Whenever I went outside, if only to swim in the sea, I tried always to wear a shirt with the sleeves rolled down. I couldn't let my tracks be seen, especially not by the MacPhersons, who, with their bourgeois pretensions, might easily do something unpleasant if they discovered a drug addict was living so close.

At the end of one particularly long and good day, spear-fishing on the reef with Alban, he said we both needed a woman. Woman as commodity. He took me to a place in Oche Rios, a dancing place, an extra-large shack of banana leaves, cocoanut matting and corrugated iron in which a sound system man operated. More than a travelling DJ, a sound system man sets up his homemade gear wherever there are people to dance, he dubs his own lyrics over the instrumentals, he is a rude boy par excellence, the apostle who says 'forget your troubles and dance'.

Alban said it would be easy to find a woman in this place. But I had none of the social skills of Jamaicans; I found it hard to understand the patois; I didn't know if you *asked* a woman to dance, *told* her or simply started dancing with her, although I suspected it was the latter and the relative clumsiness of my dancing made that difficult. After two hours with the women in their tight skirts taking little notice, I was getting desperate. Alban told me to buy us another rum. He circled, dancing through the hip-bumping bodies and back to my side.

"She the one you need, mi tinkin," he pointed to a girl of about eighteen, not beautiful, not ugly, tight dress, the usual little plaits. She was bumping gently away by herself. She pretended not to notice that Alban was talking about her. He nudged me towards her, himself close behind.

"Mi fren wan duns wit you. Him an inlishmun, but a rude boy." We danced, me embarrassed and unsure, but with the fourth record we were looking more at each other than at the floor. Some chemistry was happening.

"Shall we, um, go outside? We could get a drink. Would you like one?" It was ridiculous. I sounded so English, so uppercrust, so alien to her culture. But she came outside with me, looking up at me with limpid black eyes every now and then.

"What's your name? I'm William."

"Mi? I's Fleur. You reeli from Englun, man?" She stood so close as we looked out at the pulsating night. I told her I really was from England, and with another large gulp of rum, I had enough courage to ask her the main question.

"Fleur, will you come back to my cabin in Long Bay? We could catch the last bus." She didn't look at all surprised. She put her arm round me.

"Sure ting. You reeli is a rude boy. Come wit mi to get sometings from mi ouse, man." And she led me off through the banana trees. Her house was a wooden shack on stilts with chickens and pigs rummaging about in the dirt beneath. She emerged with a battered shopping bag.

She stayed with me for ten days. A young Englishman living on his own was an opportunity not to be missed. At best, I might take her back to England with me, and at worst, I provided her with free food and shelter and an escape from the daily grind of poverty. She showed me much affection and kindness.

It came to an end when I got a message via the PO that the owner of the cabin was coming with friends to have one last rave-up before they had to start teaching for another year. On the morning of the proposed party, I decided Fleur must go. What would all those young English people think to find me shacked up with a Jamaican girl, whom they would definitely regard as a whore, but she wasn't a whore, not really, we'd grown quite fond, she hadn't asked for any money, just to be with me, but they would think she was a prostitute, a black one to boot, and would treat her badly, not that they were prejudiced, mind. There were tears in her eyes when she got on the bus. And I did press a few notes in her hand.

When they came, the jolly teachers, they made me feel instantly apprehensive, left out, not a part of their hearty social illusion. I had to go home. I prepared a large fix, as soon as they'd left, and it produced an intense fever, sweating, shivering, head ache. I would go home. And there was New York to see on the way there.

On the day of my departure, I cleaned what was left of the ganja that Manny had sold me. The good stuff, the consistency of fine tea leaves, went into a polythene bag that I went to great trouble to strap between my legs with surgical tape.

I was stoned on one last joint and too many physeptone pills, and was in disarray when I heard the raucous hooter of the Kingston Flyer. I grabbed the newspaper that contained the seeds and stalks that I'd cleaned from the ganja and jammed it on top of everything in my suitcase and shut the lid.

Just as I was boarding the bus, Mr Williams thrust a paper bag full of avocado pears into my hands, saying they were from the tree that shaded his store. Alban gave me the firm hand slap as one brother to another, and Manny grinned a toothless grin. I was off, back to what is called civilisation.

The flight was not the ebullient wallowing in grandiosity it had been the other way. I was nervous; I worried about whether I should try to score in New York, home of the really heavy version of the junky myth surrounded by death; but there was also the jazz. I had a contact, a guy I'd met in Paris, and he'd said I was welcome to stay in his loft, even if he wasn't there, which he probably wouldn't be.

La Guardia airport was big, fast and noisy. I had my first, if rather hilarious, shock at the immigration desk. When I came to extract my passport from my hip pocket, I found it was covered in green slime. It had got right in between the pages. I had sat on the bag of avocados. The man behind the desk was not amused, but, after some argument, agreed to stamp it.

In the customs the man told me to open my bags, which I thought a bit tedious of him. As I opened the lid of my suitcase, what I saw made me want to run away. There, perched right on top was the Daily Gleaner package containing the stalks and seeds of my ganja. It was the first thing he looked at. He picked up a few stalks and looked at them as though he'd never seen anything like it before. He smelt it, rubbed it between his fingers.

At last he spoke: "Say, what *is* this stuff, anyway?"

"Oh that, well, it's, um, well it's, you know, it's," and then quick as a flash I was inspired, "it's Jamaican Herbal Tea, you know, you pour boiling water on it, let it brew, and drink the infusion with a twist of lemon, although some people prefer it with milk and sugar."

"You don't say," he answered. There was no telling if he'd swallowed the story, which wasn't, in fact, that far from the truth. You can get a nice high that way. But he told me to wait while he went over to see his superior. My heart sank even further. I watched them at the end of the hall, as my man showed the bundle to a hard looking superior and pointed in my direction. Visions of prison in New York, of being locked up with Mafia hoodlums, fear. He walked slowly back.

"That's OK," he handed the package back to me. "Sorry to have delayed you." He closed my case without searching any further.

"Have a good stay in New York." I couldn't believe it. Something was watching over me.

I peered out at the hugeness, the grittiness and felt alone, as my yellow cab barrelled across the double-decker Brooklyn Bridge, through the German, Italian and Russian quarters to stop outside a decaying brownstone walkup. As instructed by my man in Paris, I sought out Mr Brownstein in the basement, who was expecting me and gave me the key to the lockup on the sixth floor. There was a mattress, a tattered Persian carpet, a washbasin with a cold tap and one battered cupboard. It was one long room that ran the thickness of the building. The john was down the hall.

I had planned to have enough physeptone pills to last me for the two weeks I was to be in New York, but only a very meagre supply was left after Jamaica. Somehow it would have to do. I knew it would be foolish to try and score in New York. I wasn't that desperate that I would risk dicing with the Mafia.

The first thing I had to do was go and hang around the Village, around St Mark's Place and Bleaker Street, because that's what hipsters did. I tried hard to look as if I had 'no particular place to go', to look cool.

"I can't just walk up to that likely looking guy and ask to score. I don't want to, anyway, do I? Not actually withdrawing, am I? But it would be so nice, so warm," my internal dialogue ranted on.

To forestall all this I went into a record store and found myself saying slightly ridiculous things to the hip black cat behind the counter.

"I'm from England." A pause to allow him to gasp in admiration, but he didn't. "Yes, I'm over here from England and, you know, I've been digging Cecil Taylor's piano for years.

"That's great man," the cool cat replied wearily.

"Well the thing is, d'you know his address? I'd very much like to meet up with him." And the guy took me seriously, well didn't laugh.

"No man, I don't have the man's address, but it's cool you dig him in England." He played me the latest record made by the man. We got friendly and he said he'd meet me at the big Coltrane concert that weekend. I wandered back to my loft half an hour later. I was alone in New York, just like in the movies. The next day I went to the Museum of Modern Art and got sore feet looking at the Mondrians and Pollocks, reproductions of which had so excited me years before.

The concert by John Coltrane was indeed big. It was the legend playing, right there in front of my eyes. He was to die the next year. He had split up with McCoy Tyner and Elvin Jones by then and was playing with the then wild young men of jazz: Archie Shepp, Pharoah

Saunders and John Tchcai, with his new wife Alice playing the harp and piano.

One of the odd things about Coltrane* was his love of the cheesy tune from The Sound of Music, *My Favourite Things*. It was something to do with its melodic structure that attracted him. Previously it had been the rocket that his quartet would board to take off into the saxosphere, but now it was the vehicle for a big band playing what is now called trance jazz: a high-energy, ensemble improvisation that veered all the time towards a wailing ecstasy. That one piece lasted over an hour. The Village Theatre, which was full

John Coltrane

to the roof, seemed to be floating up and out of New York. The concentration, the ecstatic pulsing drew the audience into trance grins and many 'yeah man's'.

He really was a god. His music was one of the closest material expressions to spirituality there has ever been. He was black, but his sheets of sound were white hot being-lava. His wife, Alice's, reaction to the unthinkable scale and unending surprise of John's spontaneity was to elevate him to the status of avatar in the pantheon of her philosophy.

I couldn't find the dude from the record store anywhere. I went back to the loft with one of those gross American sandwiches, a submarine, and got back to my fretting. Although I wasn't actually with-

---

* On July 17th 1987, the twentieth anniversary of John Coltrane's death, there was a concert at the Bloomsbury Theatre in London by the *Coltrane Legacy Band* led by his widow Alice with her sons Ravi on tenor and Oran on soprano, Reggie Workman on bass and Rashied Ali on drums. Alice had become Turiya Aparana Satchidananda, a guru. She wore a maroon Tibetan-monk-style robe and her hair was large afro-Indian. Andrew, my brother-in-law, had long been researching a book that was eventually published in 1997 as *The Book of Enlightened Masters*. So he came to the concert, and afterwards we went back stage and met Alice. She received us with a regal dignity and readily agreed to meet again the next day at her hotel.

Wearing her maroon robe, she was sitting at a small table in the tearoom, surrounded by midwestern US tourists with their loud clothes and voices. Her back was ramrod straight; her smile seraphic. Andrew interviewed her as to her teachings. She gave us cassettes of her holy music – Sanskrit hymns of devotion in the Hindu mould with Alice on lead vocals and keyboards with a backing from her black disciples giving it strong flavours of soul, blues and jazz. Her courage, her beauty, her music! And one of her 'received' books has the best title: *Endless Wisdom, volume 1*.

drawing, having aches and pains, I was strung-out. The three pills I had successfully rationed myself to only had the effect of stopping me from feeling worse. I needed to talk to, be in common with, an American, a native. I would go and see Bruce, the man I tripped the morning glory with in Paris.

We had exchanged two or three letters since those crazy days in Paris and I had his new address in Hartford, Connecticut. He had married Leila and had thus got her back to the States. I got to Hartford, an ugly industrial town, on a Greyhound bus. They lived in a clapboard house in a street lined with worn-out trees. We were all three excited to see each other again, to be face-to-face with the stuff of our own myths.

But the heroes who had been so fired by Beckett and Burroughs, who had walked on the edge of human understanding, no longer existed. Bruce had fallen into Scientology and held that it was the only possible way forward for mankind. I was busy with my holes. The romance of our genius had been dissipated in our striving to fit in somewhere, in our maladaptions. We had no spark of anything for each other. It was like meeting up with an old school friend whom you find you don't actually like. And Bruce was insistent and boring about Scientology, a philosophy I thought unhealthy and irrelevant.

I flew home a few days later. I'd had what is called a good time in Jamaica and New York, in my outward movements anyway. It was so rare that I could break out of my shell of self-concern and find myself *involved* with something outside. The world seemed dirty and gross. But my travels would provide some good stories, proof of what an estimable hipster I was.

The prestige of government has undoubtedly been lowered considerably by the Prohibition law. For nothing is more destructive of respect for the government and the law of the land than passing laws which cannot be enforced. It is an open secret that the dangerous increase of crime in this country is closely connected with this. (Albert Einstein, *My First Impression of the USA*, 1921)

It was the Autumn of 1966. It started building on the plane back to Heathrow, the detailed logistics of going down the Dilly to score; I had it all mapped out. There was no question as to it being a bad thing to do. I'd gone for over two months without a fix of heroin and *deserved* one as soon as I could get it. I cashed a cheque at the airport, took my bags to a left-luggage locker at Liverpool Street Station and within two hours of landing in England I was outside Boots in the Dilly. I couldn't see any obvious junkies in the chemist, so I went down to the main concourse of the tube station. I couldn't help but recognise Paul, as soon as I noticed a surgical boot and callipers.

"What are you doing here?" I asked quite pointlessly. "When did you leave Cane Hill?"

"Some time back. You trying to score too?"

"There's a guy in the little cafe round the back who's selling, but he wants to unload three grains in one go. Think he wants ten quid."

"Let's go halves then. Have you got a fiver?" He hadn't, but said that if I gave him seven, he'd go and deal with the guy who was a bit paranoid and preferred to deal with people he knew. Paul would keep a grain for the three quid he put in and would supply me with a couple of syringes. Ten agonising minutes later, Paul was back, hobbling along as fast as his callipers would let him.

"Let's go then. I've got it. I know a cool place to fix." We were out in the street, heading up Shaftesbury Avenue. Suddenly he darted into the doorway of a dingy office block. We went up to the first floor, through a swing door, along a passage and into a rather smart toilet with a washbasin on the wall. Paul locked the door.

"This is a lot better than that hole in Piccadilly, isn't it?" He was proud of his secret fixing-place.

"Yeah," I replied as I pulled my belt from my trousers and rolled up my sleeve. "Let's have my stuff, then." He had taken the usual plastic phial from his pocket and was counting the jacks it contained. I was impatient.

"Jeesus!" He exclaimed. "There's only two grains here. We've been conned. The sodding bastard." But I knew his game. He was offering me a predetermined melodrama to cover the fact that he'd kept a grain of heroin for himself. I had no inclination to do anything about it. My need for that first fix was now too urgent for me to care if I was being conned. At least he'd brought me to a clean place to fix.

After more protestations about not being able to trust anyone any more, he handed over the eight pills we agreed should be my share. I put two into the syringe I had ready and drew up water from the basin tap. With my left arm strapped up with my belt, I shook the syringe until the jacks dissolved.

I got a hit immediately, the blood spurting into the clear solution. Heroin reached once more to the core with its remembered rush of euphoria. Paul was still digging around in his arm, the thin shaft of steel penetrating a festering sore, as he pulled and pushed the sharp point around the resisting vein. Then he had it; his bad leg jerked down; his surgical boot smashed on the floor; his face closed up. He too felt the rush.

Back home in Cambridge, I did nothing to ease my parents' concern that all was not well, that the cure I was supposed to have had might not be all that I made it out to be. They were learning to recognise the web of deceit that I spun around my persistently mysterious comings and goings. My first priority had been to visit the doctor and persuade him to give me prescriptions for heroin once again.

"What happened in Jamaica?" He asked. "I don't suppose you managed to get yourself off physeptone, did you?"

"Not exactly," I havered and went on to give him a biased account of my travels. Lies and embroidered truth presented the image of an incurable addict in desperate need of help.

"So you see," I concluded. "I've got to have a prescription for heroin. If I don't get one, I know I'm going to be drawn into that evil scene at Piccadilly again, and then, well... God knows what'll happen." It was emotional blackmail. I was appealing to his humanitarian and Hippocratic tendencies, hoping that his repugnance for prescribing such a dangerous drug could be overridden. But he hesitated. Something more was needed.

"If you were to give me a regular prescription, like you did before, my habit would be under your control and I wouldn't need to have anything to do with other addicts. It's my final year just coming up, and I feel pretty confident I can get a degree, but only with your help." He moved his prescription pad into a central position on the desk. My manipulation was going to work.

"I'll only need two and a half grains a day," I added as he took the top off his pen.

"OK, I'll give you prescriptions for two and a half grains a day for the next week. You must come back and see me after that. If I hear that you are in any way abusing my trust in you, I shall have to think again."

And so I was once more set up with an assured supply of heroin for the forthcoming term. It didn't take my parents long to find out but there was little they could do, other than insist that I go for a proper cure somewhere once I'd finished at Cambridge.

I gloss over the effect I was having on them. We were entering the third act of the tragedy. No longer angry at being made one, I accepted my identity as scapegoat and drug addict whose every word is devious to some degree, manipulating people and circumstance towards the next fix. My mother is a chronic worrier, and her anguish is her most powerful weapon. I couldn't bear it that I was the cause and neatly turned it round. I wouldn't have become an addict if they had not made me go to Eton, misunderstood me so completely, and so on and on. All hurting, all hurt. My father honed his stoicism.

I was given rooms in Angel's Court for my final year, no doubt, to keep me under the watchful eye of the porters whose office was close by. I started to penetrate the arcane philosophy and psychology I needed to get my Part Two. My essays, now two a week, were always done at the last minute. Not uncommon in itself, but, unlike most students, I could only manage them when I'd scored some amphetamine or cocaine to give the heroin an extra lift.

I could only give my undivided attention to the few lectures I got to if I'd had a fix of just the right amount about half an hour beforehand. My 'pataphysics and neo-dadaism kept all and sundry at a safe distance, they suited my prickly isolationism. I could be weird because I was a 'pataphysician. I was a 'pataphysician because I was downright extraordinary.

That was the public side of it. A few poems managed to escape the private hell I'd entered, poems that spoke more clearly than I then imagined of mine being the human condition *in extremis*. Of course, I could only write when nicely stoned.

In some of the poems were signs that I fantasised dying tragically young in the Charlie Parker, Coleridge, de Quincey and Cocteau tradition. It would be one way of making my mark on the world.

The only time I felt fully at ease with someone else was when we had both fixed. H was the reverse of the philosopher's stone. It turned what was, potentially, gold into the base metal of one-pointed addiction. When zapping on the effects of a fix, there was certainty, a sure knowledge that nothing mattered very much, that death was inevitable, that we could BE in the moment, but only because heroin gave us blinkers to obscure the past and translate the future into an horizon of possible further fixes.

It could be said that heroin is an *antispiritual* drug, it distorts the instinctual need for one-pointedness; it distils the complexity of human experience into something essentially simple; it channels all needs into one; but in doing this, all the addict's energy, physical and otherwise, is dissipated *out* into a nexus of fear, intolerance, suspicion and self-regarding pity.

Remembering the deliciousness of our last encounter, I was curious as to how Margareta was getting on and rang her several times but got no reply. At the last attempt, Dr Grey answered and told me she'd gone back to Fulham and he hadn't seen her since. On my next trip to London to score some cocaine, I decided to go and see if I could find her.

I shouldn't have been surprised when her husband answered the door; it was his flat after all. He wasn't too pleased to see me, but asked me in nevertheless.

"When did you last see her?" He asked aggressively.

"About three months ago, before I went to Jamaica, why?" I was genuinely puzzled at his approach.

"Because a lot's happened to her since then, and I'd like to be sure that you weren't directly involved," He looked at me curtly.

"What do you mean? Where is she? What's happened?"

"Even if you weren't the direct cause, it wouldn't have happened if it hadn't been for you." It was beginning to dawn on me why he was being so obtuse. He edged closer to the point. "Are you still hooked? No, you don't have to answer that, it's obvious just from looking at you that you are."

"What on earth are you on about?" I feigned innocence.

"OK, I'll tell you. About two months ago Margareta asked me if she could move back here from Dr Grey's. She didn't say why, and I didn't ask. It was OK though; I was still living over the road. She was terribly pale and looked ill. Said she was recovering from a bad bout of flu. I didn't see much of her for the next few weeks, until, one day, I called round to tell her about a part that sounded right up her street. She was in an awful state. The flat was a pigsty, blood on the carpet, a syringe lying on the table. Yes, William, she was using heroin, she was hooked." He paused, looking in my eyes with pitying bitterness.

"Oh no!" There was nothing I could say. I wished I wasn't there. "Oh yes! She was well and truly hooked. She'd been buying at least a grain a day from some Australian yob called Marcus. For someone who's never used the stuff before, that's quite a lot, isn't it?"

"Yes, to begin with it is. But what happened to her, where is she?" I asked, genuinely shocked.

"I did the only thing I could. I helped her pack a couple of suitcases and put her on a plane to Sweden. She agreed that it was the only way. I heard from her last week. She's more or less straight now, still finding it difficult, but grateful that I got her out before the addiction could get too strong a hold. She'll be OK, which is more than can be said for you." He kept his temper barely restrained.

"It's great that you got her back to Sweden," I said lamely, and then, as if to justify my part in the affair, I added, "Of course, I was in Jamaica when all this happened."

But he had told me what he felt I ought to know and ushered me to the door, banging it behind me. I went to Nigel's in Cromwell Road and had an enormous fix which laid me right out for several hours. Close to an overdose.

One day, not long into the first term of that last year at the university, I scored five grains of cocaine in London. By the time I got back to my rooms in College, I had used maybe a third of it and my mind was out near Alpha Centauri. I could see the world in a grain of coke. It was after midnight, my neighbours were asleep and I enjoyed the isolation.

Despite another fix with more coke than H in it, I picked up messages of hunger from my body. It hadn't eaten for twelve hours. There were some baked beans left over from the day before in my saucepan, to which I added a knob of butter. I put it on the gas ring and stirred absent-mindedly with a fork. It was then that I noticed something odd about the beans: a white mould growing right in amongst the individual beans; not a furry mould, but more like frogs' spawn. But it was no ordinary mould: when I tried to get hold of a piece on the fork, all I got was beans, and yet the longer I looked into the saucepan, the more obvious were the growths. Then it dawned on me. It wasn't mould at all. The white blobs were the eggs of some insect.

At first I wasn't put out by this discovery. My cooking arrangements had always been rather squalid. In my first year in Whewell's Court, I'd lived on raw tinned pilchards and tinned new potatoes heated up in my electric kettle. I was still hungry and started to tear open a new packet of digestive biscuits. I thrust a biscuit into my mouth. But when I glanced at what was left of it in my hand, I saw there were insect eggs right in the midst of its crumble. This was worrying! The bugs had somehow managed to penetrate the wrapping, which I found difficult enough to open myself and had then got into the centre of the biscuits without leaving any trace on the outside. I couldn't understand it. I sat down in the armchair next to my gas fire.

My gaze fell on the wallpaper. My God, they were there too! They had burrowed beneath it and their eggs could be seen as little bumps. If they had got into the biscuits and under the wallpaper, there was no telling where else might not be contaminated. The room had been perfectly all right when I left it to go up to London. Now it was infested with the eggs of some pernicious insect that could well be the carrier of some awful disease. Part of my mind told me that such a thing was quite impossible, but was overruled by the incontrovertible evidence of the eggs.

Now that I'd started to look, I found them everywhere: on the skirting board, inside the coffee jar, on the bottom of the kettle. It was bad. I would have to warn the porters about the infestation in the morning. The whole room would have to be fumigated. I thought I ought to check the corridor and put my head round the door. They were there too. The whole building would have to be evacuated. I resolved to spend what was left of the night huddled on my armchair in the middle of the room, where I'd pulled all the furniture to prevent it getting infested any further. It was a long night.

The coke kept me from sleeping. Towards dawn my legs started to itch, especially on the backs of my calves. I pulled up the legs of my jeans to have a look. The insects had attacked my body! I immediately started to dig the eggs out of my legs with a pair of nail scissors, frightened that their diseases would kill me.

I heard it strike eight o'clock while I was still busy with the scissors.

The porters would now be on duty and it was beholden on me to let them know what had happened so they could make arrangements to evacuate the building and get it fumigated. I rushed down to the porter's lodge.

"My rooms are infested," I tried to shout through my panting. "It's some insect. You'll have to fumigate the whole building." Still panting.

"I see sir, infested you say?" The porter replied in measured tones from beneath his regulation bowler hat. He remained amazingly calm, given the severity of the infestation.

"Yes, I first noticed them in the baked beans, but they are everywhere. They even managed to get into an unopened packet of biscuits. They're out in the corridor. They're everywhere. I tell you, the whole building will have to be fumigated."

"Sounds bad. And you think, sir, that it'll all have to be fumigated, do you? We'll have to get someone along to have a look at it, won't we, but meanwhile, what I suggest is," he paused briefly, as though he were saying something difficult, "that you go on home on your bike. You know, home to Chaucer Road." The porters knew that the Senior Tutor was my father and that he lived in Chaucer Road.

"And have a nice hot bath and some breakfast. When you get back, you'll find we've done whatever's necessary, and you'll feel right as rain."

"Yes, maybe you're right, but you will go and investigate, won't you?" He said he would. I went home as he had suggested.

My parents greeted me with worry. They sat me down in the kitchen. We gripped the blue and white striped coffee mugs with both hands. We didn't look at each other.

"William," my father looked at me compassionately, "it seems you have been hallucinating." I was flabbergasted. He must be talking about the insect eggs.

"You mean they're not there. Don't be ridiculous." I wouldn't believe it.

"All the porters could find was the mess you've made of your room. What drug were you on last night?" He was firm, but more sad than angry. It hadn't occurred to me to connect the two, that the cocaine could have had anything to do with the eggs, but as I told them, the connection became all too apparent: a classic example of the coke horrors, a state brought on by excessive use of the drug, known for psychotic hallucinations of insects.

I had *known* – not suspected or believed – that there was a dangerous infestation of disease laden insect eggs. I had seen them everywhere in Angel's Court. Now I had to acknowledge that the bugs were unreal, that they lived in the crevices of my mind! And my father an entomologist! In 'lucid dreams' you know you're having a dream but can do nothing to alter its course. I knew I was high on cocaine, but this knowledge in no way effected the reality of the insect eggs. When you wake up from a lucid dream, it takes a little time to adjust to what is really real. I needed a long hot bath before I could distinguish hallucination from reality. The scabs on my legs were real; the porter saying, "I see sir, infested you say?" an hallucination.

It was becoming increasingly public knowledge that William Pryor was a sick man, prone to all sorts of odd behaviour.

Not long after this episode, I met Al. We were both collecting our scrips from Pecks the Chemist next to old Addenbrokes Hospital, opposite the Fitzwilliam Museum.* Al and I eyed each other, but didn't speak. I noticed he got two phials in his cellophane package, meaning cocaine as well. As soon as I'd got my stuff, I hurried after him and introduced myself as a fellow addict.

He was in his late forties and was Canadian. He even wore a lumber jacket. He was walking through the gates of the hospital, towards a side entrance.† I sensed that he must be going to fix, so I followed him. I didn't fancy the bike ride back to college. He opened a sliding door just inside the entrance and beckoned me into a tiled room before he shut it again. A box of disposable syringes, another of medical wipes and a bottle of sterile water with a rubber top through which to stick needles were on a table in the corner. I was amazed to find these facilities laid on for us to fix and told him so.

"Yeah, man, my doctor arranged it for me. The day-sister lays it all out for me between nine and ten in the morning. Cool, isn't it?" I agreed and went ahead with my fix. Just as I was about to stick the needle into my arm, he asked me if I wanted some of his coke. I took the needle off, put my thumb over the end and took the plunger out to allow him to shovel some of the crystalline powder into the heroin solution with his special penknife.

When we'd both got a hit and the buzz had worn off a bit, we talked. He had the same doctor as me. When he'd come to Cambridge

---

* Which now houses a significant collection of my grandmother's woodcuts and paintings.

† When the old hospital building was converted into a smart business school, this part of the building became Browns, an upmarket chain restaurant. You can now drink your Chablis where Al and I once fixed our heroin.

from London, he'd asked around if there were any doctors prescribing heroin and had been told about mine. He asked me back to his bungalow in Chesterton and drove us there in his battered old Jaguar.

We were greeted by his English wife to a scene of cosy domesticity. Al, who was one of the Canadian junkies who had fled their homeland when the drug laws were tightened up, had been using for over twenty years. He despised those addicts who affected to hate society and lived in squalor. He held that his addiction was genetic and metabolic, something he had to put up with, but it didn't mean he couldn't lead a decent life. He vehemently decried those 'pimps' who gave junk to people who weren't addicted. He told me it was important that I discover if I was a real junky or just someone messing around with the stuff. The implication was that real junkies were men who faced up to carrying their crosses of metabolic addiction for the rest of their lives, while the rest were no more than pharmaceutical dilettantes.

11 NATURAL DESELECTION

In October 1966, aged 21, I started what was to be my last year at the University. Andrew and I would run into each other at some of the lectures I managed to get to. Walking back to town one day from a lecture on Wittgenstein, we talked.

"What are you up to these days. Don't see much of you?" I asked.

"Not much. A bit of meditation."

"Oh yes?" I tried to cover my embarrassment. I just couldn't see him doing something so unhip. "What sort?"

"Shabd yoga or yoga of the sound current." He replied, but I was none the wiser. I didn't press him to explain as I wasn't that interested.

Some weeks later he involved me as an unwitting third party in a successful bid to meet and go out with my sister Lucy, now at Hornsea Art College. I found this odd. Up till then I had regarded her solely as a rather tiresome younger sister who kept pestering me to be allowed to meet my friends, and now one of them was chasing after her. He gave her a blade of grass as a token of his affection.

I was needing more heroin than I was getting on my prescriptions, and Al couldn't spare more than the occasional jack. Coming away from the doctor's surgery one morning, clutching my prescriptions for the next seven days, I had a brain wave. It shouldn't be too difficult to change the '1' into a '2', to make it read '25 x 1/6 grain'. I traced a '2' from an old letter he'd written me onto Bronco lavatory paper, and, using the technique learned at primary school, transferred that on to the prescription to cover and include the '1'. I then went over it carefully in the same colour ink as he used. The result was convincing.

I presented my forgery to the chemist later that morning. There was a certain thrill at getting away with it. I told myself that I wasn't doing anything seriously wrong, just bypassing the law to get what I needed.

The next day when I presented a similarly doctored scrip to Mr Philkin, he took me by the arm to a quiet spot at the back of the shop. He had the previous forgery in his hand.

"Look, there's something funny about these prescriptions, isn't there?" He wasn't threatening.

"I don't know what you mean: 'funny'?" I tried it on.

"Well, the day before yesterday you were only getting fifteen pills, two and a half grains, and suddenly you get an extra ten pills. Bit odd isn't it?" He was a kindly man who was sympathetic to us addicts.

"Yes, well, the doctor agreed to give me more, to give me what I needed, you see." But I knew it wasn't working.

"Come on now! I'm giving you a chance to tell me what really happened."

"But it's true, what I just told you, it's true." By now, I knew that he knew, he clearly knew.

"It's a pity you couldn't tell me. I rang the doctor yesterday, when I noticed how the amount had changed, and he told me what he'd written here." He tapped the prescriptions with his finger. I was in a panic.

"Yes, OK, I did change the amount. I needed it. What's going to happen? What are you going to do?" I asked with fear welling.

"It's all right, you'll get what you're meant to have today. You give me the other prescriptions so that nothing can happen to them, and the doctor asked me to tell you to go and see him. For goodness sake don't try it again. I won't be so broadminded next time. I will have to call in the police."

The doctor was understanding. I was sick, after all, and left it that he would make it more difficult for me to forge my prescriptions in the future by writing the amount in letters as well as figures. But now I knew that I could get away with it and that compassionate professionals could not deny me their help and understanding.

A few weeks later I tried it again. The number written out made it more difficult but not impossible: eight could be changed to eighteen, for instance. To my delight, I passed three of these off successfully, which made me somewhat reckless.

And then, one grey day, my withdrawal pain was so extreme when I started my forging that I made a mess of it. I tried to use a rubber to erase a slip of the pen and, in so doing, removed the top surface of the paper. I botched it up as best I could, but the ink spidered into the paper. It was an obvious forgery.

Then I remembered that the chemist near the Round Church, who had started fulfilling heroin prescriptions, had a doddery old man as relief pharmacist during the lunch hour. I waited, sweating and aching, till one o'clock and then walked as slowly as I could to the chemist. The old man was on duty all right and he processed the prescription without any comment. Great relief, I'd done it again.

That evening – I was at home, it being the Easter Vacation – the front door bell jangled. My father answered it, with me hovering. Two men, one in a dowdy raincoat, the other a leather jacket, both deferentially businesslike, hands in pockets, both with that stocky military look. My father put on the air and voice he reserved for bank managers:

"Yerrs?" They produced their warrant cards: plainclothes policemen.

"Does a Mr William Pryor live here?"

"He does." I edged backwards so they couldn't see me.

"We need to talk to him about a certain matter." They were so correct, these servants of the Queen.

"You had better come in then," replied my father, opening the door wider. They brushed their shoes politely on the doormat.

"This is William, my son."

"I see sir." Nodding at me. "Is there somewhere private we can talk?"

"Um," replied my father, "We'll go to your room shall we, William?" Not waiting for a reply he led them up the back stairs to my room. The policemen refused the proffered chairs and indicated they wanted to talk to me alone.

"No, I'll stay," said my father grimly, "Carry on."

"If you say so, sir." The more senior of the two took out his pocket book and pulled out the prescription I'd passed off at lunchtime.

"Is this prescription yours? Was it made out to you?" Their formal game had me in its net. We all knew, except perhaps my father, exactly what we were about. Hypernervous, I went over, took the prescription and made as if to examine it carefully.

"Yes, it's mine. Why?" Some part of me still clung to a hope that they didn't know what was obvious.

"Because this prescription has been tampered with, as you will see if you look closely at it." And so followed the time honoured procedure of caution and statement.

I had been busted, something that only happened to other people. They left saying the whole matter was now in the hands of the chief constable who would decide what charges would be brought.

"Entirely off the record, you understand sir," said leather jacket, "there is no way that Bill here can avoid prosecution on at least one indictable charge." The extraordinary cheek, being familiar like that, calling me Bill! We were heading for the front door. My father opened the Victorian cast iron latch and politely showed them out.

"Thank you for not making this any more unpleasant than it had to be." That is what one did, thank them, servants of the crown and everything, only doing their jobs.

My father decided that everything must be on the table. We must go and talk over the situation with the doctor, a solicitor and Harry Williams. It must be apparent to the court that every effort was being made to deal with my addiction. He was gloomy about my future at the university.

Harry presented an open and shut case. He must have talked to my father beforehand.

"William, we have to act *before* this whole thing gets to court. You must resign from the college now, otherwise I'll find myself in a position, after the court hearing, of having to give you the sack, and that'll do no one any good. This way the bad publicity that your father and the college are bound to get can be kept to a minimum. You do see that, don't you?"

He was pacing up and down the room, his face redder than usual. I was in a black hole of despair. All light of hope had been sucked in and annihilated, so it made little difference what he said, what anyone said.

"You have to agree that we gave you a fair chance. We allowed you a leave of absence to go for your cure. We turned a blind eye to your continued use of heroin in the hope that you would get through it somehow, but now things have gone too far. The college cannot be seen to be condoning the forgery of prescriptions. You must resign and that's that." He said this with a grim finality.

"I have drawn up this letter of resignation. Will you please sign it?" I meekly agreed and signed my respectability away. There were only six weeks until my finals. It hadn't yet dawned on me that I now stood no chance of getting that essential passport to a successful career, a degree.

The doctor announced that I would go on a reducing course of heroin, which would be gradually replaced with physeptone: a few ampoules, but mainly linctus. A feeling that the state, friends, institutions and family were closing in around me was stifling. As if there were an enormous illuminated sign over my head, which read, 'this is a sick and disgusting heroin addict who has transgressed most horribly'.

When the summons finally arrived, my father and I took it straight round to the solicitor who was to act on my behalf.

"We're very lucky. He's a really good man," said my father as we hurried away from that first meeting. He meant that he was good at his job. We were summoned back when he'd heard from the police.

"Doesn't look promising, I'm afraid," said the solicitor. "They have made two charges out of the incident: 'forging a document with intent to...' and 'uttering a forged document with intent to...' The second of these charges can only be tried by a judge and jury, something we must avoid if at all possible."

"Why?" I asked.

"A judge can hand out far stiffer sentences." He had his elbows on his desk, the tips of the fingers of each hand delicately touching each other as a sign of his deep and expensive thought. "Prison in some cases."

"What I can do is this. In matters of this kind I can call on the Deputy Chief Constable. Often play golf with him. You know, explain that you will be pleading guilty and convince him that they don't want to blight the otherwise promising future of a young man like yourself. Especially one from a family like yours, if you see what I mean." I looked at my father and he me and we saw what he meant.

We didn't hear from him for two weeks, during which time I became convinced I was going to be sent to prison, a horror of the worst dimensions. It must have weighed heavily on my parents too, for the son of the senior tutor of Trinity College, Cambridge to be a worthless heroin addict who gets sent to prison, it was not tolerable.

Eventually the solicitor phoned to say that the police would use the discretion they had in these matters in my favour. They could and did agree to the second charge being tried as a summary offence, i.e. before the magistrates. But they could still send me to prison. The day of the trial loomed like a ship of doom. There was a rallying of support. Andrew and my father went with me to the court in the Guildhall (in another part of the building in which we had done *Roodmoodments*). Harry Williams and my doctor were there to speak on my behalf. My solicitor had seen to it that it was the first case and would be over quickly since I was pleading guilty and there was no need for extensive evidence to be given in court.

Then,

there I was

in the dock,

a policeman behind me to prevent my escape.

I was guilty, the detritus of society, a pathetic creature who needed to have people like Harry Williams say, on oath, that I was a fine, intelligent person *underneath,* who was now making a valiant attempt to get back on the straight and narrow.

They fined me two hundred pounds, well over £2,000 in today's money, and bound me over, or something to the effect that if I did it again I'd be in real trouble. My father went straight to the fines office and wrote them a cheque. As we emerged from the Guildhall, there were two national newspaper reporters waiting to pounce. The loyal servants of the Crown must have tipped them off. Andrew pushed them away and we escaped as quickly as we could. There was a story on page 3 of the Times the next day: 'Senior Cambridge Don's Son on Heroin Charge'. I wasn't relieved and didn't notice that I'd got away with it again, just numb and stunned.

The doctor had so engineered things that I was now getting half a litre of physeptone linctus every three days. It was made deliberately dilute so that I wouldn't be tempted to inject it. Al supplied me with fixes, some of which I had to pay for, but just as important as the heroin was the solace. He took me seriously. He didn't look down on me. He knew what it was to suffer from something you had no control over. In his eyes, I was now a proper junky.

Had we lived in or near London, I would have fallen right into the abyss that then had its entrance at Piccadilly. But still the net of environment, money and care kept me from falling. The fact that Al also struggled hard to maintain some of the bourgeois standards of house, car, wife and so on, also encouraged me not to abandon my own family. My Darwins, my family, were both my downfall and my insurance.

There is a theory that significant events happen in bunches. First, I had been spewed out of the educational system and left to find my own way through the vomit, which was, as I was frequently reminded, entirely of my own making, my spewing. And such an intelligent boy! I had no idea what I was going to do with my life. Not that I had before the disaster, but now it all took on the heightened worry that I would *not* be a graduate; I would have no degree. Chaps without degrees couldn't become something in the City, nor join the Church, nor the Army. They might have to go into trade!

The atmosphere at home was so thick you could stir it, which I frequently did with my mysterious comings and goings, usually to see Al. My parents would have suspected the worse, but had only a constant subterfuge of half-truths to go on. My mother had now to rely on her little pills to get any sleep. But my craving for heroin was undiminished: the need for the blood ritual, the taste in the bones, the pain of needle penetration, the rush to the core.

The second event in this bunch, one around which my saga has revolved, and still does, concerned my sister Lucy and Andrew, who was now her boyfriend. Up till this point, she had been a younger sister I couldn't take seriously. She was pretty. She was an art student. She was actually, had I been able to look, not totally unhip. And now she too was drawn to the meditation that Andrew practised.

It was galling that my younger sister adopted something new before I did. This implied that I was losing my grip. I remembered that I had shown no interest at all when Andrew first told me he was meditating. Other than the fact that it was nothing to do with Maharishi, whom the Beatles were in the process of making famous, I knew nothing about this Indianism of his. But how could I justify my interest in the *I Ching*, Jung, Tibetan and other Buddhism and fashionable orientalia, if I showed no interest in the philosophy my sister and her boyfriend, my friend, considered so important?

I persuaded the two of them to come on a walk. We walked down the garden, past the asparagus beds and out the back gate, over the little stream and on to the Fen, towards the river and beyond that, Newnham. It was spring. The pollarded willows were just beginning to bud leaves. The ducks were noisy.

"So what is this meditation? Why meditate?"

"It's about bringing the attention to a single point, here," he put his index finger on his forehead between his eyebrows. We walked on. I was obviously going to have to work on them.

"But why?"

"Well," said Lucy, "this," she swept her hand around to include the whole Fen, "is not where we belong. You don't feel at home here, do you William?"

"No, I suppose I don't, but it depends on what you mean by 'here'. D'you mean *this* Cambridge or *this* world? This local situation or this human condition?"

"The human condition in the world," replied Andrew, "the

unsatisfactoriness of it. That it keeps changing and frustrating us. As Jagger sings: 'I can't get no satisfaction'."

"But is there anything else?" I was cynical.

"Yes, definitely," replied Lucy, "and it's here." Her finger also went to the point between her eyebrows, "this is where we do belong: inside."

"I don't get it. What do you mean, 'inside'? I mean, where is 'inside'? Isn't that just brain in there? Grey matter?" Lucy turned to Andrew. My question had stumped her.

"Ah, well, no," said Andrew. "Let me ask you this: when you shut your eyes, what do you see?" I stopped walking and shut them.

"Darkness, blackness with streaks of activity and after-impressions of this Cambridge," I replied, intrigued as to where he was going.

"And where is this blackness with streaks? Is it outside?"

"No."

"Then it is inside. By shutting your eyes you are turning your *attention* inwards, especially when you *look* into the darkness. And that's what it's about: attention and the fact that you can turn it."

He had now most definitely got mine, my attention.

"OK, I sort of see what you are on about. But, if it's just darkness inside, what good's that?"

"Good point! It's not just darkness. Behind that darkness is light. No, the darkness is, in reality, light. When your attention is focused enough you see light, the darkness becomes light, and you hear sound and start your journey inside."

"You make it sound as though there's a lot of room inside me."

"There is."

We walked on. I didn't reply, just digested. Our conversation turned to my situation. The ducks quacked.

"And you can go there, this 'inside', without drugs?" I asked as we went back into the garden of Chaucer Road.

"Well, you can't go there *with* drugs; *only* without them," was Andrew's riposte. "Going there is the purpose of human life, of being human."

"How can I really be sure this is it, that it's not some scam?"

"That's one of the reasons you need a living teacher, someone who's completed the journey himself. Someone who has fully integrated the inside and the outside. You can look him in the eye and he you and you know it's the truth. He's called Maharaj Charan Singh."*

---

*'Maharaj' is an honorific signifying 'great soul'; 'Singh' is a patronymic taken by all Sikhs. 'Maharaj Ji' is a term of respect and affection.

Andrew and Lucy explained why you had to be a vegetarian and abstain from mind-affecting substances before Maharaj Ji would teach you how to meditate, the practice of bringing the attention inside. Andrew also outlined how the philosophy of Sant Mat fitted with what I already knew of Buddhism and reincarnation.

A fragile, disheartened, identity-searching, degree-less drug addict, I just knew this was it. No hesitation. A conviction deeper than any I had had before about who I was, why I wasn't and where I was going. This felt like the real, unalloyed, uncluttered thing, no mumbo jumbo. You might say, especially in these more cynical times, that I was drawn to what I needed: a father figure, some certainty. You would be right and you would be wrong: right about what everyone is looking for, certainty and a father, wrong to think that because I was in a fragile, damaged state it follows that I had been drawn to some cult of brainwashing weirdos.

It is not my purpose to persuade anyone of the truth of anything, nor even to protect my reputation (that should be clear from what I have written so far). But I am all too conscious that this age of the secular self encourages cynicism about anything spiritual, so I should explain. I myself, as I was then and as I am now that I write this book, knew nothing and know nothing. But that verges on the precious – what I mean is that I have little direct experience of the mysterious truths of mysticism, but I know someone who has. I can, therefore, only speak of the shapes of the truth as I have seen them. It would be futile and presumptuous for me to imagine I can persuade you of anything. But I still think it better to speak of these shapes than to keep quiet in fear of being shunned by any prejudice my reader may hold.

The early 21st century orthodoxy in the so-called developed world is the worship of the self, the self that consumes and is consumed, evolving according to its memes. The primary concern of this self is its unrelenting search for meaning, happiness and fulfilment through the consumption and ownership of things, achievements, wealth, health, knowledge and status. Many know that this is flawed, that there is more, that the self is impermanent and any happiness it achieves fades away into loneliness, depression and frustration. Knowing this they search.

I couldn't understand why more people didn't know about it. Although it wasn't advertised or otherwise promoted, it was freely available. Andrew encouraged me to write off to Maharaj Ji to ask him if

I could visit him in his ashram, the Dera, in India that coming winter. I became a vegetarian straight away, and made desultory attempts to cut down my drug intake.

In his reply, Maharaj Ji wrote: "I quite appreciate your eagerness for initiation but under the present circumstances this initiation and meditation will not give you much benefit. Try to give up your habit of heroin and do not feel disappointed. You will certainly be able to overcome it with courage and determination.

"Regarding your coming to the Dera, you can gladly come when your circumstances permit. I have no objection. But first try to give up your drug habit. It requires a strong will power and nothing else."

I was disappointed. I imagined being able to somehow meditate all my problems away. Nevertheless I stuck to the diet and did what I could to cut down my drugs; definitely no more heroin, and a valiant attempt to wean myself off the physeptone linctus. I attended the meetings that Lucy, Andrew and a few others went to when someone would read aloud from the books on the subject and we would listen to tapes of Maharaj Ji answering questions. The main thing was that he had said I could go to India 'when [my] circumstances permit', actually go and meet him.

My father picked up that I was powerfully drawn to this Indian mysticism. On my birthday he presented me with a beautiful Thai travelling Buddha. He had shown great care in finding it and great love in thinking the thought behind it. Inside him there was an understanding that all our patterns of suffering could be broken. The Buddha still graces my mantle piece. He was reaching out to say he loved me, after all that had happened.

Someone was organising a group to go in October, when the Dera Guesthouse for foreigners was open. I said I would go.

Then, some six months later, as if enough of significance hadn't happened, came the third event of the bunch. We were sitting under the blossom of one of the apple trees in the garden at Chaucer Road. Andrew was reading aloud from one of the books brought over from India. It was a bright summer day, the clouds scudded. An idyll.

We heard a car pull into the drive at the other side of the house and someone went to see who it could be. My parents had gone out for lunch with friends. No one else was in.

"It's a police car. They want to speak to you, William." Leap of adrenaline, heart pounding, I went to see them.

"There's been an accident. Your parents. You'd better go to the hospital."

We jumped into the Mini and drove flat out to the hospital. Yes, Mrs Pryor would be out of that cubicle over there shortly, but could we wait, the doctor was with her.

"What… Where's Mr Pryor? Is he all right?" Andrew managed to ask. Lucy and I were too shocked.

"I'm afraid he's in a coma. They're about to take him into intensive care now. If you go through that door, you should see him before they take him up." We went through the door. He was lying on a trolley; my father, as if dead, on a trolley.

Two orderlies wheeled him away. No tears yet. We then saw my mother. She was being kept in for the night with a broken arm and bad abrasions.

"How is Daddy? Have you seen him?" Enormous fear in those brown eyes.

"Yes, I saw him; he's unconscious. They say he'll come round soon." Her fear had to be assuaged. "Probably just bad concussion, they say. They can find no other injuries, not a scratch. Anyway, how do you feel? Does it hurt horribly?"

"No, I'm all right. Have they taken him up to a ward?"

"Yes," Lucy came in quietly, "what on earth happened? Was anyone else hurt? Was he driving too fast? It was that damned Mini Cooper, wasn't it?" Her state of shock made her sound aggressive.

"Well, I don't know, yes. We were coming round that big wide corner near Harston. We were overtaking a van. There was a motorbike and sidecar. We hit it. The man was brought in the same ambulance. Car turned right over. Daddy unconscious. Oh...." My mother started to sob just as the nurse came up to wheel her off to a ward. It was a relief. It was as much as we could do to cope with our own shock, let alone hers as well.

"We'll come and collect you tomorrow," I called after her as Andrew directed us towards the car, unable to think or act clearly for ourselves.

I rang Uncle Matthew as soon as we got home and he said he would come over the next day. As the shock wore off, self-pity and a sense of tragedy swept in. Kicked out of university as practising drug addict, my parents in a serious car crash. What was next?

Andrew had taken Lucy out into the garden to walk some of the shock out of her system. I was alone in the house. I could ring the doctor.

"I hope you can help me," I said in feeble tones, "but my parents were in an awful car crash this afternoon. They're both still in hospital, my father still unconscious. I need some ampoules of physeptone, please." No shame: addict as complete opportunist. He said he'd leave a scrip with the receptionist.

I told Andrew and Lucy that I had to ride around on my bike, just ride around, and went to collect it. I fixed two amps in the downstairs bog. A welcome escape, that is, until I thought about my promises to Maharaj Ji.

My father didn't recover consciousness the next day. We collected my mother and were allowed to see him through the window of the intensive care unit. He was wired up like an experiment. Depressed and emotionally fractured, we couldn't shield my mother from the fact that no one at the hospital knew when, or even if, my father would recover consciousness.

Matthew arrived via the hospital in the afternoon. He took me to one side to tell me that the doctors he'd spoken to suspected severe brain damage, caused both by the whiplash effect of my father's head reacting to the impact of the crash, and by oxygen starvation when he almost drowned in his own vomit that got into his lungs. Indeed, had the policeman who lived only a few hundred yards from the scene of the crash not arrived very quickly, and immediately performed artificial respiration, my father would not have survived.

Within a few weeks my mother had recovered from her injuries and was beginning to adjust to the new reality, although she would break down and weep uncontrollably at the slightest provocation. My sisters had to restrain their grief and worry as best they could for her sake, while I could suppress it through physeptone, as if I had some special permit that excused me the necessity to endure emotional pain. As weeks passed, things got no better. Ours was a house suspended on the brink of mourning for a man who was neither dead nor alive.

The date of departure for India was drawing close and, in a mood of untypical responsibility, I wrote to Maharaj Ji, telling him of the accident, and that I might not be able to come, since I felt I should be with my mother. His reply, which ended, "You have to be with your father I know, in such an emergency", heightened my sense of being the reliable man of the house. A man gaining a new father as his blood father slipped away?

We were persuaded that it was a most fortunate thing that the accident had happened near Cambridge. The new Addenbrooke's Hospital was one of, if not *the,* best hospital in Europe for the treatment of severe head injuries. They performed all sorts of innovatory tests and explorations to determine the extent of the damage. During the day they would sit him in a chair next to his bed and put lead weights round his feet to stop his legs sliding about.

He would open his eyes, but they did not see. He didn't blink when you clapped your hands. He would make noises, which, in outbreaks of optimism, we would interpret as an attempt to speak. My mother was encouraged to go in every day and read aloud to him; the theory being that it was possible he could hear and understand perfectly well and a familiar voice might help him to locate himself and regain consciousness.

By now they had him in a small ward where he could hear the babble of other voices. To sit there and talk to what had been my father, knowing that there would be no response except perhaps a dribble of saliva from his mouth, while the other occupants politely made as if not to notice, had a pronounced dreamlike strangeness. This body in front of me, with its eyes open, staring, unseeing, was my father. But it was also *not* my father, but could, according to the doctors, once more *become* my father by regaining consciousness.

12 India – an Oasis in the Desert

And so it was that in September 1967, at the age of 22, I went to India. A dazed, crushed, convicted, jobless opiate addict whose father was in a coma. Running away, you might think.

Yes, running away from the material to the spiritual world my heart pined for. In my situation there could never be a good time to go. My mother actually wanted me to. On the Syrian Arab Boeing 707 that stopped six times on its long flight to the mysterious East, I was with the core of my Cambridge peer group, nervous trainee mystics.

Paul Charrier, a school friend of my now brother in law Andrew, was on his first return visit to see Maharaj Ji. He had been a wild man in his time with hair below his shoulders. One summer day, two years previously, he had decided to take an acid trip by himself in some Norfolk sand dunes. He had a vision, an epiphany: there *is* a real teacher and he can be found in India. Immediately on his return to Cambridge, Paul went to the Public Library in the Guildhall to see what he could find on Indian mysticism.

He came across a book, *The Path of the Masters*, which he quickly devoured from cover to cover. It was written in the thirties by one Dr Julian Johnson, an American and one of the first Westerners to visit Maharaj Ji's teacher, Maharaj Sawan Singh. Its effect was such that Paul got on the first plane to Delhi.

During his several months at the Dera in 1965, Paul wrote long and urgent letters about Maharaj Ji, which had an electric effect on the larger peer group back in Cambridge. By the end of the Sixties, either directly through Paul or at one remove, some twenty people in the Cambridge area, including Syd Barrett and Nigel and Jenny, had been influenced by Maharaj Ji. Indeed Syd applied to Maharaj Ji, on his subsequent visit to the UK, to be taught the meditation, but was told to come back when he had stopped taking drugs.

India has a long tradition of living spirituality. Mystics have lived and practised there for thousands of years and still do. Not that they haven't lived elsewhere: Lao Tse was in China, Rumi in Persia, Jesus in Palestine, Meister Eckhart in Germany, Dame Julian in England.

They have all taught the same truths, whatever their religious background. But the deep inclination towards spirituality in the Indian culture has meant that that country has had a great many mystics, including the Radha Soami or Sant Mat teachers whose background has been the Sikh religion.

All religions start with one or more mystics. When they die or are killed, their teachings are taken over by priests to become mere shells of ritual and the mystical core is lost. The Dera is in the middle of the Punjab, the homeland of the Sikhs, whose religion was started by a line of ten mystics. At the beginning of the seventeenth century the fifth of these mystics felt it so important to stress the universality of the teachings that he brought together the writings of mystics from all around the then known world into one book, the *Adi Granth*. As soon as the last guru died, the priests took over and the *Adi Granth* became a scripture and guru in its own right.

Maharaj Ji was outwardly a Sikh, wearing the Sikh turban, but his teachings were identical to those of Rumi, Jesus and Eckhart (and of course to the original Sikh Gurus), but expressed in language appropriate to the times. In 1967 there were maybe half a million satsangis (as disciples are known) around the world, with less than a thousand in the UK. Today there are in excess of one and a quarter million with more than ten thousand in this country.

My first impressions of India were of course heavily coloured, or should I say discoloured, by the fact that I'd had my last physeptone on the plane as it leapfrogged its way across Europe, Arabia and on to the Indian subcontinent. I had only managed to slightly reduce my daily intake of the drug in the weeks prior to our departure and had smuggled a bottle of the linctus on to the plane with the intention of using it in tiny doses to alleviate withdrawal symptoms once we got to India. But my resolve soon broke. I kept creeping off to the toilet for surreptitious swigs from my secret bottle. By the time we got to Delhi, the bottle was empty. It *had* been a long eleven-hour flight with frequent stops, after all. Withdrawal symptoms were imminent. My suffering would be as secret, as hidden as my bottle had been.

First there was the heat, unlike anything I'd known in Jamaica, in that it seemed to penetrate everything: people, buildings, thoughts. Then, of course, the people themselves, talking, shouting, gesticulating with their heads and hands, begging, welcoming, selling. A throb of humanity. Always someone trying to sell you something, be it a 'cup chai', a samosa, a rickshaw ride or a 'very good changing' for your traveller's cheques; whatever it was, there was always someone at your side.

Maharaj Ji was due in Delhi in a few days to address the thousands gathered to hear him. We would go to the meetings before going on to the Dera, some three hundred miles to the north, in the Punjab. We were taken to Maharaj Ji's private house in Daryai Ganj and given charpoys (string beds) in a room directly beneath his own quarters.

I couldn't sleep that night, despite the fatigue of the long journey. The withdrawal symptoms had started, the aches in the arms, the sweating, the impenetrable remoteness from experience. Outside the room where the four of us lay, the noise continued regardless of the night. The cries of street hawkers, the scampering of the wild monkeys, a wedding procession led by a crazy band with someone playing the alto sax as if he had heard of Ornette Coleman. A surreal soundtrack for my restless tossing and turning.

After a day of sightseeing at the Red Fort, Old Delhi and the Quatb Menar and another restless night, we set eyes on Maharaj Ji for the first time, as he got out of his Ambassador car and went up to his rooms. He smiled in our direction and we replied with our hands together in the traditional Indian greeting. I dared to hope that for a brief moment his eyes met mine, a suggestion of something above and beyond the small aches and pains that this mind was more than prone to.

There was a crowd of maybe seventy-five thousand people waiting for him. Most sat or squatted on the parched earth with no protection from the fierce Indian sun, while we westerners were whisked into little canvas seats right at the front, under a canvas awning. The crowds sang sweet songs. There was a sudden hush when Maharaj Ji arrived, all eyes turned towards him. He greeted us with his eyes, his hands in the customary salutation. The electricity of the occasion seemed to affect my vision, to make it clearer, to make colours more radiant, especially the white of his turban and the light blue of the cloth behind the dais. I was rather surprised, when he left some two hours later, that I had been able to sit through his long discourse in Hindi, only aware of a slight stiffness in my legs. It was as though he had suspended the usual working of time.

After attending a discourse the next day and spending another tense and restless night on my charpoy, we set off by train for the Dera. The train, the Frontier Mail, was still of the Raj and pre-war travelogues. The great steam engine had a cowcatcher and searchlight on the front, and whenever it stopped, cha wallas would appear from nowhere to sell their wares:

"Nert cutterlet! Jam torst! Cup chai!" they would cry over and over again.

After eight hours on the train we arrived at the tiny station of Beas that serves the Dera. The convoy of horse-drawn tongas we'd hired to take us the last few miles crossed the Grand Trunk Road, built by the British to get troops from Delhi to the Khyber Pass. There was a yogi leading an elephant with three of his confrères on its back. This seemed the essence of India: the yogis' bedraggled appearance, their riding an elephant down from the Himalayas for the winter.

The Dera is in fact a small town. Apart from its unusual tidiness and pleasant and orderly appearance there was something else that immediately struck me: the people and the happiness. They are calm, unhurried and smiling, and greet you as though you'd known each other all your lives.

Our tongas took us straight past the domes of the Satsang Ghar, a hall used for meetings, to the compound reserved for western visitors. The tranquillity and peace were even more evident here. There were five large buildings of different vintage dotted around a tropical garden, all edged by a wall. Three of the buildings were in the post-Corbusier architecture that has developed in India since Independence, the other two dated from the pre-war Raj.

We were shown to rooms in the largest of these buildings. They were of spartan but comfortable western hotel standard, complete with their own bathrooms. We had our meals downstairs in a large dining room, eating vegetarian Punjabi food that had been adapted for western palates and constitutions. The lawns were dotted with white-painted wicker armchairs for relaxing in the sun.

The next morning we were taken to the garden attached to the Master's house. He talked to each one of us as we shuffled in.

"So you have arrived," He said to me as he shook my hand, his eyes burning into mine.

From then on, we would see him several times every day. First thing in the morning we saw him when he would give a talk in Punjabi sitting outside the Satsang Ghar under a *shamiana*, or cloth awning, with his audience sitting cross-legged in front of him. We westerners would then visit him in his garden for about twenty minutes where we'd talk and even take photos.

In the early afternoon there was *seva*. The word means 'service', which, in this context, means all and sundry of the gathered disciples, everyone from rajahs and high court judges to western hippies and the poorest peasants, doing menial work moving earth in baskets on our heads, shifting great mounds of earth to fill in ravines to give the Dera more level ground on which it could expand. The point of seva is that it is work done for no worldly gain, but only for the benefit of the community and for our spiritual selves. Maharaj Ji would sit in the middle of all this endeavour: everything *revolved* around him and *because* of him.

The final moment we saw Maharaj Ji each day was the evening meeting. It was held at 5.30 in the afternoon in a small hall on the first floor of the building my room was in. The forty or so western disciples would sit on sofas and armchairs with Maharaj Ji in the middle at one end. Usually one of his *sevadars,* someone who does seva, often a retired Indian professor of English, would translate a poem by an Indian mystic of the past and comment on it. After maybe half an hour, the professor would finish and people would ask Maharaj Ji questions. His answers were the high point of the day. So patiently, he explained how we could be mystics ourselves and fulfil the true purpose of our lives. His wisdom lay in his having done it himself, not in what he read, not in what he understood intellectually, but in what he knew first hand, inside.

I had been a vegetarian just long enough to qualify to be given instruction how to meditate by Maharaj Ji, and, for some reason he chose to disregard my recent involvement with drugs. He knew both what I had already been through, and, more importantly, what was still to unfold, the stuff I had to go through before I could wholeheartedly be the trainee mystic. When he gave me the meditation instruction on November the Sixth, I can only think that he wished to make sure I was firmly anchored before I launched on the literally death-defying escapades I was to get into later.

The *bhandara* that took place just after Christmas was Biblical in dimension and timelessness. Three hundred thousand people came from all over the Indian subcontinent and the rest of the world to hear Maharaj Ji speak. They were all fed and given shelter free of charge – that's at least 1.8 million chapattis every day. When seated, they stretched as far as the horizon.

This throng was fed in the *langar*, or free kitchen, where the *dhal* and curried vegetables were cooked in vast brass cauldrons heated by burning papyrus grass. The cooking went on twenty-four hours a day. *Chapattis* were cooked on large iron plates heated by burning rushes, and were stored in a special room, full to the ceiling, before being distributed and eaten!

My wish to be other than I was took me to new lengths when I started to wear a Sikh turban. It was taken as a compliment by the Sikh who showed me how to tie it, while the other westerners looked on it as a mild form of insanity that sometimes affects people at the Dera.

I met some lovely people: in particular Bud McKee, an epitome of hip from San Francisco and teacher of ceramics at San Francisco State. We spent a lot of time together. When we got home we were going to start an international craft business, to be called Sach Krafts.

One day we managed to sidetrack Maharaj Ji on his way through the guesthouse compound into posing for a photograph, standing next to us and two of Bud's Californian friends.

"So you want a picture of me with all the hippies?"

More hippy than mystic, the time came for me to go back to England. The torments and disquiets still boiled under my surface, though maybe more quietly. From then on, whatever the excruciations or distractions

I gave in to, I knew that the purpose of my being alive was not to be a junky, not even to be a successful writer, but to realise, to make real, the ringing truth inside me. Interestingly, once on that path, one could be whatever one needed to be. Maharaj Ji had done it and made it very clear that we could do it too. He had given me the simple meditation technique that could and would, eventually, bring my attention and consciousness into the centre of my being.

13 BOOKSELLING AND MARRIAGE

I returned to Cambridge and my responsibilities for my mother and comatose father in January 1968. I was overflowing with a need to tell any and every one some mind-blowing truths. I needed to persuade other people of the importance of what I had experienced, rather than work on my own meditation. I was returning home with good news that I hadn't applied to myself. Neither my being able to meditate nor my tenuous grasp of mysticism made much impression on my addiction. Being hooked seemed to be part of my genetic make-up in the same way that I have black hair and brown eyes.

What might have been a sign of a better future – that I didn't go to Piccadilly straight from the airport – was more a result of my being with Andrew and others than anything else. I was on the edge of a corrosive conflict of directions. My father was still in a coma in hospital, having survived two bouts of pneumonia; my mother was holding on through a suspended grief, every day hoping that he would come round and with each day that he didn't, the fear of bereavement and widowhood mounting.

I was jobless with an uncertain future. I told anyone ready to listen that there was a living mystic out there in India. Any degree of emotional pain made me yearn for a dose of something to relieve me of it. I had not sobbed, really wept, for a long time.

I was living at home, supposedly as a support for my mother. My responsible self hit upon bookselling as the career I should take up. It would make use of my brain. I started to make trips round the Cambridge bookshops, halfheartedly looking for a job.

Before long, I had made an appointment to see the doctor. He refused to give me anything but physeptone linctus, which he felt might curb any need to stick needles in my arms. So it did, for a while, but it also re-awakened all the physical pains of withdrawal.

You might say that my encounter with mysticism hadn't worked. I would question the word 'worked'. Mystical practice does not produce miraculous or outwardly measurable results. My sickness, addiction, had to follow its course. Anyway, you have to put in the effort in concentrating and bringing the attention to the centre for mysticism to 'work' – it's not something that is done to you. I didn't make the effort. And that 'working' is about finding the truth inside ourselves not about improving our lot in the world. The world may get improved as a result, but that is not the purpose.

Certainly, I was a poor advertisement for Maharaj Ji. In retrospect, I like to theorise that my time with Maharaj Ji had planted the seed of a purpose other than addiction, a seed that would eventually sprout. But first the addiction had to find its own conclusion.

Al was reluctant to give me anything at first. His 'proper junky' ethos didn't allow for someone to get right off for three months and then suddenly express a terrible craving. But, using the manipulative skills I had honed through four years of addiction, and stressing the pitiable situation I was in with regard to my father, I finally persuaded him to sell me what he could. There was no question of him *giving* me anything any more. From then on it was three or four pounds a grain.

The hospital room set aside for Al to fix in had by now become the early morning haunt of a regular band of junkies, mostly younger than myself, but all getting prescriptions for heroin. A group of them, usually including Al, would wait by the door of the chemist shop for Mr Philkin to arrive promptly at nine. I would hover in a doorway, and wait for Al to emerge, walking fast to the hospital. He would not say a word until he'd got some heroin into his bloodstream, and until he'd got that hit there was no way he could be persuaded to hand over any heroin for me to fix. I would stand there watching several junkies sticking needles into themselves. It was self-inflicted torture, but it was the only way I could be sure of scoring. If I left it till later I would have little chance of finding Al with enough left for him to be able to sell me anything.

There were far too many days when Al either didn't show up or wasn't able or willing to sell me anything. I would then plague any and all of the others with increasingly ridiculous sums of money, just to get one fix out of them. Some days I would spend hours chasing around Cambridge after one or other of the junkies whom I'd been told had a little stuff to spare.

After a while my daily pretext for leaving the house first thing in the morning to go and see someone about a job in a bookshop began to wear a bit thin. True, I had talked to a few bookshop managers, but always in a unrealistic way and looking most disreputable. The one shop, Bowes and Bowes, where I stood any chance at all of actually getting a job, I had not bothered with, almost as though I didn't want one. Marina, whose birthday party in Kings I had gatecrashed many moons before, was the unwitting provider of this opportunity. Her father was the Managing Director of the Bowes and Bowes chain of university bookshops whose head office was above the branch opposite the Senate in Cambridge. I made an appointment to see him.

Plum Warner, in checked shirt and brown handmade shoes, was most affable, which rather took me by surprise. I remembered a blustery cricketing gentleman from the time Marina had taken me home for tea.

"Dear boy, do have a seat." He had in fact been a major cricketing star. The trophies were on a shelf behind his desk. I sat nervously.

"How *is* your father? Dreadful business." He solicited.

"Much the same, I'm afraid. Still unconscious."

"Oh, I am so sorry. Please do remember me to your dear mother, won't you?"

"And your own health?" He gave me a look I didn't know quite how to interpret. Did he know? I decided to play it safe.

"Much better thanks."

"Good, good." Maybe he didn't know. "Now what can I do for you?"

"Not to beat about the bush, I want to work at Bowes and Bowes."

"I see, I see," finger tips together, "And what would you like to do here?" I was a bit taken aback. I didn't expect him to really entertain me as an employee, let alone ask what I wanted to do.

"I was thinking philosophy, sir, perhaps managing your philosophy section," said I. But he didn't seem phased.

"You see, I must be entirely frank sir, I have been thinking of opening my own bookshop and need to learn the trade somewhere. I couldn't think of a better place that Bowes and Bowes and I say philosophy because that's what I was reading."

"I see." He turned to the window. But quickly turned back.

"I would be glad for you to learn the book trade with us, William." So quickly, so positive, so strange! Whether he was giving me a break, whether strings had been pulled behind the scenes, I shall never know.

"But you have to realise I will have to start you on the lowest pay scale. I hope that isn't too much of a bore. You don't have to stick in philosophy. Work your way around all the departments, get a thorough grounding in bookselling"

My morale was boosted no end. I could now lay a small claim to being a member of the human race. I had an outer identity. I was a bookseller and could put that in my passport.

I started the following week. My colleagues in the shop seemed to know nothing of my addiction and I could be on equal terms. Well, almost.

At first I was put to work in the packing room, where we dealt with deliveries and outgoing mail-order parcels. That was good. I could relate with the two blokes down there rather well. I actually achieved some degree of work satisfaction and my intake of drugs levelled off to a regular, but small, dose of physeptone linctus. I had no time, to begin with, to go out searching for fixes. I went to satsangs more often and got my bosses to agree to stock a few books on the subject.

After a month in the packing room, it was decided that I should move on to the first floor and learn how to actually deal with customers. I was put into the section that dealt with philosophy and psychology; subjects I could give advice on. I must have been reasonable at this, because, after another month or so, I was told I could have a small section of shelves to fill with books of my own choosing on the subjects that are usually lumped together as esoterica: oriental religions and philosophy, the occult and all the fashionable quasi-philosophies.

This was only good management of course: I now had something I could enthuse over, which improved my performance all round. Or, it would have done, had not the increased stress of working with the public caused me to imagine I needed a fix once again. I would arrange meetings with Al in town and fix in one of the loos in Trinity.

One of the few regular customers for my esoterica was Nick whom I'd known in my last year at Trinity. He had then had rooms near mine in Angel Court and was quite a speed freak, always high on some kind of amphetamine.

I told him how this was it: there was a teacher in India whom one could go and visit; how I had shaken his hand. The extraordinary thing, in hindsight, is that my words reached him. Through the coverings something of the truth must have got through, something strong enough to persuade him and two friends to make the trip to India that summer.

My life as bookshop assistant had gone on its boring way all that summer and into the late autumn. My intake of drugs remained fairly constant, the need to fix stayed at the same level: whenever Al or one of the other junkies needed some cash in a hurry they would seek me out and sell me a fix. Nick and the two girls he'd gone to India with returned full of that radiance I'd had for a few weeks on my return. One of them was Mary.

I still wrote to Margareta every now and then with a lingering hope that the relationship might one day heal and become active again, but my bones knew different. She had settled back in Sweden where she was making a new life for herself.

And so it was good to meet Mary, about whom I immediately nurtured hopes. She was tall and willowy and had a debutante's clip to her voice: "yar" for "yes". She shared my feelings about Maharaj Ji; she had been involved in the London drug scene and psychedelia; she had her own struggle to escape a class background like mine. In all these respects we were compatible. But it was not love at first sight. There was none of that passion. It was more as if we shared a common destiny, as if we were fated together. I made a date with her after one of the meetings.

We'd been seeing each other for only three weeks, gone for long walks together, found conversation easy and unstrained and in that easiness there grew an attraction. We decided to get married. Quick as that. We shared a concept of being married, that of partnership on the mystical path, a loving bond on a foundation of mutual respect. This was the great adventure of life that we'd heard about.

I had told Mary about my addiction and its history. She didn't see it as a stumbling block. I would go on a gradually reducing course of physeptone right away and, with the ennobling prospect of our marriage, I would surely be able to do what had, up till then, proved impossible: get right off all opiates. For the first time since I got addicted I knew some clear blue sky, some prospect, some hope.

We set a date for the wedding in mid-January. Both family and friends were delighted when we announced our plans. We handed over the arrangements to Mary's parents when we'd been there for the weekend. They were landed gentry like the Pryors. Mary understood my feelings about Eton, the Pryors and, in particular, the stuff I'd gone through with Uncle Johnny about the fiver.

Our taxi swept up the gravel drive of the Merrison manse in Norfolk. Roger, Mary's father, had invited a close friend to meet us over dinner.

"When Roger told me you were engaged to...," he peered at Mary over his half-moon glasses, "you are engaged aren't you? Good! To a Pryor, I got awfully worried." At this my heart sank. Maybe he knew about me. "Yes, there are some dreadful Priors, spelt wrong of course, over in King's Lynn, or somewhere. All wrapped up in the wrong kind of Conservative politics. Then Roger spelt it for me. I looked you up in Debrett and Burke's and of course you couldn't be better."

"Richard, I'm *so* glad that you approve of William," answered Mary, a wry look on her face.

"Well, I got the shield, the crest you know, and made this up for you." He produced his little present, a round tin tray, on which he'd painted the coat of arms he thought was ours.

"You see, Mary's crest is impaled by the Pryor lion rampant." We saw.

But Margareta was still in my mind. I couldn't go into this marriage without being sure there was absolutely no chance of Margareta and me getting together again, that the passion that had fired us was really dead. Such was my peculiar belief in honesty, or should I say, my belief in a peculiar honesty, that I told Mary about these doubts.

Mary didn't like it one bit. If I'd decided to marry her, why on earth couldn't I put past relationships in the past and keep them there, where they belonged? The only way I could find out how things were between Margareta and myself was to persuade her to come over from Sweden. After several letters and expensive international phone calls she agreed. I later realised it was more because she wanted to visit England again than to resurrect past passions.

She knew the captain of a small cargo boat that ran between Gothenburg and Tilbury and persuaded him to give her a lift across the North Sea. The first I knew that she was actually on her way was when she used the boat's radiotelephone to tell me they were caught in storm force gales and were actually being blown backwards. But eventually she arrived, with her radiant, lived-in Nordic beauty.

Mary was staying at Chaucer Road at the time. For the first few days everything was fine. Mary and I talked endlessly about the Dera and Maharaj Ji, all of which Margareta appeared keen to know about, and she warmly enthused over our plans to marry. She was a visiting friend of the family rather than a returning lover. But the underlying tension came out when Mary and I were alone together.

"Do you still love her?"

"Yes, I think I do," said I with my weird truthfulness, but quickly added, "but it's a remote kind of love."

"But William, how can you say that?" Mary was distraught. "Do you still want to marry me?"

"Yes I think so..... Yes, ours is a safer kind of love, less stormy." So patronising.

Love: such a confusion of meanings when what is usually being said is, "I want this; it pleases me". To be honest about love – that *this* is and *that* isn't true love – is a dangerous pastime. When we feel an attachment, an attraction, even a passionate longing for someone, we call that love, but only if a variety of other conditions are met. It must accord with our need for self-esteem, it must hold out some possibility (whether real or imagined) of fruition and reciprocity. But if the meaning of the word love is in the way we use it, as Wittgenstein would have us understand, then it usually is part of some game of manipulation, which is fine as long as there is some awareness of it being a game, one of the many levels on which a relationship may operate, one of its many contexts.

Knowledge is gained by learning; trust by doubt; skill by practice; and love by love. (Thomas Szasz)

A couple of days before Margareta was due to return to Sweden I stretched things even further. Mary had gone into town on some errand and I had taken Margareta out into the garden.

"Margareta?"

"Yes, William."

"I don't know how to say this, but, well, would you marry me?" I didn't realise how outrageous this was until I'd said it. I quickly added, "I mean, if I wasn't going to marry Mary. Do you still love me enough?"

"Oh William," she sighed deeply. "Don't you ever give up? Mary loves you, that's obvious. Let's not talk about it. Anyway what would your Maharaj Ji say about it?"

"Dunno." But I did. We walked on. I put my arm round her shoulder and pulled her to me. She shrugged herself free. "Don't you love me at all? After all we went through together?" I pleaded with her as she walked ahead of me. I caught up with her.

"Damn you – of course I do," she whispered under her breath. I steered her back to the house. We went up to her bedroom and sat on the bed. My arm around her. She didn't reciprocate, but neither did she get off the bed. I persisted.

There was a light knock at the door.

"It's all right, it's only me." It was Mary, back earlier than I expected. "I wondered if you'd seen William." She put her head round the door before either of us could do anything about it.

"Oh I see. Sorry I interrupted." She said with perfect control as she saw us together on the bed. She shut the door again and we heard her walk down the passage.

"William, you must go after her, Oh dear, what *will* she think of me? You must. You must go and comfort her." I did, as best I could, but the wound was made.

The wedding was to be held in the grandest church in Norwich, right in the centre of the city. We had to have not one, but two priests, because, as far as I could understand it, Mary's mother had both a favourite priest and a favoured church and the former did not belong to the latter, and so had to double up with the incumbent. The reception was to be held in the grandest hotel in Norwich.

I had got three weeks off work and a litre bottle of linctus from the doctor to see me through the honeymoon. I think we were both rather overwhelmed by the splendour of the ceremony, lightened by Andrew. He was to read a brief mystical text, but when the appointed time in the service came there was no sign of Andrew. The incumbent priest was just announcing that instead he would read from St Matthew, when Andrew walked into the church. Quickly realising what was happening, he called out above the smart wedding hats and tailcoats of the congregation that he had arrived and would give the reading. So saying, he marched bravely up the aisle with all eyes upon him, and proceeded to read. They had had three punctures on their way from Cambridge.

We had decided to impose our own teetotalism on the guests at the reception, much to the disgust of all and sundry. What is a wedding without champers? It was all very county, very posh. As people arrived at the hotel, the master of ceremonies lined everybody up to announce them in sonorous tones as they entered the main room.

We went to a ridiculously expensive hotel in London for the first two nights of our honeymoon. A setting of pampered luxury felt like an ideal love-nest. There was even chilled apple juice waiting for us in the suite, and *two televisions*. Then we went up to stay with Lucy and Andrew who were married by then and lived in a remote farmhouse on the Lancashire fells. He was now a lecturer in Buddhism at Lancaster University. It was bitterly cold and snowed heavily soon after we got there.

To keep myself warm, to ward off the looming fear of what our married life might bring, I swallowed my linctus with abandon, only to find what had seemed an almost inexhaustible supply was all gone in a week. I tried, with Mary's encouragement, to make out without it for a couple of days, but I couldn't sleep and those old pains came rolling in.

On the third day I insisted that Lucy take me, despite the snow-drifts, to see their GP. He obviously regarded junkies as the despicable product of soft southern living and would give me nothing but some far too mild muscle relaxants. After another day with no relief, I decided we should go back to Cambridge. It was too cold for us to enjoy our honeymoon properly anyway, but we both knew that it was so I could get more physeptone.

We lived at Chaucer Road initially. Until our plans gelled we thought it a good idea for me to stay in my job at the bookshop and find a small house to rent in Cambridge. We couldn't stay at Chaucer Road for too long. My father was still in a coma some two years after the accident and the atmosphere of gloom and grief was strong. We had to get out and live our lives and my mother encouraged us in this, even though she sorely needed our support. She still followed the doctor's advice religiously and went to the hospital every day to read aloud to my father.

We found a flat in Kimberley Road and tried hard to settle into our new responsibilities, and, I fear, bourgeois way of life. I wasn't writing. I hadn't written anything for some time. And the only thing that held out any hope of preventing my life becoming too ordinary was my friend, junk, the white horse of the apocalypse.

I tried to meditate, but it was so difficult to sit still in one spot for any length of time. But I talked the walk.

That was the trouble: I could talk well*, I could present a convincing picture of myself as someone wholly committed to a spiritual way of life and could be most coherent about it, especially when I'd had my daily dose of linctus not long before, but it was the aspirations talking, not how I was. I was not even beginning to live in the way I had undertaken to at my initiation. And I knew it.

I felt the job was going well enough, even though my contacts with Al and others – sometimes actually in the bookshop – were beginning to get noticed. There were also my mysterious trips to the loo. Such was my position in the shop, given the job not by the manager of the shop, but by the chain's managing director who really had no business giving it to me in the first place, that no one said anything outright about my strange behaviour and unreliability. Instead I was transferred to work with the man responsible for liaison with the many libraries in Cambridge, where I could be kept under some kind of observation.

---

* Alan Watts was an example of this. In the sixties and seventies he established a considerable following as an inspiring writer on oriental philosophy and Zen Buddhism. After his death it was revealed that he had been an alcoholic for several years.

14 THE GEOGRAPHICAL CURE

It was 1969 and I was 24 when Mary and I were grabbed by an urge to get away from Cambridge. A new life away from the stifling history of family, relations and academia that would give me a real chance to get off all drugs*. The adventure brought us together; we talked again like we had in the beginning.

It hadn't worked before, we reasoned, because, in Cambridge, I was far too close to the origins of my addiction. For some reason or other, it had to be Devon we fled to, where I would start a specialist book business.

The Pelican trustees supported the venture and agreed to buy a house. I gave in my notice at the bookshop, and we scurried down to Devon, to Dartmouth in fact, where Mary's brother was living on a boat.

Pog, as he was known, had reinvented himself as a Berber after visiting Morocco and smoking copious kif. He wore a turban and was fiercely nomadic. Not long after helping us move to Devon where he kept his ancient sailing boat, he set sail for North Africa on his own and was never seen again.

An estate agent in the centre of Dartmouth with the eloquent name of Letcher and Scorer had what seemed to be just the thing on their books. The stream at the bottom of the steep valley babbled – it had once powered a water mill and ran under the house's sitting-room window out into a tidal creek that branched off the lower reaches of the river Dart. The nearest neighbour was in a bungalow half way up the steep lane; there was an acre of partly wooded land, with what had once been a watercress bed at the far end. The soil on the valley floor was good and black. We could visualise a quiet country life, free from pressures and drugs.

---

* This is what, in Alcoholics Anonymous, is called the geographical cure and it is always doomed to failure. It is a delusion to imagine that by removing yourself from the environment in which you practise your addiction, with a 'fresh start' or 'clean break', you can somehow cast off your addiction. You cannot avoid taking with you   yourself and all your monsters, wherever you travel, but the addict manages to so externalise his addiction as being the result of the environment and people he lives amongst, that he is unable to see this.

We went to stay with Mary's parents in Norfolk until the deal went through, and her father got me a labouring job at the timber yard he owned. Of course I had to visit my father as often as possible. Once in Cambridge I would make straight for Al's place to get a fix, and only then would I consider going to see my father, who would be sitting there in his chair, as vacant of his life as before.

On one of my visits I was telling Al of our plans to move to Devon and had an idea: "D'you think, man, there might be some way you could send me stuff in the post? What do you think? I mean, would you consider doing it?" The prospect of being cut off from all supplies was beginning to frighten me.

"Jeeesus, man. What do you think I am? It'd be too easy to get sussed out, man. They'd just have to open up one of the packets and I'd be in dead trouble. It'd be worth three years in the can at least and with my history, they'd crucify me." He didn't like the idea.

"It wouldn't have to be in packets," I persisted. "You could make a hole for each pill in a thick piece of cardboard with one of your leather-working tools. Then the whole thing could fit inside an ordinary envelope. How could anyone possibly know what was inside it. There must be millions of letters going the same route every day. I can't see what you're worrying about. And if we were to say that I'd pay you five quid a grain, how would that be?" He stared at the floor.

"I'll think about it," he replied, "but it would be me that's taking the risk. There's nothing illegal in receiving, well, in having an envelope addressed to you. I'm the one that'd be breaking the law." Eventually he came round to the idea, at five pounds a grain, insisting though, that it was always cash in advance. I stayed long enough to get given another fix before setting off back to Norfolk.

That October we moved to Dartmouth, hundreds of miles from family and the apparent bindings of history. Despite the damp patches and the rickety nature of the lean-to kitchen, the place began to resemble the cosy image we had nurtured.

On our third day in the new house, I made my excuses and set off up the long hill into Dartmouth. Behind the desk in the surgery was a sharp-faced man in his late fifties, with gold-rimmed half-moon glasses, known as Doctor Wilf, which didn't tally with his rather austere manner. I gave him the letter from my doctor in Cambridge.

"Mmm... now, let me see. You've been on heroin and other drugs for just about four years now, is that right?" He peered at me over his glasses.

"Yes." I sat on the edge of the plastic chair opposite his desk. "And you haven't been prescribed any heroin for the last eighteen months, not since you forged some prescriptions?" I nodded.

"Well," he paused to give me a piercing look, "if I'm to help you, you've got to understand I'll stand none of that kind of nonsense. You've got to tell me the truth at all times. In a small community like this there would be no way we could keep anything from the police. Any monkey business and you'll be in trouble. D'you understand?" He wagged his metaphorical finger.

"Yes, yes I do," I replied obsequiously.

"There's a good chap. Now, let's have a look at your arms. You say you haven't had any heroin for eighteen months..." He came round the desk. "Roll up your sleeves, will you?"

"Well, it's not quite right that I haven't, you see...." But he cut off my explanations.

"Come on, come on, haven't got all day you know." I rolled up my sleeves reluctantly. He held my left arm under the light. "But these punctures are all quite recent. I think you'd better tell me how these came about." I told him how my father's being in a coma made me very depressed, how moving house put a lot of pressure on me, how the world was closing in on me. It had all meant that I'd bought the occasional pill of heroin over the last couple of months. He seemed to understand, because, in the end he agreed to take me on and gave me some post-dated prescriptions for physeptone linctus.

The chemist next door was alarmed at the prescription and immediately rang Wilf to check that it was genuine. He had never handled a scrip for a practising addict before. I was one of the nastier manifestations of big city life to hit Dartmouth.

In for a penny, I sent a fiver off to Al. I calculated that there was a good chance of getting the heroin from him two days later. The postman came early, at about seven. You could hear his van approach as he changed gear to slow himself down the steepest part of the lane. I got up early on the pretext that I was going to meditate, and sat downstairs waiting, waiting.

As soon as I heard the van, I switched off all the lights. He might be suspicious if he knew I was waiting. Yes, he had stopped outside the gate and yes, he was now walking up to the front door. A letter was pushed through the flap. It had a Cambridge postmark. I could feel that it had cardboard inside. I rushed up to the bathroom and locked the door. The syringe I'd conveniently brought with me 'in case', was hidden under a loose floorboard of the linen cupboard. Al had sent me the grain as we'd agreed. It was going to work. I had my first fix for a fortnight, my first fix in Devon. The blood and the rush to the flow of my being. Now I was at home!

I may have been successful in keeping the fact that I was fixing again from Mary for the first few months. Underneath was a seething, a gradual sinking into a mud of: 'she doesn't understand how awful it is', 'she can never know how much I have suffered', 'she keeps on about the bookselling idea and the physeptone, when if only she could see…'

And then Mary found that she was pregnant. It was the good news it should have been and brought a respite of normality and love. I was drawn into the pregnancy, became involved. And Mary was as graceful as an upper-crust swan, as willowy as a Modigliani and as happy as a young woman achieving a purpose. There was a complication: Mary's blood was rhesus negative, which meant that the baby was in some danger of being born with the wrong kind of blood.

Because of this, Wilf and the hospital doctors insisted that the delivery take place in hospital, which went against our inclinations. As a concession, the midwife came down to the house and left a bottle of gas 'in case we can't get you into hospital in time'. It was nitrous oxide, laughing gas, and one could get quite a nice high from it. The bottle was empty in a couple of days.

As the birth approached my mother came down to help out. It must have been obvious that all was not well with me, or between the two of us, yet she valiantly kept her worries under control.

I was allowed to be present at the delivery. Her legs splayed, the panting groans, but a pain, I sensed, that was welcome, a pain that *worked* towards a much desired and fulfilling result: a healthy baby girl. The extraordinary sight of the nurse carrying the still silent creature by her legs to a table at the back, where she was given oxygen from a tiny mask, still silent, then held up again and slapped, more oxygen, and then, after an eternal four minutes, the first cries. And at those cries of dismay and bewilderment, great smiles all round. Another life begun.

It was a couple of days before Mary was allowed home with the as yet nameless baby, in which time my mother and I had plenty of opportunity to have concerned mother and son conversations. She had been unable to find a rather precious earring back in Cambridge. Just one of the pair was missing, but she suspected the worst. Had I taken it? I denied it. If I was going to steal something like that, I'd take both wouldn't I? Anyway what made her think I had taken it?

She'd been giving me a chance to make a clean breast of it and once again I'd let her down. While mending a tear in one of my jackets the day before, she'd come across the missing earring in one of the pockets. I couldn't deny I was still using drugs of some sort could I? Why couldn't and didn't I do something about it?

She could do nothing about my father, but *I could do something about my drug-taking if I really wanted to,* and what did I want the earring for anyway? I told her that I'd had no money in the bank one day when I desperately needed to buy myself a fix, but hadn't been able to find both earrings, nor sell the one I *had* found.

Once my mother had gone back to Cambridge and Mary had returned from the hospital with our daughter, it was soon time for me to go into Torquay to register the birth. The day I chose to go, I had only the dregs left in my bottle of linctus and the expected envelope hadn't arrived from Al in the morning post. I was withdrawing and needed some relief.

I remembered Chlorodyne. The problem was that I could hardly take some home to cook it up. I would just have to swallow the stuff raw. I bought two bottles in the first chemist I came to and hurried to the nearest public loo. Once in a cubicle I opened one of the bottles. The full horror of the stuff's smell hit me. It was an outrage to my metabolism. Eventually, my desperation gave me sufficient courage to put the neck of the little bottle as far back in my throat as I could, to tilt my head and to pour the foul liquid down my throat.

The thick, gooey poison made me gag, but I suppressed it long enough to get the contents down into my stomach. The chloroform took immediate effect, clouding my brain into a dizzy lightness, but, as that wore off, I began to feel some relief as the opium did its work. But it was short lived. The emetic effect of the ipecacuanha was too powerful. I could not hold it back and promptly vomited. I lost all that I'd put in with such difficulty, along with my breakfast.

I opened the second bottle and quickly poured that down my throat, thinking my stomach couldn't react so violently a second time. I sat as still as I could on the lavatory seat so as not to provoke my system. I read the graffiti on the cubicle door to occupy my brain: 'young man seeks interesting position here Wednesday evenings', 'Mick Jagger for God' and so on. A retching started down there somewhere in what was my body, but I found I could control it this time. The opium began to warm me all over, to wrap me in a blanket of fuzzy safety. I stuffed the empty bottles into the cistern and emerged from the cubicle and out into the daylight.

When I got to the registrar's office, I couldn't remember what we'd decided to call our daughter. I dare not ring Mary at home. She might notice something odd about my voice. I would just have to go ahead and hope the name came back to me by the time I got into the man's office. After half an hour's wait I still hadn't remembered and it was my turn to see him. The opium was making me extremely verbose and by the time we had discussed the merits of different maternity hospitals, the number of births registered in Torquay during the last month and so on, I found that the name had come back to me. It was Lydia. But I couldn't recall if we'd decided to give her a middle name, and, after much dithering, decided she wouldn't have one.

Other than make a list of the obvious titles I would sell, I had done nothing at all about the mail-order bookselling idea. I couldn't even admit to myself that I didn't know where to start. I looked around for something else to do. There was the beautiful black soil in the garden and the barn-like building opposite the house that had once housed the water mill. The land was covered with a dense jungle of brambles, nettles and bracken, whereas the barn was more or less sound. I would go in for organic mushroom growing.

I had several tons of best horse muck delivered and bought some mushroom spore through an ad in the Sunday paper. In an attempt to maintain a constant temperature, as was recommended for best results, I built a polythene tent over my bed of horse manure, which I heated with an electric fire on a cable from the house.

It took me the best part of a month just to do that, and by the time I got round to laying down the actual spore, Lydia was four months old. I had become the dutiful father in respect of nappy changing and taking the pram on walks. The heroin kept coming from Al up to twice a week and Wilf was still giving me my linctus.

One Saturday morning, I was sitting in the bathroom, about to fix two of the jacks of heroin that had arrived minutes earlier from Al. We were expecting Nigel and Jenny to stay for the weekend, and Mary was up early to make ready. She must have sensed something odd going on. Before I could do anything about it, she had burst into the bathroom – the bolt was none too strong – grabbed the envelope on which the rest of the heroin lay, tipped the pills into the lavatory bowl, and flushed it. All in one swift determined movement.

In thirty seconds she had filled the ensuing weekend with the hellish prospect of withdrawal pains. I was out of linctus. How was I going to enjoy Nigel and Jenny's company? I rushed out to the septic tank. There was just a chance that the pills might not dissolve completely amongst all the shit and lavatory paper. For twenty minutes I fished around with my arms amongst the sewage, but there was no sign of my precious heroin.

As soon as Nigel and Jenny had arrived, I suggested it might be nice for them to drive into Dartmouth for a look around. This way I would get a chance of finding Wilf and persuading him to let me have some extra linctus. The chemists in Dartmouth wouldn't dream of selling me any Chlorodyne. I was already too well known. Once I'd drunk a large dose of the linctus Wilf was persuaded to prescribe, I was able to become the affable host.

However close I thought myself to be to Nigel, I had to keep all this addiction stuff from him. I somehow needed him to see me as a straight person, not as a whimpering druggy. Addict William locked away, incapable of showing his face, of companionship, of being challenged.

That October, when Lydia was six months old and my mushrooms had failed to come up, we decided that we needed a holiday from Devon, to go back to Cambridge, visit old friends and show Lydia off to mothers. I could visit my father; his condition had shown no improvement, he was still as deep in his coma. I could also reinforce my contact with Al. We still managed to maintain a facade of contented marriage, despite frequent rows. We stayed at Chaucer Road.

One morning, very early, my mother knocked on our bedroom door.

"William, William," more tapping on the door, "are you awake?" she asked in a pale voice.

"I am now," I replied, surfacing from my drug-induced sleep. "What is it?"

"That was the hospital. The ward sister." She sounded awful.

"Come in, it's OK, you can come in."

"Daddy's dead." She sat on my bed. Mary got up and went to her. "He died last night." He had been in a coma for nearly three years. She didn't cry, just stared at the floor. "They said we can go and see him before they do whatever they do."

Mary felt it better if she didn't come, but my mother, youngest sister Nelly and I went up to the hospital as soon as we were dressed.

They had put a screen around his bed. The ward sister told us that he'd gone quietly in his sleep. We could come into the ward and pay our respects if we wanted. I preferred to stay outside while they went in. I caught a glimpse of his body through the screens. Some five minutes later they emerged, arms round each other, dabbing at tears with handkerchiefs.

We stumbled down the shock of loss. My father has gone; my daddy is dead. Now I will surely never know him.

It fell to me to ring round relations and friends with the news, and in this bringing and sharing of grief, people seemed able to put on one side the gossip they had heard about me. There was a solidarity in the face of death. It wasn't till lunchtime that I was able to get out of the house on some pretext or other and rush up to Al's to score a fix. When I was feeling a little better, I went on to my old doctor's surgery, and with shameless use of my tragedy, persuaded him to let me have some physeptone ampoules.

Uncle Matthew came over the next day, a visible desolation in his face. It was agreed that the funeral take place a few days later. First there would be a private cremation in Cambridge, the ashes would then be interred in the graveyard at Weston, the Pryor's home patch, and the process would be completed with a memorial service in Trinity College Chapel to allow his friends and colleagues in academia to pay their respects.

I went with Uncles Matthew and Johny to the crematorium at the appointed time and bore witness to the rolling of the coffin into the back room. I imagined men in overalls lifting the coffin off the rollers and dropping it into a great furnace. I was stoned. I could not feel grief.

In the days before the interment at Weston, my use of my father's death to gain sympathy and therefore heroin and physeptone ampoules started to *use* me: I was taking far more than usual. When the day of the funeral came I had only a mouthful of linctus left and no ampoules or heroin. I would be withdrawing at the funeral if I didn't do something about it.

I rushed off after breakfast and waited outside the chemist to see if Al or one of the others would sell me something to get me through. Al didn't show up but Fred let me have two ampoules and fifteen capsules of Heminevrin for five pounds. I accepted, gave him the money, fixed the ampoules and rushed back home. Heminevrin is a Swedish invention to alleviate the withdrawal symptoms of alcoholism. It is a powerful hypnotic, it sends you to sleep – quickly if in large enough doses – and its effect is quite similar to alcohol intoxication.

We had to leave at eleven. I was feeling nervous and depressed and took two of the Heminevrin. They had no noticeable effect, so I took two more. A quarter of an hour later the first two started to have their way with me. I began to talk and behave as though tipsy. When the other two pills got to me, I could hardly stand up, and had the absurd obstinacy of a drunk, refusing to admit that I was in no state to go anywhere but bed. Mary managed to get me there and I passed out.

When I came to, still very groggy, there was no one in the house. Couldn't work it out. What had happened. But wait, oh my god, the funeral. I rang for a taxi.

"Can you shend a thaxi to Chausher Road? Where do I go? Oh, to Weshton in artfodsher, near itshin. How much? Eight pounhs! Yesh awright."

The driver took some time to find the church when we got to Weston and we drove into the car park just as the congregation left the church for the vicar to perform the interment ceremony. My presence can only have heightened my family's grief. I should not have been there. At my father's funeral. Wobbling, in danger of folding up, Lucy had to hold me upright. Father and son; not there for each other.

In contrast, I behaved myself at the memorial service in Trinity ten days later. Under the influence certainly, but only to the right degree, I acted as chief mourner with decorum.

Not long afterwards, such was Uncle Matthew's grief at the loss of his brother that he wrote a letter in which he declared that I had killed my father.

Killed my father because he worried about me so much that it caused him to crash.

This is what scapegoats do.

Back in Devon, the slide down the slippery slope surrendered to its inexorable slithering. I lived in a fractured consciousness all the time. I had all but forgotten the place Maharaj Ji might have had in there.

One particularly bad day, I was sinking in to an unreachable pit and Mary and I could hardly say a word to one another. That evening I told her that I was going out. I could not explain myself.

I walked into Dartmouth and took a room at a central hotel. At three o'clock in the morning, I crept out, charged with adrenaline. There was a narrow lane at the back of Mr Williams' chemist shop, adjacent to Wilf's surgery. I scaled the wall easily and broke one of the metal-framed windows at the back of the shop. But it only got me into a lavatory that was locked.

I clambered out with some difficulty, terrified that people sleeping in the terrace close by had been woken by the sound of breaking glass. I waited once I was over the wall and held my breath, but no one stirred.

The other chemist also backed on to a narrow back street, not three hundred yards from the police station. On my way, I found a rusty right-angle bracket of the kind used to support shelves. I broke one of the small panes in the sash window at the back of the shop and thrust my hand in to release the catch. The window slid open quite easily and I clambered in. Pools of blood on the windowsill told me I'd cut my hand.

There was just enough light from the street lamps outside for me to locate the Dangerous Drugs Act cupboard. After fifteen minutes of strenuous effort with my improvised jemmy, I had bashed a hole large enough to get most of my fingers through, by now behaving like the crazed animal that the junky myth would have me be.

In went my hand and after some tortuous twisting of my wrist and fingers, I was able to extract a cardboard packet of ampoules. It was pethidine, a powerful analgesic used in childbirth. I groped in the cupboard again, but all I could reach was another packet of pethidine ampoules. It was not the morphine or heroin I had hoped for, but it would do.

I climbed out of the shop as quietly as I could and hurried back to the hotel. The first ampoule hit me like a sledgehammer: the familiar rush of heroin, but with an intense tingling all over and an almost total disorientation of my senses. I broke the top off another ampoule and injected that into my vein. It made me as stoned, as chemically altered, as I'd ever been in my life. I was deranged.

Strangely, a part of my consciousness kept track of my situation. I was in an hotel room in Dartmouth; I had just broken into two chemists; I had stolen two boxes of pethidine ampoules from one of them; I was the only known junky in Dartmouth; the police would be after me; I was in a hotel room in Dartmouth; the only known junky in ampoules; stoned so completely OUT of his mind; I had to have a plan; a plan; the empty ampoules on the floor; the cut on my wrists; must have a plan; now if I go to the police myself and say....say what?.... say...

At eight o'clock I went to the police station.

"Good morning, Mr Pryor." The friendly sergeant knew my name. The local drug addict.

"Good morning," I tried to say it normally. "I've come about the break-in at the chemist's. Just thought you ought to know that I had nothing to do with it."

"Sorry, Mr Pryor. Don't know what you're talking about. We've had no reports of any break-ins. But then they won't have opened up yet, will they?" He paused for thought, pencil to lips. "So, how would you know about these here break-ins?" I hadn't thought. Of course, the chemists didn't open till nine.

"Well, you see, it's just that, well, I heard a rumour, yes, I heard a rumour that there was going to be a break-in at one of the chemist's and I just wanted you to know that I had nothing to do with it. Wouldn't know what to do, anyway." I wobbled slightly and had to steady myself on the counter.

"I see. Well that's most considerate of you, Mr Pryor. Now, I think the best thing you can do now is get a taxi to take you home for some breakfast." Policemen, college porters, all the same when it comes to recommending drug-crazed breakfasts at home. "Don't you worry about a thing, we'll get to the bottom of this." He was humouring me. I had no option but to do as he suggested and go home.

Mary wasn't up. I sat myself down and started to pulverise the empty ampoules I had stuffed into my pocket. Mary appeared in her dressing gown. It didn't take her long to piece together what had happened from my paranoid incoherence.

Wilf rang at half past nine.

"William, the police are on their way down to see you. Now, listen carefully young chap. You must tell them everything they want to know, that's the only way out of this mess. If you co-operate with them, I'll back you to the hilt and speak up for you in court. Do you understand?"

"I don't know what you're...." I tried the bewildered innocent approach, but he cut me off.

"Come on William, that's only going to make things more difficult. Everybody knows you did it. It'll be very easy to prove, you left copious evidence. Do yourself a favour! Own up like a man! It's your only chance."

"OK, yes, OK." So quickly, they all knew so quickly.

"Right, you be a good lad when they come. I'll see you through it all."

He did. The magistrates in Totnes made me pay for the damage I'd caused and put me on probation for eighteen months. I would doubtless have gone to prison had Wilf not spoken up for me: basically a sound chap; victim of his addiction; given his word that he'll make a serious effort this time.

Now Wilf had me by the short and curlies. As his wife, who acted as his receptionist on occasion, kept pointing out, I should feel very indebted to Wilf. He had gone to no end of trouble to help me and it was up to me to prove that I was worth it. Hadn't I got a lovely wife, a beautiful baby daughter, a lovely home, a good brain.

I was put on a drastically reduced dose of linctus, for which I had to go into the chemist every day to drink on the spot. I was hammered and humiliated. I was a junky.

My probation officer was a kind man in a Gannex raincoat who made very few demands. He would drop in for tea every now and then. He was encouraging about my latest project, to clear the level land at the bottom of the valley and grow organic potatoes for sale to health food shops and the like. The summer was beautiful, I got a taste of the pleasures to be gained from hard manual work and my physeptone intake had levelled off.

My mother had sold the house in Chaucer Road, not wanting to involve me in the transaction. She had met one of my father's old friends Charles Gurney, who was then professor of engineering at Hong Kong University. She went to live with him in Hong Kong. I didn't meet him. I was her affliction. They must have debated long and hard what to do about me.

A smattering of hope returned, despite the linctus, the occasional Chlorodyne and the rare fix of heroin that I was able to persuade Al to send. Mary's parents came to visit, not in the house thank God, but in Dartmouth's best hotel, and that went off all right. Generally a year of possibilities, of fitting in with the landscape, but not actually doing very much. It was almost as though I had learnt a lesson from my second brush with the law.

My first (and last) crop of potatoes was a disaster. I got maybe thirty pounds from my extensive patch, which I managed to sell to a health food store in Torquay. The mushrooms were even worse. I got only a pound or two from the whole bed. I had to find some other way of earning a living, do something that I knew something about. My mind went back to bookselling. Had I not trained at one of the best university booksellers? I started to compile my lists of books of orientalia and the occult with more dedication, still toying with the idea of mail-order.

But I didn't know where to start. How, for instance, did one go about getting customers. Well then, why not start up a specialist, alternative bookshop? It would have to be in Torquay, the nearest town of any size. I put the idea to the trustees, and they agreed in principle.

Shortly before the car crash, my father had added a codicil to the deeds of the Pelican Trust. It stopped me having direct access to the capital, unlike my sisters who were able to spend theirs when they became twenty-one. I was given the interest as income, but any capital expenditure was made entirely at the discretion of the trustees.

My stomach had become accustomed to Chlorodyne and I would swallow a bottle every day. After a month's search, I found a good site for the bookshop. It was a lean-to, lockup shop at the back of the Market building, right in the centre of town. The rent was reasonable and I set about fitting the place out with shelves, carpets, a cash register and other accoutrements of the trade. Mary didn't want anything to do with it and I was left on my own to get on with it. The mutual distrust between us grew. I resented the fact that this real attempt of mine to get involved in the world met with indifference. She was bitter that my addiction went on and on. We rowed frequently.

When Mac, one of the Dartmouth boat people I'd hired to help me fit the place out, painted the sign to go above the window, COSMIC BOOKS, I knew my shop was going to happen. It seemed daft for me to travel from Dartmouth everyday. We would have to move into Torquay!

Mary was not pleased with this idea, and when I persisted to the extent of going to an estate agent with a view to putting the cottage on the market, she became even more steely-mouthed and clipped of speech. But the place had been bought by the Pelican, so it was my decision. She protested that it was mad to leave such peace and live in Torquay of all places.

We moved that autumn as the leaves were turning. Our new, rented accommodation was a winter let of a terraced house which we would have to vacate the following April. Our rows became more furious. Me increasingly in fear of my inadequacy as father and husband, her with decreasing appetite to share my burdens. It got so bad that Mary went home to Norfolk for a week with Lydia to let things cool off. We were back at it almost as soon as she'd returned.

Somehow, I continued to make ready for the opening of the shop. I joined the Bookseller's Association and went through all the formalities necessary to get my first stocks of books. The books started to arrive: Beckett and Burroughs, modern art (including that one from the Museum of Modern Art in New York), poetry, Buddhism, the occult, Hinduism and Western philosophy. And the place looked good: different, but appealing with its black shelves and grey carpet. It became my *raison d'être*.

Occasionally, my tame chemist in Paignton hadn't been able to replenish his stock of Chlorodyne and I would have to range further afield in search of chemists that didn't know my face too well. On my way back from one such trip to Newton Abbot, feeling pleasantly high on one of the three bottles I'd managed to get, I sat next to a hip looking lady on the top deck of the bus. She had a bandana round her forehead and some of her hair was in tiny little plaits, sure signs of hipness in those days (we're now into 1971).

We got talking. Her name was Anda. From Manchester, she had been in Torquay for the last six months. But far more important, and at that time quite devastating, was the fact that she was a junky. We had established the rough outlines of our drug taking proclivities within minutes of starting the conversation. It was devastating because I had always assumed Torquay to be as sedate, prim, palm-treed and junk-free as its image would suggest.

Anda invited me back to her pad, not all that far from the shop. The prospect was a welcome and exciting break from my pained and lonely tedium. She was good-looking too. She shared the tenement-like house with two brothers, one of whom was also a junky.

She made me a cup of coffee and bade me sit next to her on the sofa. I finished telling her the resume of my addiction that I had started on the bus. My credentials as junky were cool.

"D'you fancy a fix now. I've got plenty." She flashed her soft eyes at me, giving me a peck on the cheek. Her intentions were obvious and it was flattering, especially after all the tensions with Mary. I knew I shouldn't. It would only start things all over again, but, on the other hand, I *was* taking an awful lot of Chlorodyne every day and that was probably doing more harm to my body than just one fix would.

"Just a small one then. But it mustn't become a habit." She smiled at that and went off to fetch the apparatus: a spoon, a cup of water, two syringes and a few tiny paper packs, no bigger than about four match sticks stuck together. She opened one of them carefully.

Junk is the ideal product...the ultimate merchandise. No sales talk necessary. The client will crawl through a sewer and beg to buy. (William Burroughs· in the introduction to *The Naked Lunch* (1959))

In a consumer society there are inevitably two kinds of slaves: the prisoners of addiction and the prisoners of envy. (Ivan Illich, *Tools for Conviviality* (1973))

"This should do you. Not much left in this one. Shall I cook it up for you. Don't suppose you've done it before, not with Chinese?"

"Yeah please." She tapped the granular yellow powder gently into the bowl of the teaspoon, drew some water up into the syringe and squirted enough into the spoon to cover the powder. She then held the spoon above the flame of her cigarette lighter, and, as the water bubbled, the powder dissolved. She wrapped a tiny piece of cotton wool round the tip of the needle and drew up the solution through it into the syringe.

She handed it to me. I already had my arm tied with my belt. The veins were bulging. I got a hit, the blood. I played with it. Then pushed it home. The rush swept through. Back to good old heroin, I thought. She had a fix herself, then moved closer to me. When the fixes had worn off slightly, she led me to her bedroom.

The gates to the truly criminal world of addiction had opened. They used the real thing: 'Chinese' heroin, black market, underworld junk. This is the stuff that the gangster films are about. It is not white, but a sulphurous yellow. It is manufactured in secret laboratories from opium grown in Burma and Afghanistan and smuggled into the country by, in those days, the Mafia and the Chinese Triads and their agents. It is sold in 'packs'. A good one is enough for several fixes; a bad one hardly staves off withdrawal symptoms. It is 'cut' with an innocuous filler to increase profits along the line, and hence, you never know exactly how much actual heroin you are taking and overdoses can result.

The time came to open the shop. The first day I sold one book. I was not disheartened. It was obviously going to take time for word to get round about such a strange venture.

Mary and I could hardly bear to look at each other, let alone exchange commonplaces. All my interest in life was outside the house, away from her. She hated Torquay and I treated her with disdain and distrust. One night, when I got back from the shop, both she and Lydia were out. Puzzled, I got my own supper. They didn't return till midnight. I was furious. There was a row. She said she'd been to the cinema, but it was a transparent lie. Two days later, she went out just as I got in, to visit a friend. She didn't come home that night.

In the fight that ensued when I got home the next evening, she confessed that she'd spent the night with Bill, a very kind man who had been a great help. I found out where he lived and went round, my heart full of bitter revenge. The man was breaking up my marriage. Had he no shame? But he was much bigger than me and I had to leave. Mary was destroying me, threatening to take my daughter away from me. She was mad, that was it, she was mad. Mary stood as much of my ranting as she could, but finally my possessiveness and inability to provide any emotional or physical security was too much.

She left me for good. I was alone.

It was late March and the landlady wanted me out so that she could double the rent for the holiday season. I found someone to take pity on my plight: the kind-hearted proprietor of the only vegetarian restaurant in Torquay, just round the corner from Cosmic Books. He knew a naturopathic doctor who wanted to let the top floor of his house. I moved in and eventually got the Pelican to buy a lease on the flat.

The only thing that kept me among the living during these traumata was the shop. Despite marathon weeping sessions and hysteria for weeks after Mary had gone, I managed to keep it open most of the time and business was beginning to pick up. I saw Anda again. She offered me solace of the body and the needle.

There was a small community of junkies in Torquay, mostly tough characters from the North. On my third visit in a week, she suggested I meet one of these blokes, who would be able to supply me on a daily basis, if that was what I wanted. If I could wait for a couple of hours, he'd be sure to be round. Meanwhile she led me off to the bedroom, where we fixed and had sex.

Darryl was a sinister man with a cast in one eye and a sneering mouth. He was off to London to score and asked me to put ten pounds towards the deal. He half-convinced me that I would get twice as much that way. He kept his word and late the next day he came into the shop and handed me four bulky packs.

By this time business was picking up as more people got to know about the only alternative bookshop in Devon, in the West Country. I could afford to take on some part-time help: Anne, the vegetarian restaurateur's daughter. It meant that I could spend as much time as I liked running around after a fix.

My habit was raging again and needed one or more fixes everyday. This time, though, it was very different. My suppliers would scrape together, by fair means or foul, the hundred odd pounds necessary to score an ounce deal from a connection up in London. The atmosphere of illegality was strong. I was darting in and out of dark doorways, meeting people on street corners, endlessly waiting for the man. All this in Torquay!

The shop provided a ready supply of cash with which I could buy my stuff. In six months I got through some seven hundred pounds (that's over £3,000 in today's money).

I had a new doctor in Torquay who I was able to persuade to give me Heminevrin as a sleeping pill. The months ran into each other as a blur of the chase for relief, the wheeling and dealing, and, above all, the waiting.

One of the most striking aspects of hell is that it goes round and round; the same torments over and over again. This was the worst day of my life. There were so many of them.

In desperation, I wrote to my mother who was now in Hong Kong with her new husband, Charles Gurney. I wrote asking for help, any help, some help.

A few weeks later, rather to my surprise, my mother and stepfather turned up, unannounced, concerned at the state I was in. She hadn't seen me for a couple of years. I must have looked ill. She looked older. Nervous. Worried. We neither wanted to be with each other, but there was nothing else for it. The scapegoat came home to roost.

How like Michael Foot Charles was: Welsh, socialist, with his bad hip and highly developed eccentricities. He had views on everything from how best to do the washing up to Wordsworth. I told them about the heroin, more in the spirit of trying to convey how hopeless my situation was than anything else. They went to talk to my doctor and, I later discovered, to the police. They set up a temporary home in a holiday flat in Teignmouth.

There was a loud thumping at the front door. It was half past six in the morning. I went down to open it in my dressing gown. There was a posse of plain clothes policemen on the doorstep. I feigned anger and protested loudly as they searched the flat, even showing them the loose floorboard. Luckily there wasn't much to find. A few old syringes and needles, that was all.

They told me to put some clothes on and hauled me off to the police station. I was taken to a cell that smelt of vomit and told to strip down to my underpants so they could search my clothes. I vociferously demanded my rights, but all they were prepared to do was to phone my mother. I paced up and down the cell in my underpants.

Several hell-days later*, I was released into the care of my mother and stepfather who had now arrived and had had the foresight to collect my dose of physeptone on the way. I drank it like a man dying of thirst. I was told, through my solicitor who turned up soon after my parents, that the only way I could save myself from what could be a nasty prosecution was for me to offer my services as prosecution witness against Anda and friends who had been busted simultaneously.

From then on, I was in a tangible state of fear every waking moment. Every man in the street was a policeman. I was the centre of a multi-tentacled conspiracy that included all the other junkies in Torquay, my parents, the police, my doctor and anyone else who would fit.

---

* A hell-day is equivalent to ten minutes of ordinary time. In fact, one hell-year is roughly equivalent to 2.5 ordinary days and 146 hell-years to one ordinary year.

15 THE TRIALS OF TORQUAY

I was 29. I had been using drugs to change my emotional metabolism since I was 18.

Rosey, a mature student at the Torquay Art College was now helping Anne look after the shop in her spare time, and had invited me to come along to their end of year student concert and bring my poems. Though a paranoid ghost, I went. She knew about the bust and the forthcoming trial, and saw that I needed something that would enable me to believe in myself in some small way.

I was thrilled when, near the end of the evening, she announced that I would read some poems. It was a tonic to be listened to by an audience of art students, that my arrangements of words had some point.

One of the art students, a pretty redheaded, freckled seventeen-year-old called Joy, came to the pub with me. She was sympathetic and eager to listen to my troubles. I told her how I was persecuted on every hand, pushed about by my parents, and so on and on. She enabled me to feel credible, just slightly human, not just the debris left over after a violent clear up by the drug squad, the 'thought police'.

It was then I made a very obvious and disastrous discovery: alcohol. The warm, numbing effect of four Pernods was a welcome relief. In common with most serious drug users I had previously regarded alcohol as a gross, messy way to get high. All it did was release by suppression, and so crudely compared with heroin. Drunks were such bores: they puked and fell over. But in my present condition it was a godsend. It would be all right, I thought; there's no need to get drunk, actually inebriated, every time you drink.

There were at least six pubs within two hundred yards of my front door and the stuff was legal. More than that: it was approved of, sanctioned by society at large, not even as a necessary evil, but as what one deserves after a hard day's work/play/a sudden shock/any kind of event, good bad or indifferent. Alcohol is what one deserves. It is what lubricates the entire social function. It is a drug.

I began to see Joy quite frequently. She was such a cheerful and positive ally in the war and made so few demands. We would go out dancing in the discotheques of Torquay, largely because I could go on drinking until two in the morning, but we did also enjoy dancing away all our nervous energy. Soon I was going to pubs as soon as they opened in the morning, until it struck me that it would be a lot more convenient (and cheaper) if I simply bought a few bottles to drink at home. I would have a largish tot of rum and coke before I went down to the shop in the morning to steady my nerves and would escape to the nearest pub as soon as Anne or Rosey arrived.

I was indeed used by the police as their chief prosecution witness. My babblings would be the final straw that ensured the three 'evil pushers', Darryl among them, would get sent to prison for a few years.

Joy decided that I needed looking after and moved into the flat, which was within easy walking distance of the Art College. She came with me in the police car to the Crown Court in Exeter. The violent cut and thrust of the court rammed home my confusion, guilt and shame at seeing the three faces I knew so well surrounded by policemen. The hate in their eyes burnt into mine.

The defence counsel's main goal was to undermine my credibility as a reliable witness and he had no difficulty making me look weak, unprincipled and foolish. Naively, I expected the prosecution counsel to be on my side. But he was just as vicious as he set out to show how a basically decent chap had been brought low by these vermin, these leaches on the open wounds of society or some such. He succeeded in getting me to break into tears, standing there in the witness stand, with the whole court watching, like Romans at the death of a gladiator.

"I didn't think I was on trial here. The way you're going on, it's as though I was on trial. Haven't I got enough problems without having to put up with all this."

He indulgently let me get over my tearful outbreak with a glass of water before he continued to establish that all three of the accused had supplied this pathetic victim we see before us with their foul and despicable wares. He did this with a series of photographs taken by the police from a hide they had established in the builders merchant's yard opposite Cosmic Books showing various meetings I had had with the accused.

When the prosecution had finished, defence counsel got to his feet again.

"I should like to put it you, Mr Pryor, that you were offered immunity from prosecution if you agreed to give evidence against my clients and that, in fact, you are just as guilty as they are. Is this not true?" He stared at me.

"I don't have to answer that do I?" I turned to the judge.

"Yes, I'm afraid you do Mr Pryor," he replied over his glasses.

"Well, no, it's not true. I may be an addict." I choked back a sob. "But I never sold heroin to anyone."

The night after the trial, Joy and I went to the nearest discotheque to celebrate the end of the trial. As we made our way home at two o'clock in the morning through an underground car park, a girl wearing shiny trousers, whose face I vaguely recognised, was leaning against one of the concrete pillars.

"That's him," she screamed pointing at me. Two men stepped out from behind another pillar. One of them swung his fist at me, hate contorting his face. He got me hard in the mouth. I was knocked out, flat on the ground. Joy contrived to stop them from kicking me more than once by lying on top of me. The fist of rage had knocked my four top front teeth clean out of my head.

Joy went back to the car park the next day and found my four missing teeth, which she put in a matchbox. The police half-heartedly went through the motions of trying to find who had done it, showing us mug shots.

Within three months of my first drinking session with Joy, I was displaying the symptoms of chronic alcoholism: drinking at least one bottle of spirits a day. I couldn't begin to function without at least a quarter of that inside me by eleven o'clock. I developed tremors in my hands. I would sweat profusely at night. I got aches in my legs and hands from peripheral neuritis. My appetite disappeared. I had great trouble in not vomiting my first drink of the day straight up again.

There was still a residue of beatnik 'pataphysician in me, dimly holding on to an explanation of my auto-destruction. One of Joy's more sympathetic lecturers at the Art College was Paul. He had been at Oxford at the same time I'd been at Trinity and had known many of the same people through his involvement in poetry, jazz and R&B. He had just got back to England, after spending a few years at the University of British Columbia in Vancouver. We had a common interest in surrealism and Dada, about which he was more knowledgeable than I. He was a frequent visitor to the flat. We would smoke some grass, get nicely high (I would already be well charged from my bottle of white rum in the bedroom) and launch into endless rapping sessions, which often involved free-form word improvisations into my tape recorder.

One of these games evolved into a strange but revealing project: a script for a film about my death. It involved me observing my own funeral that was to take place in the fens, with a fleet of helicopters airlifting Ely Cathedral's organ into position for Cecil Taylor to play. There would also be a procession of all senior Cambridge academics, dressed in their finest regalia, on their way to do homage at my catafalque. This was surrealism.

Mary had got herself a small house in Dartmouth and devoted herself to caring for Lydia and healing her own wounds. I made a few abortive attempts to get back with her. Lydia seemed to be frightened of me, which was hardly surprising since I had raised my fist to Mary – though not hit her – during our last few rows. I agonised with Joy over whether I should go and see Mary, playing on Joy's amazing straightforwardness.

Eventually Mary knew she had to divorce me. She waited until the statutory two years had elapsed so she could get a divorce on the grounds of our separation. I did not, indeed could not, contest her claim for custody of Lydia and there was no wrangling about money. I was very fortunate it was so civilised.

I would wake or, more accurately, recover consciousness, after a few hours of drugged oblivion or sleep, at about six in the morning. If things had worked out well the day before, I would have some white rum left over which I would pour, as best I could with my shaking hands, into a mug. I would add enough cola to take away the sting and would then try to drink the mixture without spilling too much. As the first slug of alcohol hit my stomach, it would react, due to gastritis, by retching.

By eight o'clock I would have got sufficient alcohol into my blood for me to feel able to cope with the world. That is all I ever did: cope. I would try to eat a little breakfast, although this became increasingly difficult as the months passed. Joy would sleep through my first retchings, sweatings, gulpings and sighings and would go off to college unaware, as far as I knew, of this messy ritual.

At ten to nine I would walk down the town to Cosmic Books, timing it so that I arrived outside the off-licence just as it opened. I would buy a half-bottle of rum or vodka and then wobble into the shop and park my body behind the desk. By half past nine, I would have drunk half of the bottle and be feeling much better, even able to open a few bills and put a few books straight. Far too often I would be in a stupor by half past twelve when Joy would come down from the college and she would have to get me home as best she could, sometimes allowing me to stop off and buy more booze on the way. She would then go back and run the shop all afternoon.

I would usually be sufficiently revived by sleep and more booze in the early evening to watch television or to go out somewhere, but would always spend the last hour or so of the evening getting enough alcohol in me so that, with the help of whatever number of sleepers I had available, I could drop slowly off into the oblivious unconsciousness that passed for sleep.

My mother and Charles bought a house near Totnes. He had retired and spent his time building things out of bamboo and quoting Victorian poetry. She painted, played the piano and violin and gardened. But another constant in their lives was me, just fifteen miles down the road. I was hospitalised for what the NHS thought was the way to a cure on a couple of occasions.

I was hospitalised again. I was so bad physically this time that the other alcoholics in the ward were brought to my bed.

"That," they were told, "is what you'll be like if you go on drinking." I was 29.

But any further account of these months in hell would be tedious: that's one of the key characteristics of hell – it goes round and round and round, seeming to be for ever.

I went to two meetings of Alcoholics Anonymous. I was getting so low, so desperate, maybe a group of Bible-thumping do-gooders could do something to pull me out of the abyss. I had little idea as to what they actually were, but somehow expected them to work a miracle on me, if I paid lip service to their do-gooding ideals.

They made us wait outside while they decided if it could be an open meeting so Joy, a non-alcoholic, could attend. This I resented. It seemed a funny way to be offering help. Eventually they decided we could both attend and in we went to join the small group round the table.

I couldn't believe that everyone in the room was an alcoholic, albeit recovering, some of them looked so utterly normal. They couldn't have been to the hell I was now in. I couldn't get past my prejudice that they were salvationist do-gooders, and couldn't hear what they said. I wondered if there'd be time to get some drinks in after they'd finished.

A metabolic desperation that clouded my vision had been thickening for two years. There had to be a resolution. With some difficulty I persuaded the doctor to put me on a reducing course of Heminevrin, which Joy would dole out four times a day. It would take me a week to get right off, during which time I would stay at home. As a symbol of my good faith, as a necessary ritual, I poured the last three inches of a bottle of vodka down the sink. I made sure Joy was watching. Not because of, but despite, my lopsided plans, this was the last.

Ever. A fact that would have terrified me had I known it at the time.

Within three days, when the dose had been reduced from a massive sixteen capsules a day to a still large twelve, I was ill and in bed. I couldn't eat. I couldn't walk, not even to the bog, and had to be helped. But, worst of all, I couldn't swallow the Heminevrin and had to have them emptied into a little hot water.

I was, at last, heading for that AA-defined place, Rock Bottom. The place of no return, of the perception that there is no hope and no help but in giving up. The conclusion to the addiction meme*, when it had been drained of power.

My headlong slither downwards had not taken place in an unpeopled vacuum. Joy, my mother and, to a lesser extent, the rest of my family and what few friends I had left had all been sucked into my turmoil. In fact, this turmoil was a fully interactive drama, depending on those it dragged in to provide grist to its mill, at an inevitable cost to them.

But as my condition worsened the family got serious. Twelve years after my addiction started. Something drastic had to be done. Interestingly, it was my brother-in-law Andrew who came up with the solution. He phoned every Council on Alcoholism in the country to ask what private facilities there were in their area. The only place that offered any serious hope of recovery was a treatment centre near Bristol. My parents promptly went to have a look and were impressed with what they saw.

"William, you'll die if you go on like this. You know what the doctor said," said my mother in a cracked voice.

"Don't care. Anyway, I am doing something about it. Look, I haven't had a drink for five days now."

"But look at the state of you," she went on, "you're a zombie. You just lie in your bed all day. Apparently, at this Broadway place they

---

*See my explanation of the addiction meme in the epilogue.

deal with what it is that makes you need to take drugs and drink in the first place. They say it can be changed."

"But that's just it," I protested weakly, "why should you want me to change? You don't really care, none of you do. How could you, about this?" I waved a finger round me, the room, the empty bottles. I was in bed. I was ill.

"Well, we do, and it's because we do that we want you to go to this place." I didn't believe it. "They're very nice people and really do understand. I'm sure you'll like it when you get there, and it *would* be good not to have to drink, wouldn't it?" My mother pleaded. She sensed that my resolve was weakening.

They were determined and, when Joy joined their ranks, the easiest course was to capitulate, if only to get some peace and quiet. It couldn't be much worse than what I was going through, although I was filled with terror at the thought that they might actually stop me having my chemical support forever after. What would there be in its place?

It was arranged that my mother drive Joy and I up there the following Saturday. I had one more day and night of freedom, one more day and night of hell. For some weeks I had been having the DTs, delirium tremens. It took the form of a constantly repeating film show, the same short sequence of apparently insignificant action over and over again, which appeared on the walls and ceiling of the bedroom. I had no choice but to watch. I knew only too well that it went on, even if my eyes were shut. And it was in its insignificance, its apparent irrelevance that its horror lay. It just kept grinding on, over and over again, so that all meaning was lost.

My mind was seeing itself disintegrate. For my last night of freedom, the delirium film show developed into an aural horror: voices, distortions of known sounds, horrible creatures creeping up on me. I had to keep the radio on all night, through the witching hour, in an attempt to ward off the terrors that threatened me.

So this was Rock Bottom!

16 TOTTERDOWN AND FIRST STEPS

Man seeks to escape himself in myth, and does so by any means at his disposal. Drugs, alcohol, or lies. Unable to withdraw into himself, he disguises himself. Lies and inaccuracy give him a few moments of comfort. (Jean Cocteau)

On a May Saturday afternoon in 1975, at the age of 31, after twelve years of addiction, I finally arrived at Broadway Lodge, a kitsch Victorian convent building, previously called Totterdown Hall and stuck strangely in the middle of an aspirational Weston Super Mare housing estate.

Broadway Lodge had been set up by an ex-US marine, Jim Ditzler and his tall, blonde, British wife, Joyce. Crew cut Jim had a scar on his cheek and penetrating twinkly blue eyes, and seemed much taller than his five foot six. He had an authority that fairly cracked through the air as he oversaw his confused and dazed clients' attempts to be honest, to understand their confusion. It was the first treatment centre in Europe to use the American Hazelden Method: a group therapy amplification of the Alcoholics Anonymous Twelve Steps programme*. It had been in business less than a year when I got there.

This was the beginning of my physical recovery. Not a helpful word here, recovery, since it implies that a return to some previous state of health is underway. There was no previous state of health I could return to: I got hooked in my teens, and my childhood, pubescence and adolescence were mostly confusion, anger, despair and unease. If I went back there I would have no hope of staying sober. Addiction had been my escape from my scapegoat self. My *re*covery had to be a *dis*covery, finding a Terra Incognita where being in my skin had a balance of purpose and contentment. I would have, eventu-

---

* The relative success of the AA programme seems to be due to the fact that an alcoholic who no longer drinks has an exceptional faculty for 'reaching' and helping an uncontrolled drinker. The 12 steps describe the experience of the founders in getting sober in the industrial north west of the US in the 1930s. They were a God-fearing lot and, though they made great efforts to keep the language neutrally ecumenical, God still appears in 6 of the 12 steps. Other than baldly stating that it as an 'illness', the programme offers no further explanation of what addiction actually is and does nothing to address the underlying malaise. It is my contention that addiction is a self-medication defence against depression, the knot in the belly. It is the symptom, not the condition. [continued overleaf]

ally, to confront my holes and my gremlins, a process beyond Broadway's commitment to sobriety and one that would take a lot longer.

Under the AA dogma, Jim and his counsellors were in the business of getting their clients through the detox and basic rehab, as we made that crucial first step into self-awareness, into knowing we were addicts or alcoholics. Up to that moment we were in the thrall of denial: it's the world's/my family's/my body's/the martian's fault that I drink as much as I do. I can stop tomorrow if I want, but I don't want.

Once you *know* you are in the power of a chemical, you can begin to do something about it. You can be persuaded of the simple proposition that life without mood-altering chemicals is possible. If you cannot admit you are hooked, you can't imagine living without. Once you have admitted your slavery, you can start to change. One day at a time. One of AA's strongest ideas. Don't think further than today. That is all that matters. Just get through the day. You can do it!

AA is a 'fellowship' of recovering alcoholics, as Narcotics Anonymous is of recovering drug users. Just recovering addicts, no professionals. Like chain letters of possibility: it works for me so it will work for you – a powerful proposition. You can see apparently normal people sitting there in front of you saying they were once like you; they are as close to addiction as their next drink, smoke, fix.

The Minnesota Model, as the Hazelden method is now called, certainly does help addicts find less damaging lifestyles without any chemical support. But they are still addicted lifestyles: AA meetings become the crutch – in rooms thick with chain-smoked cigarette fumes you have to go on and on describing yourself as a recovering addict or alcoholic. This new addiction is enforced by the circular dictum: when you stay away from meetings you are heading for a drink. I stopped going at the end of my first year of abstinence. And I still haven't had a drink, 28 years later.

[cont.] The steps the founders took were: *1. We admitted we were powerless over alcohol - that our lives had become unmanageable. 2. Came to believe that a Power greater than ourselves could restore us to sanity. 3. Made a decision to turn our will and our lives over to the care of God as we understood Him. 4. Made a searching and fearless moral inventory of ourselves. 5. Admitted to God, to ourselves and to another human being the exact nature of our wrongs. 6. Were entirely ready to have God remove all these defects of character. 7. Humbly asked Him to remove our shortcomings. 8. Made a list of all persons we had harmed, and became willing to make amends to them all. 9. Made direct amends to such people wherever possible, except when to do so would injure them or others. 10. Continued to take personal inventory and when we were wrong promptly admitted it. 11. Sought through prayer and meditation to improve our conscious contact with God as we understood Him, praying only for knowledge of His will for us and the power to carry that out. 12. Having had a spiritual awakening as the result of these steps, we tried to carry this message to alcoholics and to practise these principles in all our affairs.*

AA was founded in 1935 in Akron Ohio by drinkers involved in evangelist Frank Buchman's Oxford Group, later to be called Moral Re- Armament. In 1921, Buchman, a Lutheran minister, visited England, where he preached to students at Oxford (hence the name) that you could change the world by changing your life. In 1938 he started Moral Re-Armament. Much of the AA creed comes direct from his evangelical methods of converting sinners (alcoholics) into Christians: confessing your sins before your peer group, sin (addiction) being the result of self-centredness, salvation only possible with complete surrender to Christ. Moral Re-Armament achieved a certain notoriety through Buchman's public admiration of Adolf Hitler and, after the war, for its strident anti-Communist position.

AA is a private realm. The world thinks alcoholics are simply people who drink too much, but in AA you have a disease, a condition from which there is only 'recovery', not cure. The monster broods in the background waiting to drag you back to its slimy hell at the drop of an AA meeting. They offer you a mantra: 'I am an alcoholic' which must be repeated long after you have stopped drinking, in fact, for the rest of your life.

When we arrived at Broadway, I was going through diabolical withdrawal symptoms from Heminevrin: blurred and hazy vision, disorientation, weakness in the limbs, no appetite. As soon as we got into the spartan hallway, my heart sank, and it was low enough already. It had the smell of unhappy indoctrination, not unlike Eton.

One of the patients fetched Margaret, the duty nurse, who ushered us into an office. A sensible, white-haired Irish woman who would obviously brook no nonsense, she asked interminable questions as she filled in forms about my history. My withdrawn vacancy was such that I couldn't remember how to spell anything: Torquay, my GP's name, even my own name. All I was interested in was getting the Heminevrin I'd been promised, but I'd have to wait until she could get the doctor's approval, especially for the vast dose of four capsules in one go.

After tea with the other residents, Margaret got through to the doctor who said I could have my four Heminevrin. I swallowed them in the dispensary and, despite the fact that Joy and my mother were still downstairs, went straight to my shared bedroom and got into bed in search of relief, sleep, oblivion. As I began to savour the slight effect of the pills, Margaret came in, tut tutting loudly.

"We don't go to bed in the afternoon here, you know, whatever you might do at home. Now, come along, up with you. Why don't you go down to the coffee room like a nice man and say goodbye to your mother and your lovely girlfriend?" I lifted the wet rag that was my body out of bed. Joy and my mother were just about to leave.

"You do as they say and I'm sure you'll be all right. Be good," said my mother, looking so distraught. Joy and I hugged. I was neither sorry nor glad to see them go. There was nowhere I could turn for solace. "You are now entering Rock-Bottom-super-nightMare. On our left you can see AA meetings; on our right group therapy and straight ahead is sobriety. Praise be to your Higher Power!"

"We'll have you off these pills in a week. Then you'll start to feel better," Margaret said. The prospect appalled me.

Later that evening the doctor arrived. He was much friendlier than I expected. Something remarkable happened while he was prodding my liver and testing my reflexes. He inspired confidence; he managed to persuade me my physical health was not too bad. My peripheral neuritis would ease with plenty of good food. I would sleep like a baby in no time at all, and my liver would soon make up the damaged tissue. Remarkable for someone who had so nearly drunk himself to death! He prescribed a controlled reduction in my Heminevrin to nothing, in a week*.

The other residents, some ten of them at the time, were friendly enough, but also daunting. As in any residential institution there was an unspoken hierarchy that was used as an integral part of the peer-group treatment and that led to a web of insider jokes and gossip from which I was, as newbie, excluded. I shared my dormitory with Jock, a gnarled Scotsman from Wales; Henry, a thin faced man in his late forties who had very few teeth; Rupert, a fresh-faced chap who seemed to have come straight out of public school and Mike a solid, muscular, tattooed cockney. Henry, amongst other things, was an artist and a carpenter, and I felt I would probably get on with him best.

For the first week I was withdrawn, disorientated, lost, without any hope. New arrivals were not allowed to make any phone calls or go out of the grounds, making a complete break from the past, that everything will change, but also reducing the chances of relapse before the patient has been able to find his feet.

The Group room, with ballroom-like parquet floor, had probably been the nuns' refectory. At one end was a large bay window complete

---

*I have just discovered that this confidence-inspiring doctor was, in fact, an alcoholic himself, and died, unrecovered, from the condition some years later.

with window-seat. On the walls hung Woolworths reproductions of Dutch masters. In the middle of the room was a large circle of what can only be described as uneasy chairs: upholstered, very low, no arms, with an old upright piano against the wall near the bay window.

As with a wagon-train, we would circle the chairs against marauding reality outside. The appointed one reads from a polythene-covered card, a preamble that states the aims of the group therapy: *The members of this group all share the same problems; alcoholism, chemical dependency, personality disorders, character defects... By conveying to others our problems and feelings, we find that we are not alone.*

Through self disclosure and open discussion our various defence mechanisms are recognised and resolved and we find a logical approach to our problems.

Those that tried to get sober their own way, we were told, always came to grief. They either ended up dead, or worse: with Korsikoff's syndrome (a 'wet brain'), spinning out the remainder of their lives as vegetables in the back wards of mental hospitals.

They got us to wash our own brains. Certainly it is true that when confronted with the fact that you are an alcoholic, you have two options. You can deny it flatly (and most alcoholics and addicts do) and carry on down, or you can grant that it might be true. You are only likely to do this if you've reached a crisis (Rock Bottom) that forces the realisation that you've run out of options. If this is the case, you're not likely to be in a state to work out what on earth to do about it and this is where AA comes in. They have been where you are and know a way through and out. You can trust what they say because they are people who have been through what you are going through, not experts or academics.

Broadway was concerned to speed up this process of recognition and identification, self-analysis and cleansing, assessment and change. Perhaps it would be better to call it a process of learning, rather than indoctrination. It was just the 'tough love' they practised that made it seem like the latter; 'tough love' as it was practised at the birthplace of group therapy, Esalen in California.

Diminutive, five foot two, Scottish Liz, with a no-nonsense Glaswegian determination that had to be taken seriously, was my counsellor. Short dark hair with a not pretty, not ugly face whose smile was her best feature. We met in one of the nun's cells, now a counselling room. We got straight into my induction into the AA doctrine. She set me to writing examples of my 'powerlessness' over alcohol and my 'unmanageability', as a preparation to getting my First Step.

Still going through the days, one by one, hour by hour. Hanging on. Confronting metabolic desperation.

I was asked to write thirty pages on my career as an addict. It was difficult. If only because I still had a powerful tremor in my hands that made writing a challenge, and because it was impossible to concentrate for more than ten minutes at a stretch. But the mind is a marvellous instrument. On re-reading some of what I wrote, I find it to be remarkably articulate, even if it appears to have been written by a drunken spider.

Articulate in the way it presents me as not such a bad guy after all; a few weaknesses here and there, but all in all, an interesting and active middle-class bohemian. Despite the confusion and dislocation, the shakes and the depression, my mind was still able, indeed found it imperative, to present a picture that my fellow patients might like. Because the next move, after writing the thing, was to read it to the assembled group. They would then write you letters, telling exactly how they saw you, but not before they had each been asked if they accepted your account as being honest. If they didn't, your story was rejected and you had to go back and start again.

They accepted my story. They read their letters to me the next day. It was the strong stuff that only one alcoholic can say to another. I was an inveterate snob, a lecher of the worst kind who never once considered the feelings of the women he was involved with, a manipulative and cowardly wreck who always ran home to mummy when things got tough, an intellectual dabbler who never stuck at anything, a spoilt little boy who always wanted his own way, and much more.

I had no qualities at all. I loathed and detested what I had become. What self-respect I had was a sham. I was not happy. Brutal stuff.

The Second Step of AA says: [We] *came to believe that a Power greater than ourselves could restore us to sanity.* An interesting circumlocution so that agnostics and atheists might not be put off. My 'power greater than myself' was my meditation, and I began to say so: how I had been to India where I'd had a spiritual experience. But I didn't know what I was saying. I was referring to some vague memory of a memory that something extraordinary had happened to me in 1967.

Reeling from the shock of my appraisal, I began to believe that change was possible… It is so hard *not* to sound clichéd when writing about recovery! What I mean is: change was the only option on the table. In a state of emotional, chemical and metabolic shock, I had been confronted with my awfulness, with the ghastliness that is any practising addict or alcoholic. The confinement of the institution enabled some tiny flame of hope to say this was not all I was and, well, maybe it could change. By getting out of bed five minutes earlier, brushing one's teeth twice a day instead of just occasionally; such small changes had the effect of proving that one could move on.

The next stage was for me to be confronted by my 'significant others'. My mother and stepfather were invited down one Sunday. After lunch, they were taken into Jim's study and asked to give a detailed account of what I'd said or done over the years that had hurt or damaged my mother in any way. They were at it for some two hours. I was brought in, and my mother was asked to pronounce the heinous deeds I had inflicted on her.

When she had got to the end of the list, one that included theft, deceit, blackmail, emotional cruelty, constant dishonesty, there was a heavily charged atmosphere, but silence. What could I say? Eventually Jim broke the strain.

"Well, William, what do you have to say to that?" He asked quietly.

I thought hard for a few minutes, then, "I did do some writing."

Jim suggested that she write me a letter when she got home to mop up any more deviance. It conveys the emotional charge of the situation:

Dear William,

Of course I thought of so many more things I should have said yesterday to make you realise what we have all suffered because of you. I don't say this with any vindictiveness but simply because I gather that this may be the way to help you to change.

As I said yesterday, there has been constant anxiety about you because you have not been able to live a satisfying life, because you have lied and cheated, been totally selfish in order to lead your life of addiction without thought or consideration for others; you have been no support to me in my great hours of need when Daddy was in hospital; you have used me over and over again without any return.

Of course I now realise that I should not have let myself be used and that you lied to try and stop me from worrying, but of course I always knew you were lying and so could never believe you when you told the truth. [She then gives details, which she'd forgotten the day before, of things I'd done.] Of course, all this is the blackest part of the picture but I don't think I've overstated it. I don't think I can take any more. But I can still love you, if you feel like writing, we'll be at…

"...to make you realise what we have all suffered because of you."
That's it in a scapegoat nutshell.

It felt like my mother had won. I *had* been a despicable junky alcoholic worm. The scapegoat could not escape. He had shouted, "Can't you see?" and she couldn't or wouldn't. Any inadequacies in her mothering were not relevant. They were just William making a fuss. Just William.

Joy was different. There was less guilt and more confusion, on both sides. The group and staff had been telling me I must let go of Joy, stop using and manipulating her so I could have a connection with the real world, outside Broadway. Both in letters and on the phone, she repeated her undying love for me, but I couldn't respond. I didn't know what love felt like, doubted that I had ever known and told her so.

The day she came for the confrontation ritual, I was able to go for a walk with her beforehand and prime her as to what I didn't want her to talk about. When it came to it, Joy felt almost as much under attack as I was.

But whatever the roots of her love, that it was love could not be denied: an open, encompassing, accepting love. She presented me with a warm mirror in which I could try on different attitudes and selves as I struggled out of the cocoon of addiction.

After five weeks I had such a clear understanding of the routine and purpose of the treatment that I was accused of 'complying', of giving them the performance I thought they wanted. I was feeling much fitter, as the doctor had prophesied, and was sleeping well with no chemical assistance.

One particular group was a turning point. I was feeling low. All I knew about myself was negative and despised. Ten people sitting in the circle, ranging in age from mid-twenties to sixties. Dark lines under their tense battle-scarred eyes. Both Liz and Jim were there. Roger was a recent addition, a *Telegraph*-reading accountant in his fifties from one of the smarter suburbs of Bristol. He blustered and guffawed while the broken veins in his cheeks reddened.

"Roger, your wife's coming up on Sunday, isn't she?" asks Jack, a sharp-faced, nervous character.

"Of course," snaps Roger, as if surprised at the stupidity of the question. He fingers his old school tie nervously.

"What I mean is: are you going to tell her what you told us yesterday about your first wife and the sleeping pills? How you were too drunk to stop her taking that overdose? How, in effect, you murdered your first wife?" There was a hint of smugness in Jack's voice.

"That's absolute rubbish. I did no such thing. I may have had one too many sundowners earlier that evening, but I certainly wasn't drunk. I felt rather sleepy and had an early night. Yes, Hilda had been rather depressed that week, but my company just seemed to make her worse, so it was better I went to bed. I don't know anything about any sleeping pills. The coroner said it was an accident, an accidental overdose after she'd had too much to drink." Roger went slightly red in the face.

"Shit, Roger," I exploded. "You seem to've forgotten what you told us yesterday, or rather, what we got out of you." I was now sitting right on the edge of my chair, stabbing the air between Roger and me with my finger.

"You know what I mean. All that about how you asked the doctor that week if he couldn't give Hilda some sleeping pills, and how you found one of your precious bottles half-empty at the bottom of the stairs, but were too drunk to do anything about it. You're just covering up again, trying to deny your responsibility for what happened. You're just a stupid ex-colonial drunk who can't stop lying."

With that my righteous indignation seemed to subside.

"You getting angry, William? What are you getting so angry about, William?" Jim had broken the silence. He sat sideways on, resting an elbow on the chair back, and threw a piercing glance at me with his small blue eyes. I shuffled around on my hands, looked at my shoes, brought my hands together and then onto my knees.

"I don't know… Roger, I suppose. He's being so dishonest with himself. He's almost trying to deny that he's an alcoholic."

"Yes, OK, but why does that make *you* so angry? What right have *you* got, in the light of what's been coming out about you in the last few days?" Jim almost laughed and then looked up at me with those all-seeing eyes.

"None I suppose. Anyway, I'm not angry, just want him to tell the truth, to share with us."

"Come on now William, you weren't angry? You're not trying to disappear up your ivory tower again, are you? I thought you were going to get out of that ageing hippy thing. Cum'on, why don't you tell us all how you're feeling right now?"

"I…" I stared at my shoes.

"William, how are you feeling right now?" repeated Jim in a slow, determined voice.

"I suppose...."

"Yes?"

"I suppose I feel all tied up in my guts," I crossed and uncrossed my legs. "I don't like what I feel, but I can't describe it."

"Can anyone in the room tell William what he looks as though he's feeling. Come on, we'll go round the room. Everyone tell him how he looks." At this they all found something that was not a person to stare at, mostly some detail of the parquet floor. There was silence.

"Come on. Henry, we'll start with you."

"Well, I think you look miserable," he glared at me.

"You're just putting on an act," said Enid. "It's all part of your being such a cunning snob. You think you're so clever." She was a well-built woman in her thirties. She wore a shapeless knitted dress with a scarf knotted round her neck.

"Yes, definitely an act." She emphasises her point.

"No, I think William really is upset at the way Roger has been wasting our time with his lies." Peter glanced nervously at me as he spoke, wanting my approval.

The general consensus seemed to be that I was being deceitful and was trying to draw attention away from my own problems by attacking Roger. There was a long silence after they had all had their say.

"And how do you feel now?" Jim stared at me.

"Fed up, pissed off, confused. I don't know how to do or say anything right, it seems. I'm a liar, a cheat and a vindictive wet blanket. Why on earth can't we talk about someone else for a change?" Another long silence, which Jim breaks in a quieter, more gentle voice.

"It's OK, William. What you're feeling now is real enough." Jim turns to face me directly.

"You're just getting to the stage where you can begin to like yourself." I felt both puzzled and frightened.

If that wasn't enough, the next one was more serious.

"Let's talk about your relationship with women, William." Jim broke the long silence with his quiet, penetrating voice. Everyone but me relaxed momentarily now they were able to focus on my issues.

"Why?" I was defensive, defiant. "Why do we have to talk about my relationships with women. Shouldn't we be discussing Roger in that respect. What he did to his two previous wives?"

"Because, from what you told us yesterday about, who was it, Anita and then Sheena and then Margareta and then Mary and now Joy, it sounds as though you've ponced off women all your life. You have used and manipulated them with little regard for their well being."

"Oh, I don't know about that. I was married to Mary for five years, you know." I was uncomfortable.

"Yes," snorted Roger, "but all the time you were using that heroin stuff and must have been making your poor wife's life a misery. Didn't you have a little girl? How on earth did your wife manage to bring her up living with a junky?"

"She's all right. Anyway you're a fine one to talk." I stared down at where my hands went under my knees.

"No, hang on, what I'd like to get at," Henry broke in, "What I'd like to ask you, William, is how on earth you could manage to be surprised and so hurt each time one of your ladies decided she had had enough of your insane, egocentric behaviour. The way you told it in your life story, it's as if you treated them well, that all was fine, until suddenly, for no apparent reason, they all upped and left you."

"Take Sheena," Henry edged forward on his chair. "You were telling me about her when we walked down to the shops yesterday, remember? You seem to have treated her like, like some kind of object, to be moved around and used according to your fancy."

"Hey, that's not on. That was a confidential conversation. You've no right to talk of that."

"Of course I have, it's all relevant. As I was saying, one moment, Sheena's in the way, obstructing the work of a genius with her stupidity, the next she's needed to keep you warm in bed, to stop you feeling lonely. The paroxysm of self-pitying grief you indulged in for so long after she finally came to her senses is amazing. It bore very little relation to how it was between you. Six months of self-inflicted misery after the girl you'd been manipulating and exploiting tells you to get lost, it's insane."

"Have you finished? I don't know how you think you know so much about my love life." I threw a look that wanted to kill Henry.

"Oh, it's obvious. All the women in your life have walked out in desperation, haven't they?" Henry came back smugly.

"I wouldn't say that. The relationships have just come to an end, that's all. Most relationships do, and not in the way yours did Roger. It's not usually necessary to kill them off. Anyway Joy's still with me."

"You mean, she hasn't had the guts to leave you yet." Roger paused, gathering indignation. "And you've no right to talk about my previous wives in that light. You know damn well they killed themselves." There was a brief, brittle silence.

"William," said Jim, " you mustn't try to get us talking about someone else. We're trying to find out why you have related with women so badly. If you could admit, to yourself as much as to us, how parasitical you've been you'd be on the way to having a fuller and more free relationship with Joy." Jim went on looking at me after he'd stopped talking.

"I don't see what all the fuss is about. They must have liked being with me or they wouldn't have stayed as long as they did. My scene with Joy will sort itself out when she's had time to adjust to my being sober."

"Good God, William, you're so blind." Roger was angry. "And arrogant."

So Jim thought I could begin to like myself. Just at the point where I thought this the most unlikely thing. And so began my recovery. That last group meeting had been a violent challenge to my emotions and everything I knew about myself. Any further denials and pretensions I might have had began to surrender themselves, reeling on the ropes.

The pressure was on to make commitments both to the group and to myself: first that I get rid of Cosmic Books and second that I should join Mike in a halfway house in Chester. To give up the shop would be tough. To have to go to Chester, when I had a perfectly good home and girlfriend in Torquay, would be tougher. The theory was that halfway houses give the recovering alcoholic time (months rather than weeks) to find his feet in a supportive environment with other alcoholics with the same needs, and with some professional help on hand. I was to throw away the past and write my future on a blank slate.

I had a glimmering that a complete break *was* necessary, but wished it didn't have to be quite so drastic. Liz agreed that I could go to Torquay for a weekend to get the sale of Cosmic Books moving, but insisted that I make contact with someone in AA before I go. The advertisement Joy had put in the *Bookseller* had brought no response and we had to begin thinking of selling off the stock, rather then selling the shop as a going concern.

Joy met me at the station, a nervous man with a vivid awareness of the present and little opportunity to ponder my sobriety. She had the house looking very smart, very welcoming, but I didn't feel at ease. Too much of the past crowded in, too much uncertainty as to the state of our relationship, too much that was unknown. There was love, but so confused, so fractured.

My AA contact, Trevor, came over to see me. He was emphatic that he would do nothing to help if I started drinking again, but would do everything in his power while I remained sober. Fair enough. It was strange going back to the bookshop, the scene of so many of my drunken fantasias, and I was immediately glad that I was getting rid of it. I phoned a few people who I thought might be interested in the stock at half price or less. The next day I returned to Broadway as agreed.

I told the group I had made arrangements to meet some booksellers in the shop a week later to sell them the stock at a knockdown price. Unlike my first trip, I was tense and nervous when the day came round. I had a taxi booked to pick me up after the morning group. To my irritation, Henry noticed something.

"William, how do you feel about going to Torquay today? D'you think you're going to be all right?" he asked.

"Yeah, fine. I'll be fine. I've got to meet this bloke in the shop at three and then another at seven this evening. They're both coming to buy stock, I hope. It's very important I be there."

"Will you ring that guy from AA?"

"If I get time, but this business is very important and I may not have the time."

"William, I don't think you're in a fit state to go, myself. You seem to be forgetting what your priorities are." Henry had delivered his judgement.

"What do you mean, 'not in a fit state'? Of course I am. Anyway it's essential that I be there." I was defensive and angry.

"Hmmm, I'm not so sure, William," said Liz. "Let's see what the group has to say. Roger?" This was ridiculous, my taxi was due in ten minutes, and they were debating whether I was in a fit state to go!

The consensus was that I was too uptight to risk it. I was dumbfounded. I was doing well in the treatment, and they were telling me

I couldn't go to sell my business, which had been their idea in the first place! Hadn't I been perfectly all right the time before? Hadn't they agreed that I could go this time?

I went despite their misgivings. I committed the cardinal sin of Doing It My Way and not listening to the group. I felt guilty, but still I went. I was later told that had I not returned on time, I would have been asked to leave, and that would have had dire consequences for my chances of staying sober by casting a shadow of disapproval over me.

I had graduated from Broadway. I was officially 'in recovery'. I had been to Torquay one last time to collect a few things and say my goodbyes to Joy who was going to wait for me there. Mike, who had left Broadway two weeks earlier, was already in Chester and met me at the station.

I was getting through, surviving each day as it came. That's all. The unseen scapegoat hole of my adolescence put its head over the trepidation several times every day. My father's death, my mother's remarriage, my loss of contact with most of my old friends – all these had shifted the locus of the hole, but it was still black, throbbing and incapacitating.

I found myself in a bleak North peopled with grim alcoholics hanging on to a grim sobriety by their grim fingernails and daytime television. At the age of 32, my personality was of an emotionally volatile teenager who had once, many hells ago, been a beatnik and now needed to find how his adult self worked and what it did. Other than Mike who was going through similar confused explorations, the other blokes in the house seemed to regard life without drink as simply that: life without a purpose. Whereas I was a volatile mixture of fear, excitement, nerves, teenage angst and wondering what my spirituality was about.

I had to keep going to AA meetings. It wasn't just the power of the 'stay away and you're heading for a drink' double bind, but the undoubted fact that everyday life was raw, frightening and confusing. None of my aspirations, none of my discoveries, could amount to anything if I started using again. But this halfway house sobriety wasn't a great deal of fun.

It was urgent that I find a role, preferably as a poet or writer. My explorations led me to the local Arts Centre, where Chester Poets met once a week. I had brought my poems with me from Torquay and set about proving my poetic credentials to the circle. It wasn't difficult. The underlying dynamic of the group, as with most such circles, was that I'll listen to, read and praise your poems, if you'll do the same for me. I was relying mostly on poems written above the Hang Chow some fourteen years previously to prove what I was, but it didn't matter. They accepted me to such an extent that I found myself on the editorial panel of their next anthology in which I had four poems published.

There was a jazz club at the Arts Centre on Saturday nights that I couldn't resist, despite it having a bar. The first group I heard was downright exciting, returning me to early raptures with jazz, especially the tenor player. Yes, he was interested in doing some poetry and jazz and I was invited to sit in at a couple of the practice sessions to try some things out. We ended up doing gigs in Chester and at a leftover of the Arts Lab movement in Liverpool where I managed to resist the most enormous joints of dope that were being passed around

Graham, the tenor player, was the first new, non-addict friend I had made since getting hooked. When I went to his home to listen to records and to talk, I was swamped with new sensations. It was as though I had just emerged from a long stretch of total solitary confinement, unsure of the fashions and manners of the day, unsure, indeed, that I would be acceptable as company or how to speak.

Here was a guy my own age, living comfortably and with a wealth of experience both as a painter and musician, while I was just emerging into the harsh light of day. I had not hung out with ordinary people for over ten years. I was a blank, a vacuum. I was envious and insecure. It felt like a good idea to explain exactly what I was doing in Chester, what I'd been through, the whole thing, but briefly. It was a way of relating with them. I tried on the 'brave, noble, recovering drug addict' suit of clothes.

They showed respect. To have come through heroin addiction *and* alcoholism, wow! Charlie Parker couldn't manage that. I wallowed in the glory, even assuming a self-deprecating modesty. This way I could gain some kind of esteem, and that was what I thought I wanted. Trouble was, in my 32-year-old puberty, there was so little, other than getting sober, that I could respect myself for. I just needed to be loved.

I visited my sister, Lucy, and her philosopher husband, Andrew, whose remote farmhouse near Lancaster was not that far from Chester. I remembered that Mary and I had gone there on our honeymoon.

It was an AA 'making amends' mission, meeting them on an equal footing for the first time. They were my main connection with an inner life, so I could begin to explore how my sobriety meshed with my spiritual purpose.

Their farmhouse, high up on the moors, at the end of long bumpy track, had views many miles long. The curlews sang their sad songs. The kitchen was decorated as if it were one of Lucy's paintings with manikins in stripes and bright blue walls. There were goats in the barn outside to be milked, a horse for the Gipsy caravan. Andrew went off to lecture on Buddhism, while Lucy painted.

Broadway and the half way house had indeed made me a blank slate – I was envious of the solid establishment and nitty gritty of their lives and family (their four intense children were still at home). Again we talked about Maharaj Ji – how you can never escape him, once he's opened that window in your mind.

After four months in Chester I was ready to leave. Broadway's idea was that I stay there for a year, but I rebelled again. I went home to a snug, warm, welcoming reality in Torquay. On my third day home there was a letter from the Bristol bookshop I'd applied to for a job. I'd been frank about being a recovering addict. No job.

And so started my life. I was now like any one else, an ordinary mortal. I could not hide from the struggle of life in the counterfeit heroism of addiction. I must now earn a living. I must now discover how to be a human being and how to be *with* other human beings. Now it couldn't hide in the addiction, the pain at the core of me was more apparent than before, ricocheting around my various attempts at being an adult, my various stratagems at distracting my attention.

Our relationship is so unlikely and so familiar, Joy and I find a loving comfort in each other's company. By 1979 we knew that getting married was inevitable and did the deed at Paignton Registry Office. A harmonious marriage is a partnership, not a merger. When I began to let go of her, to let her be the glorious heart that she is, only then have we relaxed into respecting each other and loving each other. Marriage, the social ritualisation of it, is important: the two of you make a declaration to family, friends and yourselves that you are committing yourselves to make it work.

A central tenet of AA's Twelve Step model is that addiction is a progressive illness that cannot be cured in the ordinary sense of the term, but that can be arrested through total abstinence. The problem for me is this idea of 'arrested progressive illness', one that cannot be cured. The primary precursor of addiction – the pain that demands the comfort of the drug in the first place – doesn't get a look in. The condition of addiction, the day-to-day taking of the stuff with all the attendant psychological and physical damage and mess is the symptomatic result of desperate self-medication for depression and for something bigger and deeper, the original pain. A symptom that quickly gets out of control, but symptom none the less. It is progressive because addiction feeds on itself, because the precursor pain has been subsumed into the pain of addiction, and the greater that pain, the greater the quantity of stuff needs to be taken, causing greater pain.

The Twelve Step method of dealing with the illness model works, no doubt. It got me to a state of not-drinking sobriety and not-fixing straightness. But it could not touch the precursor pain. The power of AA to get millions of addicts out of the self-fulfilling double bind of taking stuff to mask the pain of taking stuff was one of the twentieth century's great discoveries. But an old discovery: when you want to practice mysticism you go to a practising mystic, not a priest, theologian or academic. When you want to get straight, you listen to people who have got straight, not doctors, psychologists or therapists.

But what of that original pain? This is something mysterious. We all have a pain at the root of us. It's been called original sin. It's the burden of being here. Or the longing that gets us out of here. Most of us manage to develop complex shells to keep it hidden, to distract our attention. Freud codified it as an irrational force lurking in our unconscious, something his immediate successors developed rigorous controls for.

If the new child is loved sufficiently he can hold the pain, can stroke the head of this pain, sing it lullabies and hint at sagas of salvation. If not, the pain engulfs, and the message learnt from his parent is, "I cannot bear this," and "Make it better!" This is the beginning of addiction: "Can't you see?" and "Make it better!"

My recovery, my going back to a state of health, has revolved around the position this pain holds in my inner life, around how I hold it, what I do with it. It cannot be made better, but it can be either grasped or shrunk from. It is the source of creativity. It is not painful, this pain – it goes beyond to the purpose of life. Grasp it and you're in love and living dangerously. Deny it and you're merely existing. So, my recovery reached through creative meanderings and entrepreneurial fumblings to being a whole vulnerable human, standing there making a speech to a family gathering. Being seen.

I had stopped taking chemicals to change how I felt, but it wasn't the end of my addiction. There's a bigger shift in the mind-body nexus required. A modicum of happiness, equilibrium and satisfaction must be found. Did it end when I left the halfway house to become an everyday human? No, not as long as I was on the edge of the hole, keeping dry one day at a time. Did it end when I stopped going to AA meetings because the 'keep coming to meetings or drink' threat (with its hints of Christian hellfire) had lost its charm? No, the golem of melancholia often appeared stronger as my emotions stabilised. There has not been an *end* to the addiction, with its many subjects and objects, but a *metamorphosis* of the cocoon of dependency into a fully-fledged, fractious and fractured dragonfly.

e.e. cummings wrote:

> *when man determined to*
> *destroy*
> *himself he picked the*
> *was*
> *of shall and finding only*
> *why*
> *smashed it into because.*

My dragonfly is free to fly when it smashes the why and transcends the because, to buzz into the thickness of today.

Twenty seven years have passed since I was in Broadway. It has taken me that long to be able to look back with sufficient balance to be able to write this book. It didn't cross my mind when I first emerged into abstemiousness that I could, with some application, become a professional writer. I can ask myself now: Why not? How that failure of imagination has wasted time! Not enough 'you can do it' messages as a young man? Had I been a proper Darwin or Pryor, I would, by now, have had a string of meticulously researched tomes to my name. But then I wouldn't have been an addict, a free improviser or groundbreaking entrepreneur. Nothing is a waste of time, especially not zeitgeist crystallising.

John Cage tells the story of the Indian Guru who was asked by a disciple why, if God was all about love and compassion, he allowed so much suffering in the world. Surely it couldn't make any sense for God to allow sweet little children to die from cancer, to wipe out thousands of innocents in war and natural disaster? Where was the love and compassion in that? Why did God allow it?

The guru chose to ponder this deep question at length.

"You see, it is very simple. It thickens the plot," he answered.

Outside one of the double-glazed windows of my writing shed is a wire-frame bird feeder full of peanuts. It has an outer cage to keep squirrels and crows out. Watching our bravest local squirrel learn how to get the lid off reminds me of myself. He didn't sit there and size up the problem before getting out his screwdriver. No, he simply scrambled around and pushed and shoved until, somehow, the lid came off. My scrambling kind of entrepreneurism has been the thickening of my plot, the avoidance of writing, the getting the lid off the money thing.

For 25 years I attempted to make myself into a post-industrial, anti-capitalist capitalist, green entrepreneur. With others or on my own, I've started a few companies: amongst them Clear, Calm and Company, Airlift Book Company, The Whole Thing, The Green Catalogue, Arq and Floot.com. Their names hint at my inclinations. I have raised in excess of a million pounds to fund them all. Some of them have been profitable, some not.

Now that I have given up trying to imagine myself as a businessman I can acknowledge there are aspects of commerce I have never been comfortable with or good at. When I want to present a heroic picture I say that I am useless at being ruthless, but that's a cover. Really, I'm no good with the need for precision and analysis, and the attention to, and affection for, money and the bottom line offends some part of my Darwin genes. The final straw is profit's insistence on the sacrifice of creativity.

It has been a bumpy road learning to live with, enjoy and be nourished by family and friends. I didn't know how to be with my only child Lydia, now a grown woman. I was the first of three fathers for her and maybe the worst; my need to talk about my difficulties and to show her success that I didn't have; all this kept me away. Eventually I discovered what a straightforward, unmessed-up woman she is. And have begun to know the delights of being a grandfather to her beautiful daughters Esme and Bette.

Another fulfilling circle. Maybe recovery reaches reconciliation through the turning of circles?

Anger with my family has spilled over into my recovery on a few occasions. I had been the devoted scapegoat for the family silence, the incapacity and inability for discourse of the emotions. I had screamed, created, performed and become addicted and in so doing I had spent my inheritance, drained my Pelican of blood. All my three sisters have had to do is keep their heads below the parapet. Now I was straight I expected natural justice to award me my inheritance all over again. Most unreasonable!

I also wanted some approval, some back patting, some concern and some love as I tottered down the unknown territory of my newfound sobriety. Money *and* love – completely unreasonable!

The addiction myth that held me in its grip could not have metamorphosed as completely as it has without the meditation I attempt. My purpose in the world is not the cutting of the path through the jungle. Certainly, we have to get through the undergrowth, but the purpose of life is internal: to be in the centre while cutting the path. Being an addict, even being a recovering addict, does not make this path-cutting any easier: your attention keeps getting stuck on the many jungle thorns that addicts are drawn to.

Meditation has shown me that the discomfort, unease and vexation that has gnawed at me for fifty years can be held differently. I do not need to hold them as proof of my addiction; they don't need to be seen as lack or absence. They are, rather, the ultimate blues or *bireh* in Sanskrit: the pain of separation from the source, an elemental reminder of the origins of my being.

So far it has all been about change. First the cultural revolution intending to change everything. Then chemicals used to change my mood. Then the changes of Totterdown. Then the ducking and diving change of my strange entrepreneurial sobriety.

> *Bebop was about change, about evolution. It wasn't about standing still and becoming safe. If anybody wants to keep creating they have to be about change. (Miles Davis)*

I would have liked to have said: "Only the coolest survive to be the bebop. Only those who turn dysfunction into compost will know the early worm."

As we edge crabwise towards the denouement, the speech, the complete change that is death is something I must consider. The sixties are well known for their casualties and deaths. It is the one certainty of where we are, of our physicality. I might die just getting up from my computer; my heart might just throw up its hands in horror and say, "enough, already". But I am not dead; I am gone beyond sobriety and glad of it.

A small selection of the better known users of opiates for creativity in the recent past include: Antonin Artaud, Chet Baker, Graham Bond, William Burroughs, Eric Clapton, Gregory Corso, John Coltrane, Miles Davis, Marianne Faithfull, Jerry Garcia, Billie Holiday, Janis Joplin, Anna Kavan, Charles Mingus, Nico, Charlie Parker, River Phoenix, Lou Reed, Will Self, Alex Trocchi and Paula Yates. Of these 20 people, 13 died before their time, while the other 7 have found ways of living with or without.

With Julian Hough, the hobo, one-time boy friend of my sister Lucy and founder of the National Theatre of Brent, months would pass when no one knew where he was or what had happened, and no one got alarmed. Then in 1995 word started to percolate that his body had been found on the Kingston bypass. Dead. Not surprising, but shocking none the less. Apparently it had taken the police three months to identify the body, and then it had only happened through dental records.

The Guardian gave him a half page obituary which recorded that he was seen cantering past the Horseguard's barracks on an imaginary charger barking orders. He was wearing battered brown brogues with paper thin soles and a stained rust-coloured jacket. His hair was wild and he hadn't shaved.

For any old actor, Julian's funeral service would have been moving, but for someone who had been a hobo for years, it was extraordinary. The dark Victorian church in Pimlico was packed with a wonderful range of people including a sprinkling of rock and stage stars, including Dave Gilmour of the Pink Floyd. There were two priests conducting the service, one each side of Julian's coffin.

The highlight was the performance by his old partners and friends of the National Theatre of Brent's funniest piece: the Visitation. The priests looked on, forcing benign smiles, as the archangel Gabriel appeared and had the funniest discussion with the Virgin Mary. The church wept with laughter.

Imagine the pain in him! A hobo!

Another fatality was Ponji, who had much the same wandering rootlessness as Julian. On his return from India, he had been persuaded to have LSD therapy (i.e. therapy that revolved around taking LSD) with one of the angry young therapists of the sixties. Ponji never recovered. He would never settle down anywhere for more than a few days. We didn't see him for a while. Then bang, news came that he had jumped under a tube train at Finsbury Park Station.

What desperation is this? Can it have been a casual jumping?

And Johnny Johnson, the coolnik who shared his dope with Nigel and me above the Hang Chow. Rumour has it that he was the heir to the Lea and Perrins Worcestershire Sauce fortune, with his sisters in the William Hickey gossip column every other week, and was not American at all; his accent an affectation.

One day in London, he could take it no longer. He jumped out of a third floor window. He did not die but was left a paraplegic. A few months later, he dragged himself to another window and, this time, he successfully killed himself.

Why the American accent? Why the second jump?

And Margareta died of stomach cancer. Joy and I spoke to her on the phone from India just ten days before she died: a ghostly morphine voice talking of light.

That pain that cannot be expressed, released. It is the longing, the creative juice, also. Physical death is not the solution. The only comfort, the total comfort is to be found by being here now, in the centre. And this is only possible by dying daily.

Since the day of my birth, my death began its walk. It is walking toward me, without hurrying. (Jean Cocteau)

Given that the pain of being a devoted scapegoat was entirely to do with the family and the Darwin orthodoxy, and given that this pain was what pined for comfort, for annihilation in drugs, it is right, it is good, that the final evidence of resolution should come through a family gathering.

There was talk at my mother's eightieth birthday party that a biography was being written about my grandmother, Gwen Raverat, by art historian Frances Spalding. When a publication date was announced, my mother and I organised a lunch to celebrate its publication for Gwen's descendents, cousins and friends at a hotel in Cambridge, a few hundred yards from the Old Granary where she had lived.

We invited Hambros, Pryors, plus some Cornfords, Keynes's and Darwins. Some seventy people; many oohing and aahing reunions. Joy and I had taken some of my Norwegian cousins on the river that morning. One fine young daughter of one of my aunt Elizabeth's daughters told me how she is a therapist in a woman's prison. She responded openly to my curiosity, interested to discover a cousin with a similar attitude to family dysfunction. Becoming a therapist in such an extreme environment was the only way she could begin to transmute the Hambro variety of the family devils.

I was to give the main speech. The full circle. I took risks, I was funny, but I also raised a tear or two. I held forth about the problem of being a Darwin and the family's ambivalence to family, quoting Gwen's *Period Piece* on the subject:

It was a grey, cold, gusty day in June. The aunts sat huddled in furs in the boats, their heavy hats flapping in the wind. The uncles, in coats and cloaks and mufflers, were wretchedly uncomfortable on the hard, cramped seats, and they hardly even tried to pretend that they were not catching their deaths of cold. But it was still worse when they had to sit down to have tea on the damp, thistly grass near Grantchester Mill. There were so many miseries which we young ones had never noticed at all: nettles, ants, cow-pats… besides that all-penetrating wind. The tea had been put into bottles wrapped in flannels (there were no Thermos flasks then); and the climax came when it was found that it had all been sugared beforehand. This was an inexpressible calamity. They all hated sugar in their tea. Besides it was Immoral. Uncle Frank said, with extreme bitterness: 'It's not the sugar I mind, but the Folly of it.' This was half a joke; but at his words the hopelessness and the hollowness of a world where everything goes wrong, came flooding over us; and we cut our losses and made all possible haste to get them home to a good fire.

They smiled and tutted in appreciation as we huddled in Gwen's charm. I suggested that she would have agreed with Frank Zappa when he said that art is making something out of nothing and selling it. Though nervous, I had them in the palm of my hand. After the coffee we milled. I was thanked for the speech with warmth and an affection that surprised me. The scapegoat had escaped. One lovely cousin, a sculptress, told me, with a mwa kiss, that I was her hero. Taken aback, I asked why.

"Oh, you know, all this, and what you've done with your drug problem." I had had no idea.

Maybe it wasn't the drugs they minded, but the folly of the addiction. Maybe, this wasn't the end, but the metamorphosis of my addiction into a creativity they could appreciate.

I didn't need to plead: "Can't you see?" any more.

They *could* see. Well, one or two could.

Epilogue

I have two proposals to make: 1) recovering addicts can, and therefore should, move beyond mere sobriety, and 2) all drugs should be legalised and licensed. The proposals are intertwined: a new understanding of what addiction is and isn't will lead to a more fruitful attitude to its treatment, while the legalisation and licensing of drugs will bring an end to the suffering and criminality caused by their current illegality. Neither of my proposals will stop people getting hooked, but they will move the problem into a civilised 21st century context, start to clear the extreme moral confusion surrounding the pleasure and pain of drugs and alcohol, and may enable more people to develop beyond recovery.

The concept of 'addiction' is a rich example of a meme, a notion invented by Richard Dawkins, the ardent disciple of my great great grandfather, to explain how evolution operates in society and the mind. A meme is a unit of the social DNA. It is an element of a culture, or system of behaviour, that is passed from one individual to another by non-genetic means, especially imitation. You catch them, like viruses.

The addiction meme has many levels. It whispers: addiction is an incurable illness. You know you've got it when you can't control yourself, when you get withdrawal symptoms from a lack of the substance. They hurt and are the real and visible sign of the devil that is the illness. You won't catch the illness if you have a free, strong, democratic, consumer self – only seven-stone weaklings and inadequates get infected with addiction. You can only be redeemed, saved by the New Church of AA and Medicine, if you confess your sins to your Higher Power, before the congregation of other addicts. Dare to think you can be responsible for your own life and you will be damned to eternal withdrawal.

I just got a junk email with these words in red: *Another amazingly addictive and fun game from the creators of…* The meme is ambivalent: 'addictive' seems to mean 'exciting fun', as well as 'slave making'.

I am not against the fundamentals of what AA does. Within the confines of the meme, where addiction *is* an illness, the Twelve Step treatment does work. I would not have been able to stop taking alcohol, Heminevrin, heroin, methadone, whatever, without it. Through the various Twelve Step programmes millions are able to stop indulging in their destructive behaviour. This peer group chain letter of possibility and change does work. It is personality surgery, cutting out the rotten bits and grafting in hope and possibility. But like physical surgery, there is no call to go on and on about it.

The addiction-as-illness meme may be comforting in the detox process, but it can only deliver the addict into a mere staying-clean sobriety that has a new dependency: AA. To move beyond, an addict must grasp the full implications of being a human being with all the vulnerabilities and vexations everyone else has to endure – the very thing that mood-altering substances seemed to offer an escape from.

Addiction is like pregnancy in that it is all or nothing. You can't be slightly pregnant or slightly addicted. But also like pregnancy, there comes a moment when you are no longer addicted, when it has changed shape, when the 'I am an alcoholic' mantra of AA is no longer true. I am not a negative, and both 'alcoholic' and 'addict' are negative. I can now mother the child my addiction gave birth to, the child of creativity. The only incurable illness I have is the great nostalgia, the longing for the yearning, and this I welcome!

In the Vietnam War, many US soldiers used heroin to get them through. When they got back to the utterly different environment of home, many stopped using – just like that, with no withdrawal symptoms. The addiction meme was overwhelmed by the trauma of war. Withdrawal symptoms are only dreadful while the meme infects you. Otherwise they are no worse than a dose of flu. Addiction is not what it seems when we get out from under the meme.

When the doctor tells you that the particular pattern of suffering you are enduring is an illness, you sigh with relief, knowing it will be easier to deal with. It has a label. You are not responsible. You can hand over to the doctors, psychiatrists and self-help groups – they understand your weaknesses and deficiencies. Treatment can be prescribed.

"What have I got Doctor? What is it?"

"You have a bad case of addiction, I'm afraid. It's incurable."

"You mean I'm going to die!"

"Not necessarily. If you do what I say, it can be arrested. I am going to have to send you to a treatment centre."

"But how did I get it?"

"Have you had any flaws recently? Any attacks of moral ambiguity? Have you ever eaten any dangerous ideas?"

"Well, doctor, yes – how did you know? I've got this flaw – right here, through the middle of my brain."

"There you are. Addiction always finds our imperfections. As soon as it finds a crack, in it goes and you're hooked."

"Hang on, a minute. If I've got addiction, does that mean I'm specially immoral?"

"No, not really. It's OK. It's an illness, like AIDS. It's not your fault. It has made you do the things you've done. The illness made you mug that old woman."

"I don't understand: how can an illness make me do something?"

"Well, it's an illness of the self, you see. Your self is diseased. It has gone bad, and must be corrected. Mugging that old lady was a symptom of your illness."

I do not mean to make light of the seriousness of what we must call addiction, just to throw some light on how the medical profession has developed and taken ownership of the meme. In its pursuit of improvement and fulfilment, the 21st century self is increasingly unlikely to find a coherent way of holding the craving pain that is the core of its humanity. Consciousness-altering substances appear to answer this inadequacy – the hole is filled, the pain becomes that of being hooked. Addiction starts here; the meme kicks in.

In the West the majority have not been in the thrall of organised religion for the last fifty years. We no longer trust priests to tell us what is good or bad. We have given doctors, psychiatrists, psychologists, psychotherapists and peer groups that role. So many new phenomena have been pathologised into addiction illnesses: sex, gambling, eating, thrill-seeking, that a majority of the population are 'addicted'. Morality has become medicine. Doctors are priests. We fear to know what is right and what wrong. Government hypocrisy over the huge taxes they reap from alcohol and tobacco sales while waging the fantasy 'war on drugs' muddies the moral waters even further.

A Chinese Proverb has it that people in the West are always getting ready to live. Addiction is the postponement of living through condensed suffering in the illusion of the self. Perversely, we get addicted because we find life painful – we need to postpone it. The self can't stand living, but craves it. We take suffering to doctors. That's what they are for and that's how they control the meme. Addiction is compacted desire, protracted lust, the craving that Buddhists talk about as being an essential of the human condition, made into a way of life.

But you can't cure the suffering of the self by medical means – however touchy feely. Once in a balanced sobriety, each addict must discover how to be a human being for themselves, and how the suffering of the self, at the root of the addiction in the first place, can be held in a fruitful, non-harming way.

I am a complete abstainer. For 28 years I have chosen not to put any mood altering chemicals in my body other than tea and coffee. But I am in favour of the legalisation and licensing of drugs. I was a licensed addict to begin with and was able, more or less, to carry on as a student, but when I was hooked on street heroin, I nearly died a couple of times because of its very illegality.

An MP told me recently, with a strange pride in his voice, that illegal drug use is estimated to cost the UK £28 billion a year; strange pride, almost as if it were a good thing. He would not listen when I suggested this would be seriously reduced if drugs were legalised. He said he could not entertain a "vision of Britain" that contained drug addicts sitting around, doing nothing, while being supplied by the state. What about the millions of alcoholics costing the NHS billions to nurse through their self-destruction? Why is the suffering and death of hundreds of thousands of addicts and the torture inflicted on their families, why is this more acceptable than the development of a tolerant attitude to drug dependence? If Prohibition in early 20th century America was such a debacle, why do we imagine that the War on Drugs can be any more successful? History tells us that all government attempts at control and regulation have failed. All that Prohibition delivered was crime. All that the War on Drugs delivers is billion dollar revenues for the crime syndicates and the CIA. Let people chose what state they want their consciousness in.

Let us put an end to the enormous suffering and criminality that the illegality of drugs causes round the world. The police in the part of England I live in have just announced that burglary rates are up by 75% and they lay this squarely at the door of the increased availability of class A drugs. Nowadays you have to steal to fund your habit. The beginning of a solution: take back control of the supply of drugs by licensing and legalising them.

In March 2002 a survey estimated that thirteen million people, 28% of the UK population over 16 (51% between 16 and 24), had taken illegal drugs at some point. Of the 72% that hadn't, a high proportion are drinkers of alcohol and smokers of tobacco. And 99% of banknotes in circulation in London have traces of cocaine on them. These statistics are echoed throughout the West.

Legalisation won't stop misuse but it will stop the damage caused by the criminalizing of drug supply. And it might start to clear up some of the moral confusion, to show that individual responsibility is the key, not state finger-wagging. To prohibit something in law only encourages curiosity. Fifty-one percent of young Britons break the law to take drugs – drug taking has become normal.

Let me reiterate: I am NOT advocating the use of any mood-altering substance. I prefer life without them, indeed I cannot fulfil the purpose of my life *with* them. But no one can stop people using them, not governments, not priests, not any kind of moralists. Individual attitudes to pleasure and pain is what it comes down to: real, personally-discovered morality.

Plato said that to be overcome by pleasure is ignorance in the highest degree. This is an ignorance that has frequently plagued me and which I can only ward off through meditation. Addiction always starts in pleasure. Out of the group of five young friends exploring the pleasure of the opium in Chlorodyne in my mother's kitchen all those years ago, I was the only one who got hooked. If the pleasure meets your pain, then the addiction meme is likely to be spawned.

When all else is done, we crave life itself so that we may fulfil our purpose. When we are focused, all desires get subsumed into that one-pointed purpose.

SOME OTHER CLEAR BOOKS TITLES
ALL AVAILABLE AT HTTP://WWW.CLEARPRESS.CO.UK

PERIOD PIECE
The Victorian Childhood of Charles Darwin's Granddaughter
by Gwen Raverat
This anniversary edition of a classic work, presented as a facsimile
of a 19th century book is a delightful, quirky account — beauti-
fully illustrated with the author's famous line drawings — of her
quintessentially English childhood growing up as a Darwin at the
end of the 19th century.
Cloth 1-904555-12-8 272 pages 7½x 9¾ in £25 Autobiography

VIRGINIA WOOLF & THE RAVERATS
A Different Sort of Friendship
Trade Hardback Edited by William Pryor
An extraordinary relationship between one of the greatest writers
of the 20th century and Gwen and Jacques Raverat. She is the
granddaughter of Charles Darwin and he a French painter dying
of MS. This poignant friendship is portrayed in their complete correspondence (much never before published) and other writings and
illustrated by photos and the Raverats' wood engravings, paintings
and drawings.
Cloth 1-904555-02-0 212 pages with 8 in colour 7x 9 ½
£25 Literature, Biography

THE COLOURS OF INFINITY
The Beauty, the Power and the Sense of Fractals
Edited by Nigel Lesmoir-Gordon
The world's founders and leaders of Fractal Geometry — the
biggest names in the field gathered in one book for the first time
— describe how the science has developed in the ten years since
the making of the ground-breaking TV documentary *The Colors of
Infinity*, seen in over 50 countries around the world. Contains a
DVD of the original documentary with soundtrack by David
Gilmour, PLUS a half hour fractal animation chillout movie.
paperback with DVD 1-904555-05-5 160 pages with 16 in colour
7½ x 9¾ £25 Popular Science

Some Other Clear Books Titles

ALL AVAILABLE AT HTTP://WWW.CLEARPRESS.CO.UK

Blowing the Blues

Fifty years playing the British Blues

by Dick Heckstall-Smith and Pete Grant

The autobiography of Dick Heckstall-Smith, master sax player, who has long been at the centre of British Blues. He played with all the greats including: Ginger Baker, Eric Clapton, Colosseum, Alexis Korner and John Mayall. The book comes with a CD of previously unreleased tracks by Dick Heckstall-Smith.

Paperback with CD   1-904555-04-7   224 pages with 16 of b/w pictures   6 x 9 £16.95   Music / Autobiography

Rickshaw

Madras to London by Motor-Assisted Rickshaw

by Oliver Higson

The multifarious adventures of a quintessentially "mad Englishman" as he sets out on Leg One, from Madras to London, of the first cyclerickshaw trip around the world.

Paperback 1-904555-09-8 224 pages with 16 in colour   6 x 9 £12.95   Travel

Cookham and Gwen

The Complete Correspondence between Stanley Spencer and Gwen Raverat

Edited by William Pryor

Stanley Spencer (whose nickname was Cookham, the village he always lived in) and Gwen Raverat were at the Slade School of Art in London together in the first decade of the 20th century. They became friends, Gwen being one of the first to recognize the genius in Stanley Spencer's strangely obsessive art. To support him, she bought his pictures when few others were. Now he is recognized as one of England's greatest painters of the 20th century, meriting the recent major exhibition at Tate Britain. This book is the vapor trail of their friendship left in their letters.

Cloth 1-904555-08-X   160 pages with 8 pp colour wrap   7x 9 ½ £20   Literature/Art